John Ferguson McLennan

Studies in Ancient History

Comprising a reprint of primitive marriage

John Ferguson McLennan

Studies in Ancient History
Comprising a reprint of primitive marriage

ISBN/EAN: 9783744751353

Printed in Europe, USA, Canada, Australia, Japan

Cover: Foto ©ninafisch / pixelio.de

More available books at **www.hansebooks.com**

STUDIES IN ANCIENT HISTORY

COMPRISING A REPRINT OF

PRIMITIVE MARRIAGE

STUDIES IN ANCIENT HISTORY

COMPRISING A REPRINT OF

PRIMITIVE MARRIAGE

AN INQUIRY INTO
THE ORIGIN OF THE FORM OF CAPTURE
IN MARRIAGE CEREMONIES

BY THE LATE
JOHN FERGUSON McLENNAN

A NEW EDITION

London
MACMILLAN AND CO.
AND NEW YORK
1886

PREFACE TO THE PRESENT EDITION.

THIS volume is a reprint of *Studies in Ancient History* as published in 1876, with notes added only where they appeared to be indispensable. It is proposed to follow it up with a second volume containing other writings of the author—writings for the most part hitherto unpublished, and prepared for a work which was left unfinished—from which it will be possible to gather, in a considerable measure at least, how far the author's views had grown or been developed, how far they had changed or been added to, subsequently to the appearance of *Primitive Marriage*. It seemed best therefore to attempt no statement about this at present. And there was equal reason against doing the same thing fragmentarily in notes. The notes have accordingly been confined to certain matters on which the author had announced a change of view; and to some others—*e.g.* Mr. Morgan's speculations— where circumstances had made an additional statement imperative. No better opportunity could occur, however, for doing what (as appears from the Preface to the former edition) the author had felt to be very desirable—making a pretty full collection of examples of the form of capture; and this has been done in the Appendix to *Primitive Marriage,* upon the basis of a collection which the author published in 1866. The examples thus brought together suffice, at least, to show an extraordinary diffusion for this marriage custom.

A reminder may be given that *Primitive Marriage* was a first essay in a new field, and that the author (always hoping to be able either to supplement or supersede it) never revised it with a view to freeing it from defects that are unavoidable in such a case. There is, therefore (to say nothing of more important things) a minor proposition or two, casually laid down and unrelated to the main purpose of the book, which he probably would not have repeated. There are cases, no doubt, in which he would have amended his language; sometimes for exactness' sake, and sometimes on account of misconceptions which he had not foreseen as possible. There are cases, too, in which, with the fuller knowledge he subsequently had, he would have supplemented, or amended, or re-arranged his facts—and, indeed, our knowledge of some barbarous and savage peoples has been much enlarged since 1865. There is nothing, however, he could have added to or varied in the facts which would have much affected the argument of the book; and, for the peoples whose customs are most likely to be helpful in reasoning about early societies, the facts will be gone into pretty fully in the projected volume already spoken of.

Of misapprehensions as to his language there is one which should be noticed here. This is a misapprehension as to the words exogamy and endogamy. These terms were introduced on account of two particular things—two laws relating to marriage—for each of which a name seemed to be wanted. One of these laws, when at its widest, forbids marriage between all persons of the same blood-connection or kindred — whether such kindred forms a local tribe by itself; or whether it is one of several different kindreds which together form a local tribe; or whether (as often happens) it occurs, along with other kindreds, as an element in more than one local tribe. This law was, when *Primitive Marriage* was written, unnamed; and the author termed it exogamy. It is not prohibition of marriage between persons of the same tribal community because of tribesmanship, or of anything that is necessarily involved in tribesmanship. When at its widest, it is prohibition of marriage between all persons recognised as being of the same blood, because of their common blood—whether they form one community, or part only of a community, or parts of several communities; and, accordingly, it may prevent marriage between persons who (though of the same blood) are of different local tribes, while it frequently happens that it leaves persons of the same local tribe (but who are not of the same blood) free to marry one another. Such is this law, and all the author had to do was to find a name for it; the sense of the term was not in his choice. That it was convenient the law should have a name will scarcely be disputed. Whether the term exogamy might have been applied with more propriety to something else is, no doubt, a different matter; but that to which, whether by choice or through misconception, some later writers have applied it, does not seem to be much in need of any special name. The second marriage law for which a name was wanted, allows marriage only between persons who are recognised as being of the same blood-connection or kindred; and if, where it occurs, it confines marriage to the tribe or community, it is because the tribe regards itself as comprising a kindred. This law the author termed endogamy ; and here again it is not his choice, but the nature of the law which had to be named, which makes the term as proposed by him inapplicable to local tribes in general. For the law occurs in those local tribes only which regard themselves as one blood, and restrict intermarriage to men and women of the tribe because of their blood; and it need not be said that a multitude of tribes are known in which those two conditions are not combined. The tribes which do present them are numerous enough nevertheless, to make it inconvenient that their marriage law should have no name. No doubt there is again the question whether the term proposed might not have been applied with more propriety to something else ; but that to which some later writers have applied it might be left unnamed—even with advantage. For they have used endogamy to denote the mere fact that marriages occur between persons belonging to the same local tribe ; thereby combining under one name the results in working of the marriage law last spoken of, with certain of the results of the marriage law which had been named exogamy—things which, being of different origin and of entirely different significance, it seems best to study apart from one another. With the uses to which the two words, exogamy and endogamy, have been turned, moreover, marriage laws have been forgotten altogether.

In so far as this has been the result of misconception, the author must have been in fault, no doubt. It seems, nevertheless, to be made perfectly clear in *Primitive Marriage* that it was two marriage laws he found in want of names, and that it was for them he proposed the terms exogamy and endogamy.

The notes written for this edition are distinguished from the author's notes by being inclosed in brackets—the notes on Mr. Morgan's system being also placed at the end of the Essay to which they refer.

D. McLENNAN.

SAN REMO, *April* 1886.

PREFACE TO THE ORIGINAL EDITION.

[*Dated* 20*th January*, 1876.]

I SHOULD have brought out a new edition of *Primitive Marriage* long since had it not been my purpose to supersede it by a more comprehensive work, —a purpose defeated by circumstances, which have, for several years past, and till within the last few months, made literary work impossible for me. I now bring out a reprint, because the book, which has long been rare, is, for a work of its class, much in request; and because, though I am again free to resume the studies necessary for its revision, it is uncertain whether I could soon revise it in a satisfactory manner—so that I am without an answer to representations made to me, that it is better it should be made accessible to students with its imperfections than that it should remain inaccessible to them. I have done this the more readily that, on the whole, I still adhere to the conclusions I had arrived at more than eleven years ago, on the various matters which are discussed in *Primitive Marriage*.

With a little trouble, I might make a paper on examples of the form of capture, which I published in the *Argosy* in 1866, take the place of Chapter II. But that would be to depart from the idea of a reprint; and, besides, the paper I refer to has itself ceased to be complete, so many examples of the form have since been collected. The speculation is accordingly reissued with the rather meagre list of cases which originally prompted me to it.[1]

With *Primitive Marriage* I reprint a paper on *Kinship in Ancient Greece*, which was published in April and May, 1866, in the *Fortnightly Review*. It is the result of a special research to test, in the case of the Greeks, the correctness of the scheme of the evolution of systems of kinship propounded in *Primitive Marriage*, and was undertaken on a challenge from Mr. Gladstone, who believed that the scheme was inconsistent with Homeric facts. The reader will judge how far the evidence supports my views. I think myself that the case is made out to such an

---

[1] [The contents of the paper referred to in this paragraph have, in this edition, been included in the Appendix to *Primitive Marriage*.]

order of probability as to demand an answer; and that, having regard to this case alone, Sir Henry Maine, and others who agree with him, are no longer entitled to say, that the proposition that kinship through mothers only preceded kinship through fathers, rests upon the observation of scattered savage communities of other than Aryan race.

I hope yet to be able to throw some fresh light on the structure of the primitive human groups by an induction of the facts of Totemism, and exact analysis of the conditions under which Totemism arose. What I have already written on this subject of Totemism will be found in a brief article on Totemism in *Chambers's Encyclopædia*, published in 1867; and in a series of articles on "The Worship of Animals and Plants," published in the *Fortnightly Review* in the numbers for October and November, 1869, and for February, 1870.[1] A proof of the isolation and independence of the original stock groups,

---

[1] By a misprint, or slip of the pen, no doubt, Sir John Lubbock is made to state in the third edition of his *Origin of Civilization* (footnote, p. 252), that the articles above mentioned appeared "since the last," *i.e.* the second, edition of that book. The words should have been "before the first." The first edition of the *Origin of Civilization* was published in 1870, some time after the *last* of the series of articles referred to had appeared. The preface to the first edition of the *Origin of Civilization* bears date February, 1870.

while as yet the idea of stock alone had appeared as the germ from which systems of kinship were destined to be evolved, will add fresh interest to the discussion of the influence of exogamy and female kinship on the progress of civilization.

The Essays which follow *Kinship in Ancient Greece* are here published for the first time, and, taken together, are of the nature of a criticism of the principal works treating of early marriage law that have come to my knowledge, or been published, since *Primitive Marriage* appeared. These are—Professor Bachofen's *Das Mutterrecht*, Mr. L. H. Morgan's work *On the Systems of Consanguinity and Affinity of the Human Family*, and, lastly, Sir John Lubbock's *Origin of Civilization*. The account I have to give of the origin of the classificatory system of relationships forms the most important portion of the new matter; and next to this in interest will be found, I think, the explanation I offer of the fourfold division of the ancient Irish family, which Sir Henry Maine, in his recent work on *Early Institutions*, has, in my opinion, failed to account for. These Essays were originally intended to serve as an Introduction to the reprint of *Primitive Marriage*. Their scope and bulk making them unsuitable for that service, I issue them in their present form, and I have given the book a title suited to its varied contents. It will be perceived that I have not included Darwin's *Descent of Man* amongst the works I have noticed. Having carefully studied all that this great thinker has had to say of the primitive state, I feel that I must postpone the consideration of his views till after the completion of fresh investigations, the chief of which, relating to Totemism, I have already referred to. The excellent work, *Les Origines de la Famille*, by Professor A. Giraud-Teulon, of the University of Geneva—welcome as a proof that the study of early history makes progress on the Continent—raises no questions which I have felt called on to discuss in the present volume. Of the series of remarkable articles recently published in the *Nuova Antologia* (Florence, 1875-76), which bring to bear on the primitive state of man facts respecting the various "family" systems existing throughout the animal world, it must suffice to say here that they will have to be well considered by any writer who shall hereafter treat of the origin of the Family among men.[1]

[1] [Two paragraphs which followed, bearing upon the appearance of the form of capture in connection with endogamy—a matter fully discussed in *Primitive Marriage*—are omitted, as having served the purpose for which they were written.]

Extract from the Preface to the Original Edition of "Primitive Marriage."
[*Jan.*, 1865.]

IN the course of some inquiries which I had been making into the early history of civil society, the meaning and origin of the form of capture in marriage ceremonies fell to be investigated. The subject being in itself curious, as well as obscure, and one which has never hitherto, so far as I am aware, been handled, I venture to lay the result of my investigation before the public, hoping that it may to some extent interest by its novelty. To the philosophic reader I humbly submit my little book as an exercise in scientific history. If I am right in my conclusions as to the origin of the symbol of capture, my essay must be accepted as throwing new light on the primitive state. For it will be seen that the symbol is not peculiar to any of the families of mankind. The frequency of its occurrence is such as strongly to suggest—what I incline to believe—that the phase of society in which it originated existed, at some time or other, almost everywhere. Indeed, so far as my inquiries into early social phenomena have extended, I have found such similarity, so many correspondences, so much sameness in the forms of life prevailing among the races usually considered distinct, that I have come to regard the ethnological differences of the several families of mankind as of little or no weight compared with what they have in common. The most that can be attributed to those differences is, that they have affected the rate of development of the families, and the character of the development itself, in some of its secondary aspects.

Apart from the interest attaching to the form of capture as pointing out what most probably was the primitive form of human association, it will be found to have an important bearing on several social problems which have hitherto remained unsolved. I think that the most important portions of my work are Chapters VIII. and IX., in which the solution of some of these problems is attempted. These chapters, it will be seen, are strictly pertinent to the main subject of inquiry. In order to explain the appearance of the form of capture among endogamous peoples, it was necessary that I should examine the systems of kinship which anciently prevailed, and their influence on the structure of the primitive groups, so as to obtain a true view of the rise of caste and of endogamy.

ANALYTICAL TABLE OF CONTENTS.

PRIMITIVE MARRIAGE.

CHAPTER I.

Legal Symbolism and Primitive Life.

Method of the inquiry set forth and justified.—Study of races in their primitive condition and study of legal symbols the chief sources of information as to early history of society.—Failure here of usual methods of historical inquiry.—Connection between facts from savage life and legal symbolism.—How the two may be used in combination for classification of social phenomena in order of growth.—Value for general historical purposes of legal symbolism. — Illustrated from history of Roman law, pp. 1—8.

CHAPTER II.

The Form of Capture in Marriage Ceremonies.

Extent to which this symbol has been overlooked.—Two cases in which it has been noticed.—Explanation by Festus of its observance among the Romans.—Müller's explanation of its observance among the Spartans.—Cause shown for rejection of Müller's view.—Nature of the symbol set forth.—Instances of its occurrence.—Inference that may be made as to the extent of its former prevalence, pp. 9—21.

CHAPTER III.

The Origin of the Form of Capture.

This symbol must imply something more than the mere lawlessness of savages.—It does imply that wives were at one time systematically obtained by theft or force.—That women of foreign tribes could be got for wives only by theft or by force cannot, by itself, explain occurrence of symbolism.—That the symbol could not have originated among endogamous tribes.—When symbol of capture used by an endogamous tribe, inference that tribe had at one time not been endogamous.—If exogamous tribes existed, and a state of war usually prevailed between neighbouring tribes, each tribe could get wives only by theft or force.—How this, supposing it fact, would originate the symbol of capture, pp. 22—30.

CHAPTER IV.

On the Prevalence of the Practice of Capturing Wives, de facto.

Its prevalence among Indians of South America.—And of North America also.—In the Deccan and in Affghanistan.—In old times, in Muscovy, Lithuania, and Livonia, and other parts of Northern Europe.—Among Kalmucks, Kirghis, Nogais, Circassians, and other tribes who observe the form of capture. Among the Australasians.—Constantly referred to in legends of New Zealanders.—Conjoined, it seems, in New Zealand, Feejee, and other Pacific islands with cannibalism.—Capture among modes of constituting marriage enumerated in Institutes of Menu.—This the prototype of the Roman and Spartan forms.—Inference as to origin of symbol.—Marriage of captured Gentile women allowed by the Mosaic code.—Additional evidence of capture supplied by observance of the form of capture.—How far evidence of it is also supplied by Greek traditions.—By the rape of the Sabines.—The Irish traditions.—The Scriptural account of carrying off of the daughters of Shiloh.—Summing up of evidence, pp. 31—49.

CHAPTER V.

OF THE RULE AGAINST MARRIAGE BETWEEN MEMBERS OF THE SAME TRIBE.—OF THE COINCIDENCE OF THIS RULE WITH THE PRACTICE OF CAPTURING WIVES DE FACTO, AND WITH THE FORM OF CAPTURE IN MARRIAGE CEREMONIES.

Exogamy and the form of capture coincident among the Khonds, among the Kalmucks, among the Circassians.—Exogamy among the Yurak Samoyeds of Siberia, the Kafirs, the Sodhas, and other tribes.—Among the Warali.—The Magar tribes.—Dr. Latham on prevalence of exogamy.—Provision of Institutes of Menu. — Theory of its origin.—Social state of tribes of Munniepore, and tribes of Australia, America, and Pacific Islands examined with reference to that theory.—Exogamy in New Zealand and among the Feejees.—Exogamy and capture of women among the Picts. Conclusion, that exogamy has been a widely-prevailing principle, and usually coincident with capture of wives, or the form of capture, pp. 50—71.

CHAPTER VI.

ON THE STATE OF HOSTILITY, pp. 72, 73.

CHAPTER VII.

EXOGAMY: ITS ORIGIN.—COMPARATIVE ARCHAISM OF EXOGAMY AND ENDOGAMY.

That connection between exogamy and both the systematic capture of women for wives and the form of capture has been established.—Origin of exogamy to be referred to female infanticide.—It cannot be referred to a feeling against marriage with kinsfolk.—Grouping of the less advanced races of men according to their rules as to marriage, which shows a series, with exogamy and endogamy as extremes.—Facts which suggest that endogamous tribes have been exogamous. Conversion of an endogamous into an exogamous tribe inconceivable.—Either, then, exogamy is more archaic than endogamy, or the principles are both original and independent of each other.—Propositions to be maintained, in which it is involved that exogamy preceded endogamy in order of appearance, pp. 74—82.

CHAPTER VIII.

ANCIENT SYSTEMS OF KINSHIP AND THEIR INFLUENCE ON THE STRUCTURE OF PRIMITIVE GROUPS.

Growth of systems of kinship.—The fact of consanguinity a fact of observation, and, therefore, it must at one time have been unobserved.—The social state while it was unobserved.—The first effect of it being perceived would be the conception of stock, or the common kindred of the members of a group.—That the most ancient system in which the idea of blood-relationship was embodied, was a system of kinship through females only. — How the idea of blood-relationship must have originated a system of kinship through females.—Uncertainty of fatherhood would prevent acknowledgment of kinship through males.—And nothing else could have that effect.—Appropriation of a woman to a particular man, or to men of one blood, as wife, the condition of the requisite certainty of fatherhood.—How it is probable that such appropriation of women to particular men cannot have existed in the earliest times.—Effect of conditions of subsistence on balance of the sexes.—Males must have been in a majority.—Promiscuous or polyandrous arrangements therefore a necessity.—How the rise of a system of kinship would simplify the formation of them.—That systems of polyandry have existed, and still exist.—Polyandry a form of promiscuity, and seemingly an advance from a grosser promiscuity.—Its connection with kinship through females only, and that the latter may be inferred from it.—Two types of polyandry.—The prevalence of polyandry.—The Nair-type of polyandry, which leaves paternity uncertain, described.—The Deega and Beena marriages of Ceylon.—Incidents of Nair polyandry remaining amongst the Kocch.—Progress seems to have been from the lower, or Nair, to the higher, or Tibetan, polyandry.—Tibetan type of polyandry described.—It admitted of kinship through males.—Tibetan polyandry in a state of decadence in Ladak.—A test of the former prevalence of polyandry obtained in the Levirate.—Inference as to former prevalence of polyandry from existence of the Levirate.—Evidence of existence of kinship through females only, and inference therefrom, where the two are not found together, as to former prevalence of polyandry.—Philo's report as to marriage law of Sparta considered.—Evidence that kinship through females only the first system of kinship summed up.—It must, at any rate, have prevailed wherever exogamy prevailed.—Sir H. S. Maine's views of ancient kinship.—That the primitive groups were, or were assumed to be, homogeneous.—That the system of kinship through females only tended to render the exogamous groups heterogeneous, and thus to supersede the system of capturing wives.—That the system of kinship through females only was succeeded by a system which acknowledged kinship through males also, and which, in most cases, passed into a system which acknowledged kinship through males only.—Attempt to sketch the history of this revolution.—That the system of kinship through males tended to rear up homogeneous groups, and thus to restore the original condition of affairs among exogamous races, as regards both the practice of capturing wives and the evolution of the form of capture.—That under the combined influence of exogamy and female kinship, there might be, within a tribe, a balance of men and women regarded as of different descent, and, therefore, free to marry each other, consistently with exogamy.—That, this stage reached, a tribe grown proud through successes in war might become a caste.—That caste may appear while a people is still polyandrous.—That, on kinship becoming agnatic, the members of a caste might feign themselves to be descended from a common ancestor, and so become endogamous.—Inference from observance of form of capture by an endogamous race. Effects on early society of the law of blood-feud, pp. 83—146.

CHAPTER IX.

The Decay of Exogamy in Advancing Communities.

Causes of break-down of exogamy, where it perished gradually and without endogamy succeeding it, to be inquired into, for example's sake, in the case of the Greeks and Romans.—Reasons for holding that Greeks and Romans were exogamous.—The composition and organisation of their tribes and commonwealths.—The old theory of the composition of States.—Reasons why it must be rejected.—New theory suggested by results of this inquiry.—If this theory be admitted, area in which exogamy prevailed may be greatly extended.—Breakdown of exogamy intimately connected with evolution of clans and families, and of clan and family estates, within the tribe.—Effect of laws of succession in limiting the acknowledgment of relationship.—Exogamy died out, because relationship was thus narrowed.—Effect of the law of testaments.—Motive for violation of rule of exogamy in the case of female heiresses, pp. 147—158.

ANALYTICAL TABLE OF CONTENTS.

CHAPTER X.

CONCLUSION, pp. 159—161.

APPENDIX TO PRIMITIVE MARRIAGE, pp. 165—191.

KINSHIP IN ANCIENT GREECE.

Purpose of the inquiry to test, in case of the ancient Greeks, scheme of development of systems of kinship propounded in *Primitive Marriage*.—Scheme set forth, and, as explanatory of it, outline given of scheme of development of systems of marriage propounded in same work.—First, of Greek kinship as it appears in the Homeric poems.—Position of the wedded wife.—Blood-ties acknowledged through both father and mother.—Homeric pedigrees traced through fathers.—Inference from shortness of those pedigrees.—Evidence that blood-ties through mother held more sacred in that period than those through father.—Secondly, of the post-Homeric history of kinship in Greece.—Growth of opinion unfavourable to idea of kinship through mother, and close approach made to agnation.—Evidence of this.—Thirdly, of the traditions of the Greeks and the customs of their congeners.—(1) Incestuous connections among ancient Persians.—Xanthus' account of the Medes.—(2) Xenophon's account of the Lacedæmonians.—Polyandry prevailed among the Lacedæmonians according to Polybius.—Corroboration of this in legend of Lycurgus.—(3) Suggestions of the Levirate in legends of the house of Priam.—(4) Evidence of female kinship, and therefore of some degree of promiscuity in the sister-marriages allowed at Athens, and in a provision of the laws of Solon.—(5) Indications in Greek legends of high position of women in ancient times, and of kinship through females only.—Facts indicative of ancient supremacy of women in families.—The system of kinship through females only traced through the custom of naming children after the mother.—Tradition that ancestors of Greeks emerged from the savage state, and had no marriage.—Facts relative to kinship among the Greeks, previously adduced, consistent with the tradition.—Inference made that polyandry preceded monandry, and that kinship through females only preceded kinship through males as well as through females, pp. 195—246.

THE CLASSIFICATORY SYSTEM OF RELATIONSHIPS.

CHAPTER I.

Mr. Morgan's Conjectural Solution of the Origin of the Classificatory System of Relationship.

Mr. Morgan's first impression as to the Iroquois relationships.—Origin of his work on the Classificatory System of Relationships.—Its contents.—Objects of his inquiry.—His conjectural solution and series of stages in social development involved in it.—Conjectural solution examined in reference to the three most primitive forms of the classificatory system.—If these explained, origin of classificatory system is explained, and less primitive forms easy of explanation.—First, as to the origin of the Malayan system of relationships.—Main features of that system set forth.—Customs or "stages" assumed by Mr Morgan to explain it, viz., brother and sister-marriages, the communal family, and the Hawaiian custom.—What Mr. Morgan claims to have shown about it.—That it is a system of blood-relationships assumed by him.—Brother and sister-marriages the only "stage" actually required for the solution.—Defects and oversights of Mr. Morgan's explanation.—Conjectural solution examined next, as to origin of the "Turanian" and "Ganowánian" systems of relationships.—Distinctive features of those systems set forth.—Mr. Morgan's explanations of them tested at two leading points. Were his Reason at the first point well founded, the Hawaian custom would have given Turanian and Ganowánian instead of corresponding Malayan relationships.—Supposing it failed to do this, exogamy supervening upon it, could not have had effects ascribed to it by Mr. Morgan.—The additional limitation on marriage that would have been imposed by exogamy superinduced on Hawaian custom.—Reason insufficient on Mr. Morgan's own ground, and inconsistent with Mr. Morgan's assumptions.—And insufficient whether we start from the "Communal Family" or from the "Hawaian custom."—Mr. Morgan's Reasons at second point.—Both rest on pure assumption.—What they assume, and a "slight variation" between assumptions made in them.—What involved in them.—They cannot be accepted.—Two radical mistakes which have vitiated Mr. Morgan's attempt at explanation.—Remarks on assumption that the classificatory system is a system of blood-ties.—Maintained, that it is a system of mutual salutations merely, and not a system of blood-ties.—Observations on the "stages" of the conjectural solution, pp. 249—276.

CHAPTER II.

The Origin of the Classificatory System of Relationships.

Origin of the classificatory system to be looked for in some early marriage-law.—Systems of addresses and systems of blood-ties must have originated in the same set of circumstances, and must have had, for a time, a common history.—Proposed to test the hypothesis of rise of systems of kinship contained in *Primitive Marriage* by its fitness to explain the classificatory system.—And, first, as to the Malayan form of that system.—Further explanations given as to Malayan relationships.—A household or family of the Nair type, and the nomenclature required for it.—How the type of such a family must have been altered in the transition to Tibetan polyandry.—Effect of that transition in extending application of nomenclature.—How the terms used in it as extended would acquire definite signification as if relative to descents.—How they would become applicable to relatives at law.—Tibetan polyandry not essential to explanation of Malayan relationships. — Explanation summarised.— Next, as to the "Turanian" and "Ganowánian" forms.—Extent of difference between these and the Malayan form.—The main difference is introduction of cousinry, and those who are each other's cousins are persons accounted of different blood.—Varieties of blood introduced into families by exogamy, and the differences between forms of classificatory system are all referable to the extent to which among different peoples the pressure of the notion of blood was yielded to.—Assumed, but for convenience only, that "Turanian" and "Ganowánian" forms developed out of Malayan.—The five distinctive features in which the "Turanian" and "Ganowánian" forms agree accounted for.—Not inevitable that exogamy should produce all these effects, and peculiarities of nomenclature of some North American tribes thus explained. —How the differences between the "Ganowánian" and "Turanian" forms may be accounted for.—Cousin marriages, and marriages made by cousins which would have the same effect as cousin-marriages as regards blood of cousins' children. —Tibetan polyandry essential to explanation of "Turanian" and "Ganowánian" forms.—Esquimo form of the classificatory system may be similarly explained, pp. 277—301.

BACHOFEN'S "DAS MUTTERRECHT."

Das Mutterrecht, an inquiry into the gynaikocracy of the ancient world.—It first announced that kinship through females only everywhere preceded kinship through males.—Account of Bachofen's scheme of human progress.—At first, human beings lived in a state of hetairism.—This put an end to, and marriage (monogamous) introduced by women under the influence of a religious inspiration.—Marriage established by force (Amazonianism), and women, whose combination introduced it, accordingly became the heads of families.—Children named after mothers, and rights of succession traced through women.—Improvement of religious faith came along with the triumph of women, and, for a time, fostered their cause.—Their position, however, lost through a religious influence.—Dionysos promulgated that fatherdom alone was divine, and a mother a nurse only.—Amazonian risings against this gospel ineffectual.—Bacchanalian excesses, by restoring hetairism, laid fresh basis for gynaikocracy.—It finally disappeared under influence of a new religious growth, the "Apollonic," "Solar" conception of fatherdom.—With Bachofen religion is a mere expression of the circumstances of a people, but of what circumstances never explained, and causes of progress therefore left undisclosed.—His explanation of kinship being traced through women only remarked upon.—Extent of his contribution to knowledge, pp. 319—325.

"COMMUNAL MARRIAGE."

"Communal Marriage," the starting-point of a scheme of social progress propounded by Sir John Lubbock.—As used by him, it means two distinct things.—Sense in which he regards it as initial stage in social progress.—His history of the growth of marriage.—The evidence offered by him for his initial stage in two branches.—Progress from initial stage shown by general reasoning.—General reasoning and second branch of evidence turn on principles contradictory of each other.—First branch of evidence adduced by him of communism in women, being cases in which communism reported to have existed.—That evidence examined.—Amount of it small.—Wanting in relevancy.—Second branch of evidence of communism in women, being cases in which communism inferred to have existed.—Expiation for marriage.—Conditions on which, from the facts alleged to imply that, inference of ancient communism might be drawn.—Those conditions not satisfied, and inference of communism conferring "communal rights" having existed not maintainable.—Of the contradictory principles set up by Sir J. Lubbock, which to be preferred and which rejected.—That to be decided on facts relating to capture of women for wives. —As to most ancient nations, our knowledge of this matter entirely derived from the form of capture.—That in almost all cases represents a group-act, a siege, a battle, or an armed invasion.—All cases of capture in its transition to a symbolism have that character also.—And so, mostly, have the facts of actual capture of wives.—Inference made that the capture of women for wives has usually been the act of a group or of a detachment from a group.—And, accordingly, that there could have been no system of appropriation of women by individual captors, such as could have broken up the "communal marriage" system had it prevailed, and introduced monogamous marriage.—The principle on which Sir J. Lubbock's account of social progress is based must, therefore, be rejected, while the existence of his initial stage itself had not been made probable.—Inference made thereupon, pp. 329—347.

DIVISIONS OF THE ANCIENT IRISH FAMILY.

Account of singular arrangement of the family among the ancient Irish.—Sir H. S. Maine's theory of this arrangement.—That theory refuted.—Text (in two branches) illustrating this family arrangement cited from the Book of Aicill.—Inference as to nature of family arrangement made from first branch of text. —Authority in favour of this inference.—Organization of family arrangement according to new reading of text further explained.—Features of it which are intelligible on this view. —Construction of second branch of text.—The organization operated a departure from ordinary succession law.—Object of

forming it, its functions, and its relation to the family.—The
organization a division of the Fine or Sept.—Within a sub-
group of the Fine, and therewith connected by sameness of
stock.—Limits of recognized consanguinity.—Geilfine tribe
relationship and Geilfine tribe terms of double meaning, and,
in wider sense, extended to all within recognized consanguinity.
—Limits of recognized consanguinity in ancient Wales.—
Geilfine tribe (in wider sense) and its chief answered to the
"kindred" and the "chief of kindred" of the Welsh, and the
Geilfine tribe, or body of kinsmen within recognized consanguinity, was the sub-group of Fine which organization
represented.—Use of divisional organization in levying assess-
ments for crimes of kinsmen.—Its primary purpose, more
probably, to regulate possession of and succession to property.
—This, at any rate, its most striking effect.—It was not
confined to the chieftain class, but probably originated with
them, to regulate succession to ancestral lands, and spread, by
imitation, among tribesmen.—Rights of succession between
the divisions.—Apportionment of divisional property among
members of division. Working of organization, as to succession, illustrated.—How such a system of entail of ancestral
lands may have arisen.—Resemblances in Welsh laws of
succession to ancestral lands.—And in rules of succession to
ancestral land in Western India, pp. 351—387.

PRIMITIVE MARRIAGE.

CHAPTER I.

INTRODUCTORY.

Legal Symbolism and Primitive Life.

The chief sources of information regarding the early history of civil society are, first, the study of races in their primitive condition ; and, second, the study of the symbols employed by advanced nations in the constitution or exercise of civil rights. From these studies pursued together, we obtain, to a large extent, the power of classifying social phenomena as more or less archaic, and thus of connecting and arranging in their order the stages of human advancement.

None of the usual methods of historical inquiry conduct us back to forms of life so nearly primitive as many that have come down into our own times. The geological record, of course, exhibits races as rude as any now living, some perhaps even more so, but then it goes no farther than to inform us what food they ate, what weapons they used, and what was the character of their ornaments. More than this was not to be expected from that record, for it was not in its nature to preserve any memorials of those aspects of human life in which the philosopher is chiefly interested—of the family or tribal groupings, the domestic and political organisation. Again, the facts disclosed by philology as to the civil condition of the Indo-European race before its dispersion from its original head-quarters,—the earliest, chronologically considered, which we possess respecting the *social* state of mankind, —cannot be said to tell us anything of the origin or early progress of civilization. Assuming the correctness of the generalization by which philologers have attempted to reconstruct the social economy of the Aryans, we find that people, at an unknown date before the dawn of tradition, occupying nearly the same point of advancement as that now occupied by the pastoral hordes of Kirghiz Tartary, and leading much the same sort of life. They had marriage laws regulating the rights and obligations of husbands and wives, of parents and children; they recognized the ties of blood through both parents; they had great flocks and herds, in defence of which they often did battle, and they lived under a patriarchal government with monarchical features. It is interesting—a short time ago we should have said surprising—to find that such progress had been so early made. But in all other respects this so-called revelation of philology is void of instruction. Those Aryan institutions are—to use the language of geology—post-pliocene, separated by a long interval from the foundations of civil society, and throwing back upon them no light. Marriage laws, agnatic relationship, and kingly government, belong, in the order of development, to recent times.

For the features of primitive life, we must look, not to tribes of the Kirghiz type, but to those of Central Africa, the wilds of America, the hills of India, and the islands of the Pacific; with some of which we find marriage laws unknown, the family system undeveloped, and even the only acknowledged blood-relationship that through mothers. These facts of to-day are, in a sense, the most ancient history. In the sciences of law and society, old means not old in chronology but in structure: that is most archaic which lies nearest to the beginning of human progress considered as a development, and that is most modern which is farthest removed from that beginning.

And since the historical nations were so far advanced at the earliest dates to which even philology can lead us back, the scientific investigation of the progress of mankind must not deal with them, in the first instance, but with the very rude forms of life still existing, and the rudest of which we have accounts. The preface of general history must be compiled from the materials presented by barbarism. Happily, if we may say so, these materials are abundant. So unequally has the species been developed, that almost every conceivable phase of progress may be studied, as somewhere observed and recorded. And thus the philosopher, fenced from mistake, as to the order of development, by the interconnection of the stages and their shading into one another by gentle gradations, may draw a clear and decided outline of the course of human progress in times long antecedent to those to which even philology can make reference. All honour to philology; but in the task of reconstructing the past, to which its professors declare themselves to be devoted, they must be contented to act as assistants rather than as principals.

We have said that the preface of general history must be compiled from materials presented by barbarism. Some may account it illogical to prefix a scheme of early progress formed on a view of societies that have not yet advanced far, if at all, from savagery, to a scheme of further progress deduced from the written histories of nations whose origin and early training we are unacquainted with. But, in point of fact, it is not so. It is the best proof of the propriety of such a course—as well as of the continuity and uniform character of human progress—that we can trace everywhere, disguised under a variety of symbolical forms in the higher layers of civilization, the rude modes of life and forms of law with which the examination of the lower makes us familiar. Indeed, were these remarks not merely general and introductory to the investigation of the origin of one particular symbol, many instances of this correspondence between the higher and lower levels might be cited, to show that the symbolism of law in the light of a knowledge of primitive life, is the best key to unwritten history.

Of the value of that symbolism—of that reverence for the past to which it owes its origin—there will be occasion to say something hereafter. Meantime, we observe that, wherever we discover symbolical forms, we are justified in inferring that in the past life of the people employing them, there were corresponding realities; and if, among the primitive races which we examine, we find such realities as might naturally pass into such forms on an advance taking place in civility, then we may safely conclude (keeping within the conditions of a sound inference) that what these now are, those employing the symbols once were. History is thus made to ratify conclusions derived from the observation of rude tribes; while such observation, again, is made to furnish the key to many of the enigmas of history.

For it is not as regards unwritten history merely that the two sources of information specified at the outset are of importance. Apart from the tests of truth afforded by the minute knowledge of primitive modes of life and their classification as more or less archaic, nothing could be more delusive than written history itself. In Roman law, to take a convenient example, Confarreatio has the foremost place among the modes of constituting marriage. Usus is just mentioned in the twelve tables, which contain a provision against the wife coming into the Manus of her husband through Usus. Coemptio does not appear in the old law of Rome at all, nor is there any mention of it earlier than that by Gaius. But it can easily be shown that Usus and Coemptio come first in order of age, and Confarreatio later; that is to say, the two former are more archaic than the latter. Yet have recent learned writers, overlooking this fact and the meaning of legal symbolism, represented Usus and Coemptio as forms invented and introduced by the legislators of Rome, whereby the plebians might have their wives in Manu, and enjoy the other advantages of Justæ Nuptiæ; Usus as an invention; and the fictitious sale in Coemptio as merely a device of legislative ingenuity. The true explanation of the late appearance of both Usus and the fictitious sale in the Roman law, is this—that the law at first was not that of the whole people but of a limited aristocracy, who, with a Sabine king and priesthood, adopted the Sabine religious ceremony of marriage; that the law long totally ignored the life and usages of the mass, and that *their* modes of marrying and giving in marriage began to appear, and to make their mark in the law, only on the popular element in the city becoming of importance. Instead of marriage *per coemptionem* being the invention of legislators, it was of spontaneous popular growth, and must have been as old as the establishment of peaceful relations between tribes and families. All fictions, or nearly all, have had their germs in facts; became fictions or merely symbolical forms afterwards. And that the fictitious sale was originally an actual sale and purchase, cannot be doubted by any one who knows that marriage by the form of actual sale has prevailed almost universally among rude populations.

We see in the case of the Roman law how incomplete must necessarily be the history of the law of a country, as written on the face of it. The law is at first that of the dominant and presumably the most advanced classes —the literates, warriors, and statesmen; the rest of the community are beyond its pale, a law unto themselves. When the levelling processes, by which the lower classes succeed in the long run in acquiring rights more or less equal, have gone on for some time, then the ruder customs followed by them before and since the commencement of the State appear in a modified form in what is now for the first time really becoming the law of the people. Civility seems suddenly to assume the garb and the air, and to use the gutturals of barbarism; legal processes are gone through with the frantic howls and gesticulations of armed Ojibeways; and while all this, to those who are ignorant of primitive times, seems mere idle pantomime, sometimes silly, sometimes odd, sometimes puzzling by its intricacy, to those who are prepared to receive their suggestions, the forms employed are pregnant with meaning and instruction. Fortunately all the nations in the world have not advanced in civility *pari passu;* and what is pantomime with one people, we discern to be grimmest reality with another. Were it not for this inequality of development, in what mysteries would the history of the race be enveloped! What Michelet calls the poetry of law would have to be received as such simply; as so many grotesqueries or graces introduced into the ways of life to satisfy the popular fancy. As it is, however, the so-called poetry of law, the symbolic forms that appear in a code or in popular customs, tell us as certainly of the early usages of a people, as the rings in the transverse section of a tree tell of its age.

The Libripens, with his scales, officiating at a will or act of adoption, seems out of place; but his presence illustrates the source whence all ideas of formal dispositions were derived—the sale of fungibles. So does an old form of process preserved by Gaius—the Legis Actio Sacramenti of the Romans—prove that cultivated people to have been at one time *in pari casu* as regards the administration of justice with many races which we find ignorant of legal proceedings, and dependent for the settlement of their disputes on force of arms or the good offices of neutral parties interfering as arbiters.

So far, briefly, of the importance of the symbolism of law and of the study of races in their primitive condition. What follows is an attempt at a practical exemplification in a new direction of the aid derivable from these sources in the task of unveiling the past.

CHAPTER II.

THE FORM OF CAPTURE IN MARRIAGE CEREMONIES.[1]

IN the whole range of legal symbolism there is no symbol more remarkable than that of capture in marriage ceremonies—the origin of which it is our purpose to investigate—nor is there any the meaning of which has been less studied. So far as we know, neither has the extent to which it prevails been made the subject of inquiry; nor its significance the subject of thought. In two cases, indeed, the occurrence of the symbol could not fail to receive some attention. But naturally, it did not lie in the way of the historians of either Greece or Rome to examine the matter very minutely, or to follow up the suggestions which, upon examination, it might have yielded, as to the early condition of the Dorians or Latins. Accordingly, the custom has been accepted as meaning no more than Festus said it did among the Romans, than Müller says it did among the Spartans; as indicating nothing at Rome but the popular appreciation of the good fortune of Romulus in the rape of the

---

[1] [A fuller collection of examples of the Form of Capture than could be made when this chapter was written will be found in the Appendix to *Primitive Marriage*, Note *A*.]

Sabines;[1] as indicating, at Sparta, the feeling that a young woman "could not surrender her freedom and virgin purity unless compelled by the violence of the stronger sex."[2] It is surprising that writers so acute should have rested content with such explanations, and that their views should have been so generally adopted. The theory of Festus we shall have occasion to notice hereafter: of that of Müller we observe that before we can entertain it, we must suppose that in the exceedingly lax community of the Spartans, or at least within certain of the tribes composing that community, there had been an early period of austere virtue, the tradition of which was still so influential as to compel the Spartans to observe in their marriages this custom as the shadow of their former delicacy. Now, of the existence of such a period of prudery among the ancient Dorians, or among the Pelasgi, or the Achæans, there is not a tittle of evidence. On the contrary, such evidence as we have, points to the Lacedæmonian customs as having been an improvement on ancient practice. Savages are not remarkable for delicacy of feeling in matters of sex, and the wandering hordes, who in succession overrun the Peloponnesus, were no better than savages when they first come under our observation.[3] Again, no case can be cited of a primitive people among

---

[1] Festus, *De Verborum Significatione*—Rapi.

[2] Müller's *Dorians*, Book iv., c. iv., sec. 2; and see Rawlinson's Notes, Herod., Book vi., 65.

[3] They were certainly as savage as the Khonds, with whom they agreed in cultivating a religion requiring human sacrifices.

whom the seizure of brides is rendered necessary by maidenly coyness. On the contrary, it might be shown, were it worth while to deal seriously with this view, that women among rude tribes are usually depraved, and inured to scenes of depravity from their earliest infancy. In this state of the facts, it is remarkable that any one should have been satisfied with so improbable an explanation.

Rejecting, then, the primitive prudery hypothesis, which requires for its basis a declension from ancient standards of purity—of the existence of which we have no evidence—we proceed to examine the various phases in which the symbol of capture is presented. We shall find it in places far from classic ground, and pointing, in all its varieties, so steadily to the true theory of its origin, that the mere exhibition of its phases will lead the reader to anticipate much of what we have to say on the subject. In order to see what is the precise state of the facts with which we have to deal, it is necessary to say something of the nature of the symbol, and to adduce at some length such accounts of it as we find in our authorities.

The symbol of capture occurs whenever, after a contract of marriage, it is necessary for the constitution of the relation of husband and wife, that the bridegroom or his friends should go through the form of feigning to steal the bride, or carry her off from her relations by superior force. The marriage is agreed upon by bargain, and the theft or abduction follows as a concerted matter of form, to make valid the marriage. The test, then, of the presence of the symbol in any case is, that the capture is concerted, and is preceded by a contract of marriage. If there is no preceding contract, the case is one of actual abduction.

So far of the nature of the symbol. We proceed to examine some instances of its occurrence. That the form was observed in the marriages of the Dorians, and was, equally with betrothal, requisite as a preliminary of marriage, rests chiefly on the authority of Herodotus and Plutarch.[1] The evidence of Herodotus is indirect, and is contained in the well-known passage in which he explains how Demaratus robbed Lestychides of his bride Percalus, to whom he had been betrothed—*forestalling* him in carrying her off and marrying her.[2] The case was one of actual abduction; but the language of Herodotus implies that it remained for Lestychides, in order to make Percalus his wife, that he should go through the form of carrying her off. With this must be conjoined the express statement of Plutarch,[3] that the Spartan bridegroom always carried off the bride by feigned violence. He says, indeed, *by violence;* but at the same time he shows that the seizure was made by friendly concert between the parties. These passages must be held sufficiently to prove that the custom existed at Sparta. It is equally certain that it was observed at Rome,[4] in the plebeian marriages which were not constituted by Confarreatio or Coemptio. The

---

[1] Müller's *Dorians, ut supra.*
[2] Herodotus, Book vi. 65.
[3] *Life of Lycurgus.*
[4] Festus, *ut supra*—Rapi: Pothier, Pandectæ, etc., App., Title II., Book xxiii.

bridegroom and his friends — the time agreed upon having arrived—invaded the house of the bride and carried off the lady with feigned force from the lap of her mother, or of her nearest female relation if the mother were dead or absent. The seizure is vividly described by Apuleius[1] in the story of the "Captive Damsel," in which he is understood to have had the plebeian form of marriage in view. The lady, narrating how she had been carried off, says that her mother having dressed her becomingly in nuptial apparel, was loading her with kisses, and looking forward to a future line of descendants, when on a sudden a band of robbers, armed like gladiators, rushed in with glittering swords, made straight for her chamber in a compact column, and, without any struggle or resistance whatever on the part of the servants, tore her away half dead with fear from the bosom of her trembling mother. The custom is said still to prevail to a great extent among the Hindus.[2] It may well do so, for we find what must, as we shall show, be held to be the form of capture, prescribed as a marriage ceremony to the Hindus in the Sutras.[3] It prevails among the Khonds in the hill tracts of Orissa. The marriage being agreed upon, a feast, to which the families of the parties equally contribute, is prepared at the dwelling of the bride. "To

---

[1] Apuleius, *De Asino Aureo*, Book iv.
[2] M'Pherson's *Report upon the Khonds of the Districts of Ganjam and Cullack*, p. 55. Calcutta, 1842.
[3] *Indische Studien*, p. 325. By Dr. Weber. Berlin, 1862.

the feast," says Major M'Pherson,[1] "succeed dancing and song. When the night is far spent, the principals in the scene are raised by an uncle of each upon his shoulders, and borne through the dance. The burdens are suddenly exchanged, and the uncle of the youth disappears with the bride. The assembly divides into two parties; the friends of the bride endeavour to arrest, those of the bridegroom to cover, her flight, and men, women, and children mingle in mock conflict, which is often carried to great lengths." "On one occasion," says Major-General Campbell,[2] "I heard loud cries proceeding from a village close at hand. Fearing some quarrel, I rode to the spot, and there I saw a man bearing away upon his back something enveloped in an ample covering of scarlet cloth; he was surrounded by twenty or thirty young fellows, and by them protected from the desperate attacks made upon him by a party of young women. On seeking an explanation of this novel scene, I was told that the man had just been married, and his precious burden was his blooming bride, whom he was conveying to his own village. Her youthful friends—as, it appears, is the custom—were seeking to regain possession of her, and hurled stones and bamboos at the head of the devoted bridegroom, until he reached the confines of his own village.[3] Then the tables were

---

[1] M'Pherson's *Report, ut supra.*
[2] *Personal Narrative of Service, etc., in Khondistan,* 1864, p. 44.
[3] The hurling of old shoes, etc., after the bridegroom among ourselves, *may be* a relic of a similar custom. It is a sham assault on the person carrying off the lady; and in default of any more

turned, and the bride was fairly won; and off her young friends scampered, screaming and laughing, but not relaxing their speed till they reached their own village." The custom may be presumed to prevail among the Koles, the Ghonds, and the other congeners of the Khonds; but we are without authority on the subject.

According to De Hell,[1] the form of capture is observed in the marriages of the noble or princely class among the Kalmucks. The price to be paid for the bride to her father having been fixed, the bridegroom sets out on horseback, accompanied by the chief nobles of the horde to which he belongs, to carry her off. "A sham resistance is always made by the people of her camp, in spite of which she fails not to be borne away on a richly caparisoned horse, with loud shouts and *feux de joie*." Dr. Clarke describes the ceremony differently, and it is possible that it assumes different forms in the different nations of the Kalmucks. "The ceremony of marriage among the Kalmucks," he says,[2] "is performed on horseback. A girl is first mounted, who rides off in full speed. Her lover pursues; if he overtakes her, she becomes his wife, and the marriage is consummated on the spot; after this she returns with him to his tent. But it sometimes happens that the woman does not wish to marry the person by whom she is pursued; in this

plausible explanation—and we know of none such—it may fairly be considered as probable that it is the form of capture in its last stage of disintegration.

[1] Xavier Hommaire de Hell, *Travels in the Steppes of the Caspian Sea.* Lond. 1847, p. 259.

[2] *Travels*, etc., vol. i., p. 433.

case, she will not suffer him to overtake her. We were assured that no instance occurs of a Kalmuck girl being thus caught, unless she have a partiality to the pursuer. If she dislikes him, she rides, to use the language of English sportsmen, 'neck or nought,' until she has completely effected her escape, or until her pursuer's horse becomes exhausted, leaving her at liberty to return, and to be afterwards chased by some more favoured admirer." This ride for a wife is never undertaken until after the price for her has been fixed between the friends of the parties, the lover having to pay for as well as to catch her. The custom is not mentioned in the account of the Kalmucks by Pallas, who knew of their marriage customs only by hearsay. But it favours the supposition that there are varieties of the form in use among this people, that Bergman [1] describes the ceremony somewhat differently from both Clarke and De Hell. The necessity for the appearance of using force is satisfied, according to Bergman, by the act of putting the bride by force upon horseback when she is about to be conducted to the hut prepared for her by the bridegroom. And, indeed, we find the form reduced to this minimum of pretence in not a few cases. Thus in North Friesland,[2] a young fellow, called the bride-lifter, lifts the bride and her two bridesmaids upon the waggon in which the married couple are to travel to their home.

---

[1] Bergman's *Streifereien*. Riga, 1804, vol. iii., p. 145, *et seq.*

[2] Weinhold, pp. 250, 251; and see the other authorities for like cases noted by Dr. Weber, *Indische Studien, ut supra.*

Among the Tunguzes and Kamchadales, a matrimonial engagement is not considered to be definitely concluded until the suitor has overcome his beloved by force, and torn her clothes—the maiden being bound by custom to defend her liberty to the utmost.[1] Also among the Bedouin Arabs it is necessary for the bridegroom to force the bride to enter his tent.[2] A similar custom existed among the French, at least in some provinces, in the 17th century.[3] In all the cases just mentioned the form assumed by the custom was analogous to the rule prescribed in the Sutras, where it was provided that at a certain vital stage of the marriage ceremony, *a strong man* and the bridegroom should forcibly draw the bride and make her sit down on a red ox-skin.[4]

There is good ground for believing that the form of capture is observed in the marriage ceremonies of the Nogay Tartars. The rule which prohibits a Kalmuck bride from entering the yurt of her parents for a year or more after her marriage, and which is undoubtedly connected with the form of capture, prevails among the Nogais, as it does also among the Kirghiz. At any rate, we find the custom in the Caucasus in the immediate neighbourhood of the Nogais. The form which it

---

[1] *Travels in Siberia*, Erman, vol. ii. p. 442, 1848 (Cowley's trans.).

[2] Burckhardt's *Notes on the Bedouins and Wahabys*. Lond. 1830, vol. i. p. 108.

[3] *Marriage Ceremonies, &c.*, Gaya, 2nd ed. Lond. 1698, p. 30.

[4] *Indische Studien, ut supra*.

assumes among the Circassians, indeed, closely resembles that observed in ancient Rome. The wedding is celebrated with noisy feasting and revelry, " in the midst of which the bridegroom has to rush in, and with the help of a few daring young men, to carry off the lady by force; and by this process she becomes his lawful wife."[1] The custom also prevailed till a recent date in Wales. Lord Kames[2] says that the following marriage ceremony was in his day, or at least had till shortly before, been customary among the Welsh : " On the morning of the wedding day, the bridegroom, accompanied by his friends on horseback, demands the bride. Her friends, who are likewise on horseback, give a positive refusal, upon which a mock scuffle ensues. The bride, mounted behind her nearest kinsman, is carried off and is pursued by the bridegroom and his friends, with loud shouts. It is not uncommon on such an occasion to see two or three hundred sturdy Cambro-Britons riding at full speed, crossing and jostling to the no small amusement of the spectators. When they have fatigued themselves and their horses, the bridegroom is suffered to overtake his bride. He leads her away in triumph, and the scene is concluded with feasting and festivity." Some such picture we should have had from De Hell had he expanded his account of the mock scuffle among the Kalmucks of the hordes of the bride and bridegroom.

[1] Louis Moser, *The Caucasus and its People*, Lond. 1856, p. 31; and see Spencer's *Travels in Circassia*, Lond. 1837, vol. ii. p. 375; and *Bell's Journal*, vol. ii. p. 221, Lond. 1840.

[2] *Sketches of the History of Man*, Book I. sec. 6, p. 449, Edin. 1807.

We have now found the custom in various parts of Europe and Asia; it occurs also in Africa and in America. Lord Kames vouches for the custom among the Inland Negroes.[1] "When the preliminaries of the marriage are adjusted, the bridegroom with a number of his companions set out at night and surround the house of the bride, as if intending to carry her off by force; she and her female attendants pretending to make all possible resistance, cry aloud for help, but no person appears." Speke[2] mentions an incident which he observed in Karague, and which *may* have been the sequel to a capture. "At night," he says, "I was struck by surprise to see a long noisy procession pass by where I sat, led by some men who carried on their shoulders a woman covered up in a blackened skin. On inquiry, however, I heard she was being taken to the hut of her espoused, where bundling fashion she would be put to bed; but it is only with virgins they take so much trouble." Traces of the custom are indeed frequently met with in Africa, but in so distinct and marked a form as that mentioned by Lord Kames we have not found it. His lordship has not given his authority. He mentions the custom, however, merely for its singularity, and apparently in ignorance of its connecting itself with any widespread practice of mankind, which demanded investigation. Among the primitive races throughout the whole continent of America traces of the form of capture (that is, customs seemingly of no significance,

---

[1] *Sketches, &c., ut supra.*
[2] *Journal of the Discovery of the Source of the Nile*, 1863, p. 198.

except in the light of this form) are of frequent occurrence. Among the people of Tierra del Fuego, however, the form itself appears almost in perfection. "As soon," says Captain Fitzroy, speaking of the Fuegians,[1] "as a youth is able to maintain a wife by his exertions in fishing or bird-catching, *he obtains the consent of her relations,* and does some piece of work, such as helping to make a canoe, or prepare sealskins, &c., for her parents. Having built or stolen a canoe for himself, he watches for an opportunity, and carries off his bride. If she is unwilling, she hides herself in the woods, until her admirer is heartily tired of looking for her, and gives up the pursuit; but this seldom happens."

These are among the best marked instances of the form with which we are acquainted. The instances fix our attention especially upon a few geographical points. But nothing in nature stands by itself. Each example of the form leads us to contemplate a great area over which the custom once prevailed, just as a fossil fish in rock on a hill-side forces us to conceive of the whole surrounding country as at one time under water. Were we to enumerate and examine all the customs which seem to us connected with the form, we should be led into discussions foreign to our purpose, and there would be few primitive races with which we should not have to deal. Suffice it, that the form which of old appeared so well defined in the peninsulas of Italy and Greece, may be traced thence, on the one hand, northwards through France and Britain, south-westwards through

[1] *Voyages of the Adventure and Beagle,* vol. ii. p. 182; 1839.

Spain, and north-eastwards through Prussia; on the other hand, northwards through ancient Thessaly and Macedonia, into the mountainous regions on the Black Sea and the Caspian; again, that the form which is perfect among the Kalmucks shades away into faint and fainter traces throughout almost all the races of the Mongolidæ; that we may assume it of frequent occurrence in Africa, as it unquestionably was among the red men of America; that it occurs among the Hindus, and may be assumed to have been common among the aboriginal inhabitants of the plains of India, of whom we have a well-preserved specimen in the Khonds of Orissa.

CHAPTER III.

THE ORIGIN OF THE FORM OF CAPTURE.

THE question now arises, what is the meaning and what the origin of a ceremony so widely spread, that already on the threshold of our inquiry the reader must be prepared to find it connected with some universal tendency of mankind?

Those who approach the subject with minds undisturbed by the views of Festus and Müller will most naturally think, in the first instance, of an early period of lawlessness, in which it was with women as with other kinds of property, that he should take who had the power, and he should keep who could. And it is a trite fact, that women captured in war have universally, in barbarous times and countries, been appropriated as wives, or as worse. But little consideration is needed to see that the symbol implies much more than this; for it is impossible to believe that the mere lawlessness of savages should be consecrated into a legal symbol, or to assign a reason—could this be believed—why a similar symbol should not appear in transferences of other kinds of property. To a certain extent, indeed, the first impression must be held to be a correct one. We cannot escape the conclusion that there was a stage in the history of tribes observing this custom when wives were usually obtained by theft or force. And unless the practice of getting wives by theft or force was so general where it prevailed that we may say it was almost invariable, it is incredible that such an association should be established in the popular mind between marriage and the act of rapine, as would afterwards require the pretence of rapine to give validity to the ceremony of marriage. It must have been *the system* of certain tribes to capture women—necessarily the women of other tribes—for wives. But we may be sure that such a system could not have sprung out of the mere instinctive desire of savages to possess objects cherished by a foreign tribe; it must have had a deeper source—to be sought for in their circumstances, their ideas of kinship, their tribal arrangements.

The fact that among savage tribes—whose normal relations with each other are those of war—a man could get a woman of a foreign tribe for his wife only by carrying her off, cannot, *by itself*, explain a symbolism which is so well established, so invariable, where it occurs at all. Where savages had women of their own whom they might marry, captive women would naturally become slaves or concubines rather than wives; the men would find their wives, or their chief wives, within the tribe; and the capture of women could never become so important in connection with marriage as to furnish a symbolism for all marriages to a later time. It may be doubted whether, in the circumstances supposed, the form of capture would, in a great number of cases, be bequeathed to more peaceful and friendly generations, even in the case of intertribal marriages—in which only the form could be expected to appear; and at any rate these, when first made subjects of friendly compact, would be too infrequent for their ceremonies to override those which were indigenous, and to be transferred into the general marriage law. Much more likely is it that indigenous marriage forms should be employed in the celebration of intertribal marriages when they occurred. It is *a fortiori*, that in the circumstances which we have been considering—those of tribes among which, as among civilised peoples, the law of marriage is *matrimonium liberum*—no *system* of capturing women for wives could have arisen.

What circumstances then, what social idea, existing among rude tribes, could produce a system of capturing the women of foreign tribes for wives? It will be convenient that, before we make the answer we have to offer to this question, we should consider the condition, in respect of marriage, of a class of tribes with which we believe this system did *not* originate.

It is clear that, if members of a family or tribe *are forbidden* to intermarry with members of other families or tribes, and free to marry among themselves, there is not room for fraud or force in the constitution of marriage. The bridegroom and bride will live together in amity among their common relatives. With the consent of her relations, a woman will become the wife of a suitor peaceably. If a suitor forces her, or carries her off against her will or that of her friends, he must separate from these to escape their vengeance. It follows that, among tribes of this class, which we shall call *endogamous tribes*,[1] betrothal followed by cohabitation at first, and, at a more advanced stage, betrothal and a religious or other formal ceremony of appropriation of the spouses to one another, are the natural modes of marriage. To the practice of such tribes are to be referred the two modes of constituting marriage of which the Roman Usus and Confarreatio may be taken as the types. These are at any rate the forms appropriate to marriages between members of the same family-group or tribe; and, so far as appears at present, they could only have originated among endogamous tribes, or—in the case of marriage within the tribe—among tribes which allowed their members to marry among themselves or into other groups indifferently.

The form of marriage by gift, or that by sale and purchase, could never have originated with purely endogamous tribes. A tribe, in a primitive age, is just a

[1] As the words endogamy and exogamy are new, an apology must be made for employing them. Instead of endogamy we might, after some explanations, have used the word caste. But caste connotes several ideas besides that on which we desire to fix attention. On the other hand, the rule which declares the union of persons of the same blood to be incest has been hitherto unnamed, and it was convenient to give it a name. The words endogamy and exogamy (for which botanical science affords parallels) appear to be well suited to express the ideas which stood in need of names, and so we have ventured to use them, taking care in the text to make their meanings distinct.

group of kindred—more or less numerous, with common interests and possessions, where they have any other property besides their women; living together as an ungoverned fraternity, or under the headship of a paterfamilias. Obviously within such a group there can be neither barter nor sale—neither the selling nor the buying of wives. On a marriage between two of its members, there is no foreign interest to be consulted or satisfied.

It is different if we conceive a number of such tribes aggregated in a political union to which the caste principle of its parts is extended; so that, while formerly the members of each could only marry among themselves, the members of all have acquired the right of intermarrying with one another. In forming this conception, we pass from marriages within the tribe to intertribal marriages. In an intertribal marriage one tribe loses a woman, the other acquires one; or, as sometimes happens, one loses a man, the other acquires one. In either case there is room and a necessity for compensation. Such a marriage must be a subject of bargain, a matter of sale and purchase. And we may now perceive that the marriages of which coemptio may be taken as the civilised type, have their origin in intermarriages between distinct family-groups or tribes.

But it is not in a primitive age, not until after a very considerable advance has been made in civilisation, that tribes are ever found joined in a political union. Such union indicates a state of friendliness between the tribes. And should intertribal marriages come to be permitted among endogamous tribes, they could from the first be carried through by friendly negotiation. On the other hand, the degree of political union presupposed to explain the intermarriages must be such as to exclude the idea of the members of any tribe resorting to violence to obtain wives from any other. We conclude that, among this class of tribes, marriage by capture could have had no place. Still more certain is it that they could never come to form such an association between marriage and the act of rapine as would lead them to adopt the symbol of capture in marriage ceremonies; on the contrary, we should expect to find that they would, out of respect to immemorial usage in the case of marriages within the tribe, celebrate even their intertribal marriages—though really brought about by sale and purchase—by such ceremonies as had been customary among them in marriages between members of the tribe. And if the symbol of capture be ever found in the marriage ceremonies of an endogamous tribe, we may be sure that it is a relic of an early time at which the tribe was organised on another principle than that of endogamy.

And now let us postulate the existence of tribes, organised on what we shall call, for the want of a better name, the principle of exogamy—that is, which *prohibited marriage within the tribe*—and whose tribesmen were thus dependent on other tribes for their wives. It is obvious that intertribal marriages could only be peaceably arranged between tribes whose relations were friendly. But peace and friendship were unknown between separate groups or tribes in early times, except when they were forced to unite against common enemies. The sections of the same family—when it fell into sections—became enemies by the mere fact of separation. And while this state of enmity lasted, exogamous tribes never could get wives except by theft or force.

If it can be shown, firstly, that exogamous tribes exist, or have existed; and secondly, that in rude times the relations of separate tribes are uniformly, or almost uniformly, hostile, we have found a set of circumstances in which men could get wives only by capturing them—a social condition in which capture would be the necessary preliminary to marriage. And if it be shown in a reasonable number of well-authenticated cases that these conditions—exogamy as tribal law, and hostility as the prevailing relation of separate tribes towards each other—exist or have existed, accompanied, as might have been expected, by a system of capturing wives, we shall be justified in concluding—failing the appearance of any phenomena inconsistent with such an explanation—that the same conditions have existed in every case where the system of capture prevailed, or where the form of capture has been observed as a ceremony of marriage. Nothing more than this is necessary to satisfy the conditions of a sound hypothesis.

We are in a position to do this and more. We shall be able to point to many tribes which habitually capture or captured their wives from foreign tribes; to show that exogamy is or was the law of these tribes; also, that there are cases of exogamous tribes whose tribesmen, marrying women by compact, always go through the form of capturing such women; that in all the modern instances where the symbol of capture is best marked, marriage within the tribe is prohibited as incestuous. We shall also find various circumstances common to exogamous tribes, and traceable in their case to the principle of exogamy, appearing more or less marked in the case of historical tribes which have used the form of capture, supporting the conclusion that such tribes had once been exogamous.

It may easily be conceived how, among exogamous tribes, out of respect to immemorial usage, when friendly relations came to be established between tribes and families, and their members intermarried by purchase instead of capture, the form of invasion and capture should become an essential ceremony at weddings. It was unheard of from the remotest times that a woman became a man's wife except through being made his captive, forced or stolen away from her friends by him or for him. Surely something shall be wanting if there is not at least the appearance of a capture! So the Roman youths rush in with drawn swords, and feign to enact a tragedy; so the Kalmuck girl rides, as if for life, from her lord and master by pre-arrangement!

We now proceed to treat of the matter, in order, under the three following heads:—Firstly, The prevalence of capturing wives *de facto;* secondly, Whether, where that practice prevails, marriage between members of the same family-group, clan, or tribe, is forbidden, and the prevalence of that limitation of the right of marriage; and, thirdly, How far the state of war prevails among primitive groups?

CHAPTER IV.

ON THE PREVALENCE OF THE PRACTICE OF CAPTURING WIVES, DE FACTO.

The tribes amongst which prevails or has prevailed, the practice of getting wives by theft or force, are both numerous and widely distributed. We shall find them in America, in Australia, in New Zealand, in many of the islands of the Pacific, and in various parts of Asia and Europe.

It is among the tribes of American Indians that the practice is to be found in the greatest perfection. In particular, we find it fully displayed on the Orinoco, on the Amazons, everywhere in fact, from the Caribbean Sea to Cape Horn. The abject Fuegians, as we have seen,[1] have the practice in a modified or symbolised form in the marriages of men and women belonging to groups at peace with one another. But they have the reality as well as the fiction. Between many of their tribes there is a chronic state of war. "*Strangers*," reported Jemmy Button to Captain Fitzroy on one

---

[1] See *ante*, p. 20.

occasion,[1] "had been there, with whom he and his people had 'very much jaw'; they fought, threw 'great many stone', and stole two women (in exchange for whom Jemmy's party stole one), but were obliged to retreat." The Horse Indians of Patagonia also, tribe against tribe, are commonly at war with one another, or with the Canoe Indians, the issues of victory, in every case, being the capture of women and the slaughter of men. But the Oens or Coin-men would appear to be the most systematic of these savage marauders, for every year at the time of "red leaf" they are said to make excursions from the mountains in the north to plunder Fuegians of their women, dogs, and arms.[2] Farther north still than the Oens men, we come successively on the tribes of the Amazons and of the Orinoco, all of which, excepting those reduced into missions, are continually at feud with one another, and in turns rich in women or impoverished; feelings of mutual hate and the desire for means of subsistence being concurring causes of war. Of the tribes on the Amazons the accounts are not very distinct; but the habits of the Manaos in the Rio Negro district—which, as reported by Mr. Bates,[3] are similar to those of the Coin-men—may be assumed not to be exceptional. There is no doubt, however, that the primitive habits of most of the Indian tribes have been much changed by the slave-hunting expeditions, at one time fostered by the Dutch

---

[1] *Voyages of the Adventure and Beagle, ut supra,* vol. ii. p. 224.
[2] *Voyages of the Adventure and Beagle,* vol. ii. p. 205.
[3] *The Naturalist on the Amazon.* Second Edition, 1864, p. 199.

and Portuguese. On slave-hunting being introduced in America, as in Africa, a market was found for captives of both sexes, and men as well as women became spoils of victory. No argument is needed to show that when women are systematically captured as in the above-cited cases, they are captured with a view to the raising of children—in fact with a view to their performing the part of wives. The fulness of the idea of a wife, according to our conceptions, is not, we need scarcely say, to be looked for amongst such savages. That idea can nowhere be fully realised till the circumstances of a people enable men and women to enjoy, or at least to look forward with confidence to, a permanent consortship.

Of the tribes of the great Caribbean nation we have happily a pretty full account from the pen of Alexander von Humboldt.[1] The Caribbees fall into small tribes or family groups, often not numbering more than from forty to fifty persons; Humboldt, indeed, takes frequent occasion to say that an Indian tribe is no more than a family. Where groups break up into sections, as they tend to do, and live apart from one another, the sections are found, though of one blood, and originally of one language, soon to speak dialects so different that they cannot understand one another. Become strangers, they are enemies except when forced

[1] *Personal Narrative of Travels, &c.* (1826). The passages bearing on the capture of women among the tribes of the Orinoco, from which our account is taken, will be found in vol. v. pp. 210, 293, 422, 425, 548, 565; vol. vi. pp. 20, 21, 26; vol. vii. p. 449.

to unite to make common cause against some powerful tribe which has proved a scourge to them all; enemies, and being at least at the time when Humboldt wrote, cannibals, not only disposed to slay but to eat one another. In their wars, we may imagine, that while their male captives furnished means of subsistence, the women were preserved to be wives and luxuries.[1] To such an extent, indeed, did all the tribes of the Caribbean nation practise the capture of women—depend on aggression for their wives—that the women of any tribe were found to belong to different tribes, and to tribes of other nations, and that to such an extent, nowhere were the men and women of the Caribbean race found to speak in one tongue.

Going northwards—to the wild Indians everywhere, as far as we follow them, the same account is applicable in varying degrees. It would indeed be misleading to omit to notice that in both North and South America tribes are to be found occupying much more elevated platforms of civility than those to which, for obvious reasons, we have given our attention. As among friendly groups of the Fuegians we find marriages of consent and of purchase (by labour commonly),[2] so also among friendly Patagonians; so also with the nations of the Huron tongue and the Attakapas, among whom the position of the women is exceedingly good. Indeed, all the processes have been going on through which every species of marriage would in time be

---

[1] Compare Erskine's *Pacific*, p. 425 (1863).
[2] See *ante*, p. 20.

developed. Even the red men of America are far from being primitive. A *really* primitive people in fact exists nowhere. For many thousands of years now, the various races of men have been in the school of experience, all making progress therein, though under different masters and in different forms. Hereafter we shall see how the old law of the red men, and of the natives of Australia, which counts blood relationship through females only, operates as an agent of civilisation, and tends to supersede the barbarous practices of early savagery, and especially to obviate the necessity of capturing wives.

The capture of women for wives is found to prevail among the aborigines of the Deccan,[1] and in Affghanistan.[2] It prevailed, according to Olaus Magnus, in Muscovy, Lithuania, and Livonia.[3] The form which it assumed among the peoples last named, so closely resembled what Kames describes as the custom among the Welsh, that we must quote the Archbishop's account of it:—
" Quicunque enim paganorum, sive rusticorum, filius suus uxorem ut ducat in animo habet, agnatos, cognatos, cæterosque vicinos in unum convocat, illisque talem isto in pago puellam nubilem versari, quam rapi, et suo filio in conjugem adduci proponit: hi commodum ad hoc tempus expectantes, ac tunc armati, equites suo more unius ad ædes conveniunt, posteaque ad eam

---

[1] Colonel Walter Campbell's *Indian Journal*, 1864, p. 400.
[2] Latham's *Descriptive Ethnology*, vol. ii. p. 215.
[3] *Historia de Gentibus Septentrionalibus*, Book xiv. cap. ix. p. 481, Romæ, 1555.

rapiendam proficiscuntur. Puella autem quoad matrimonii contradictionem libera, ex insidiis opera exploratorum ubi moretur per eos direpta, plurimum eiulando opem consanguineorum amicorumque ad se liberandam implorat: quod si consanguinei vicinique clamorem istum exaudierunt, ipso momento armati adcurrunt, atque pro ea liberanda prœlium committunt ut qui victores ista in pugna extiterunt his puella cedat." The difference between the Welsh and the Muscovite practice lay in this, that in Wales, in the celebration of the marriage, betrothal came first and the (sham) fight afterwards; while among the Muscovites an actual invasion came first, and if the bridegroom's party succeeded in carrying off the lady, there followed the consent of parents and the sponsalia:—" Nec ante completam hanc celebritatem mutua carnali copula, pacto parentum interveniente, se commiscere solent conjungendi; quia immane cunctis gentibus crimen apparere dignoscitur si ante sponsalia sacra stupri illecebris virgo temeratur; immo summopere cavent puellæ ne copulam anticipent quia perpetuam cum prole sic suscepta infamiam luent."[1] The intervention of the sponsalia and consent of parents before the consummation of the marriage, marks this as a transitional form of the practice. But it is none the less a case of actual capture. Another advance and the sponsalia will precede the capture, and the fight be a farce.

According to Seignior Gaya,[2] this transitional form

---

[1] Olaus Magnus, *ut supra*, p. 482.
[2] *Marriage Ceremonies, &c., ut supra*, p. 35.

of the practice prevailed in his time in Poland, parts of Prussia, Samogithia, and Lithuania. A lad's father having found where a girl lived, who would make a suitable wife for his son, he assembled his kindred and carried the lady off, after which application was made to her father for consent to complete the marriage.

There is ample reason to believe that the practice was general among the nations in the north of Europe and Asia. Olaus Magnus,[1] indeed, represents the tribes of the north as having been continually at war with one another either on account of stolen women, or with the object of stealing women, "propter raptas virgines aut arripiendas." His brother Johannes[2] dilates on the same topic, and mentions numerous cases in which the plunderers were of the royal houses of Denmark or Sweden. As did the kings, so did their subjects. Among the Scandinavians, before they became Christians, wives were almost invariably fought for and wedded at the sword-point. In Sweden, even long after the introduction of Christianity, women were often carried off when on the way to the church to be married. A wedding *cortége* was a party of armed men, and for greater security, marriages were generally celebrated at night. A pile of lances is said to be still preserved in the ancient church of Husaby in Gothland, into which were fitted torches; these weapons

---

[1] *Ut supra*, p. 328.
[2] *History of the Goths*, Book xviii.; and see Kames, *ut supra*, vol. i. p. 393.

were borne by the groomsmen, and served the double purpose of giving light and protection.[1] Such a prevalence of lawlessness existing after the introduction of Christianity and comparative civilisation, helps us to conceive what the habits of these people were in a more primitive age.

We find capture *de facto* co-existent with capture as a form, and not unfrequent, among most of the rude tribes observing the form; its frequency depending partly on the degree of friendliness established between the tribes, and partly on the degree of fixity given by usage to the price to be paid for a bride. Where the parties cannot agree about the price, nothing is more common among the Kalmucks, Kirghiz, Nogais, and Circassians, than to carry the lady off by actual force of arms. The wooer having once got the lady into his yurt, she is his wife by the law, and peace is established by her relations coming to terms as to the price, after the thing has gone so far that they cannot help themselves. It is important to observe, that among these races the capture, though an irregular proceeding, makes marriage, even previous to terms being made between the capturer and the friends of the lady, and whether they are made or not.

That the practice of getting wives by capture *de facto*, prevails among the natives of Australia, is a fact familiar to most readers. It is not, however, *now*

---

[1] *Book of Days*, vol. i. p. 720. The groomsmen are said to have been called " best men " in the North from the strongest and stoutest of the bridegroom's friends being chosen for this duty.

the sole or regular mode of getting a wife among the Australian tribes; and we do not claim to do more than show that there at present exists among them a practice of capturing wives so common as almost to be a system. And as we shall hereafter show that they are exogamous, and also that exogamous tribes which begin with a system of capturing wives, may progress—consistently with exogamy—to a system of betrothals, we shall ask the reader, conceding to us for the present that we shall be able to do so, to agree with us that so general a practice of capture, subsisting as it does among the Australians alongside of a system of betrothals, points unmistakably to a previous stage when wives were usually captured.

Among the Australasians, according to one account, when a man sees a woman whom he likes, he tells her to follow him, and when she refuses, he forces her to accompany him by blows, ending by knocking her down and carrying her off.[1] The same account (somewhat suspiciously) bears that this mode of courtship is rather relished by the ladies as a species of rough gallantry. The cases must indeed be rare in which a man finds a woman detached from her lord and protector, or the other members of her family; nor is it in human flesh and blood to take kicks and cuffs as compliments, in whatever spirit they may be administered. The following is the account given by Sir George Grey—a good authority:—"Even supposing a woman to give no encouragement to her admirers,"

[1] Turnbull, *Voyage Round the World*, 1805, vol. i. pp. 81, 82.

he says,[1] "many plots are always laid to carry her off, and in the encounters which result from these, she is almost certain to receive some violent injury, for each of the combatants orders her to follow him, and in the event of her refusing, throws a spear at her. The early life of a young woman at all celebrated for beauty is generally one continued series of captivity to different masters, of ghastly wounds, of wanderings in strange families, of rapid flights, of bad treatment from other females, amongst whom she is brought a stranger by her captor; and rarely do you see a form of unusual grace and elegance, but it is marked and scarred by the furrows of old wounds; and many a female thus wanders several hundred miles from the home of her infancy, being carried off successively to distant and more distant points."

As an Australian woman is always a wife, being betrothed after birth to some man of a different tribe or family-stock from her own, a stolen or captured wife is always stolen or taken from a prior husband. And as men do not readily part with their wives, and their tribesmen are bound to make common cause with them for the reparation of injuries, the capture of wives is a signal for war; and as the tribes have little property except their weapons and their women, the women are at once the cause of war, and the spoils of victory.[2] The tribes, as might be expected, are exceedingly

[1] *Travels in North-Western Australia*, 1841, vol. ii. p. 249.

[2] Turnbull, *ut supra*, p. 82.

numerous, and exceedingly small,[1] being a species of family groups, and, chiefly from the causes specified, they are continually at war with one another.[2] The reader may imagine the extent to which, among these myriad hordes of savages, the women are being knocked about, and the men accustomed to associate the acquisition of a wife with acts of violence and rapine.[3]

The native songs make frequent allusion to the practice of capturing wives. Here is the burden of one, sung by a heavy-hearted woman, upbraiding her lord, whose affections some recently acquired captive has drawn away from her:—

> " Wherefore came you, Weerang,
> In my beauty's pride,
> Stealing cautiously,
> Like the tawny boreang,
> On an unwilling bride.
> 'Twas thus you stole me
> From one who loved me tenderly.
> A better man he was than thee,
> Who having forced me thus to wed,
> Now so oft deserts my bed.
>   Yang, yang, yang, yoh.

---

[1] Sir George Grey says that the largest number of natives his party ever saw together, "numbered nearly two hundred, women and children included," *ut supra*, vol. i. p. 252.

[2] Grey's *Travels, ut supra*, vol. i. p. 256.

[3] The reader will find, p. 318, vol. ii. of Grey's *Travels*, a curious illustrative instance of the way in which a war about women may arise.

> "Oh, where is he who won
> My youthful heart;
> Who oft used to bless
> And call me loved one?
> You, Weerang, tore apart
> From his fond caress
> Her whom you desert and shun;
> Out upon the faithless one!
> Oh, may the Boyl-yas bite and tear,
> Her, whom you take your bed to share.
> Yang, yang, yang, yoh." [1]

Concerning the New Zealanders, it must suffice to say that the theft or capture of women plays a leading part in their popular legends, testifying to the prevalence of the practice, at least in their early history.[2] In New Zealand, and in the Feejee and other islands of the Pacific, the capture of wives appears to have been conjoined with cannibalism—the object of intertribal war being at once to procure women for wives and men for food, except in some districts where there was a special relish for the flesh of females.[3]

In the Institutes of Menu we have marriage by capture enumerated among "the eight forms of the nuptial ceremony used by the four classes."[4] It is the marriage called Racshasa, and is thus defined:

---

[1] Grey's *Travels*, vol. ii. p. 313.

[2] *Polynesian Mythology, &c.* Sir George Grey, 1855, pp. 138, 147, 207, 235, 301.

[3] Erskine's *Islands of the Western Pacific*, and Jackson's *Narrative*.

[4] Chap. iii. p. 33 (Jones and Houghton).

—"The seizure of a maiden by force from her house while she weeps and calls for assistance, after her kinsmen and friends have been slain in battle or wounded, and their houses broken open, is the marriage called Racshasa." Elsewhere [1] in the code it is mentioned as appropriated to the military class. "For a military man the before-mentioned marriages of Gandharvas and Racshases—whether separate or mixed, as when a girl is made captive by her lover, after a victory over her kinsmen—are permitted by law." The full scope and effect of this provision we shall have to consider hereafter. Meanwhile we notice that we have here the exact prototype of the Roman and Spartan forms, embalmed in a code of laws a thousand years before the commencement of our era; not as a form, but as living substance. This we hold to exclude any hypothesis except that which we are maintaining.[2]

We may notice, as further illustrating the subject, and as being in itself curious, that by the Mosaic Code the military class were, in defiance of the general law which declared that there was no connubium between Jews and Gentiles, allowed to take to wife women whom they captured in war, to whatever races they belonged. In Deut. xx. 10-14, the reader will find forms and regulations provided for the constitution of this species of marriage, and if

---

[1] Chap. iii. p. 26 (Jones and Houghton).
[2] For the probable origin of the name Racshases, see Appendix B.

interested to know the meaning of the rules, he will find a copious and learned discussion of them in the works of Selden.[1]

Thus far we have been dealing with facts. If we are right in our theory of the symbol of capture, it must be held that the Dorians, or at least some of the tribes composing the Spartan nation, and the Latins, or at least some of the tribes forming the commonalty of Rome, long had experience in the capturing of wives by force or stratagem. We leave to our Hellenists to consider how far the Doric legends may have new light thrown upon them by our view of the Spartan custom. How far, for instance, may the slaughter by Hercules of Eurylus and his sons, and the carrying away of Iole to be the wife of Hyllus— of Hyllus, who never occurs in mythology except in connection with the Dorians—be a mythical tradition of a rape of women from another tribe? How far may the genealogies of Doric heroes connected with the taking of Ephyra,—the capture of Astyocheia,—the feat of Hercules at Thespiæ—the stories of Pluto and Proserpine, and of Boreas and Orithya—be but traditions of a quasi Caribbean prowess? It must be kept in mind, too, that the case cited from Herodotus in proof of the custom at Sparta is one of actual violence. At least, the lady was not carried off in terms of arrangement. Further, to judge by what is reported of Theseus—even accepting the tradition as fabulous—

---

[1] *De Jure Naturali et Gentium juxta Disciplinam Ebræorum*, lib. v. cap. xiii. fol. 617.

we may conclude that the ancient Greeks generally were very lawless in this matter. To that hero's charge are laid numerous rapes of women whom he carried off to be his wives—his crimes of this description culminating in the seizure of Helen. Plutarch, indeed, in describing that affair, mentions a compact as having been entered into between Theseus and his companion in the seizure—Tyndarus—to the effect that he who should gain Helen by lot should have her to wife, but be obliged to assist in procuring a wife for the other; which shows that these worthies trusted to their prowess to procure them wives,[1] As to the Romans—upon our theory—the story of the rape of the Sabines must be accepted as a mere mythical tradition of the ancient method of getting wives. The story, as might be expected, is reproduced in the traditions of many tribes, in many places, and in many forms. For instance, in the Irish Nennius[2] there is a tradition of such a rape of wives by the Picts from the Gael. In the very old poem, "The Cruithnians who propagated in the land of

---

[1] There is no evidence that the Doric hordes who overran and established themselves in the Peloponnesus, were accompanied by their wives or children. It is most unlikely that they were so attended; and, except a surmise founded on the degree of influence enjoyed at a subsequent period by the women of Sparta, there is nothing in favour of the supposition. But that surmise proceeds on the ground that wives of a race alien to that of their husbands are not so likely to be well treated as they would be if they were of the same blood. Against this we must simply pronounce as being contrary to evidence.

[2] Pp. 245—251.

noble Alba,"[1] the Irish are represented as giving three hundred wives to the Picts, on the condition that the succession to the crown among the Picts should always be through their females :—

> "There were oaths imposed on them,
> By the stars, by the earth,
> That from the nobility of the mother
> Should always be the right to the sovereignty."

The story of the oaths is no doubt a fable to explain the descensus per umbilicum of the Picts. But, in "Duan Eiranash,"[2] a poem on the origin of the Goedhel, reciting the same event, the Picts are represented as stealing the three hundred wives :—

> "Cruithne, son of Cuig, took their women from them—
> It is directly stated—
> Except Tea, wife of Hermion,
> Son of Miledh."

And in consequence of the capture, the Gael, being left wifeless, had to form alliances with the aboriginal tribes of Ireland.

> "There were no charming noble wives
> For their young men;
> Their women having been stolen, they made alliance
> With the Tuatha Dea."

We have the same story in the history of the Jews. Chapters xx. and xxi. of the Book of Judges contain

---

[1] Vv. 115—120. The Irish version of Nennius, 1848, p. 141.
[2] Vv. 178—180, *ut supra*, p. 245.

highly instructive matter on this point, in a story, which, though laid in the time of the Judges, we must hold to be of very old date—a Jewish tradition belonging to the earliest history of Israel. The women of the tribe of Benjamin had been destroyed, and certain of the tribes of Israel had sworn not to give their daughters as wives to the men of Benjamin, who again could not take wives to themselves from the Gentiles, as by law they could marry only into one or other of the tribes of Israel. The difficulty of procuring wives for Benjamin—which Israel made its *own* difficulty—was solved by the wholesale slaughter of the inhabitants of Jabez-Gilead, whose population yielded 400 virgins: and next by the men of Benjamin enacting a rape of the Sabines for themselves, each man seizing and carrying off one of the daughters of Shiloh to be his wife, on an occasion when the women met for a festival in certain vineyards near Bethel.[1]

We can now say we have found the capture of women very extensively practised; and there can be no doubt that in most of the cases cited, the women captured were kept to be used as wives. In a number of well-marked cases we have found a system of capture

---

[1] See *Smith's Bible Dictionary*—Art. MARRIAGE—where it is remarked that the phrase in the Old Testament (*e.g.* Num. xii. 1, 1 Chron. ii. 21), "taking a wife," would seem to require to be taken in its literal meaning in the run of cases; "the taking" being the chief ceremony in the constitution of marriage. If the writer of that article is correct, we must believe that the Jews observed the *form* of capture, for in many cases where the phrase occurs we know the marriages were preceded by contracts.

—in the case of the Caribbean tribes of America, a system so general, that the women of a tribe were commonly not only not of the same tribe with the men, but did not even speak the same language. We have seen among tribes in a transition state, in some cases, capture almost systematically practised, alongside of more civilised institutions; and in other cases, the practice of capture in various stages of progress towards a symbolism. We have seen the marriage by capture embodied in the code of India as an institution in favour of the only class which could be benefited by it—the warrior class; and no argument is needed to show that such a rule must have been a generalisation founded upon practice. A similar rule subsisted in favour of warriors among the Israelites. The former of these cases is, perhaps, chiefly valuable as presenting in a distinct shape the antetype of the form of capture—a description of marriage by an actual capture so vividly recalling incidents of fictitious capture, as practised at Rome and elsewhere, as (in our opinion) to set at rest the question in what way the fiction originated. The latter case shows a provision made for marriage with foreign women, if captured, among tribes which, in no other case, allowed of marriage with foreign women; a provision indicating a very remarkable association between capture and marriage. It is not easy to believe that such a regulation, existing among endogamous tribes, is referable to the feeling that a victorious warrior should have the full disposal of spoils of war; it is much more likely that it was a relic of a time when the tribes—or rather the race from which they sprang—were not endogamous; and, if so, it carries us back to a remote antiquity when marriage and prowess in war were closely associated. We have seen that the mythic legends of various races, of which hitherto no rational explanation has been given, can, with great appearance of probability be, referred to the existence amongst such races in ancient times of a systematic capture of wives.

Further research, and the observation of tribes hitherto unreported upon—at present we have not been able to say anything that would be satisfactory of the races of the continent of Africa—will, we confidently expect, afford much additional evidence of the prevalence of this practice. But we have done enough to entitle us to affirm that there has existed amongst various races of mankind *a system* of capturing women for wives.

CHAPTER V.

OF THE RULE AGAINST MARRIAGE BETWEEN MEMBERS OF THE SAME TRIBE—OF THE COINCIDENCE OF THIS RULE WITH THE PRACTICE OF CAPTURING WIVES DE FACTO, AND WITH THE FORM OF CAPTURE IN MARRIAGE CEREMONIES.

WE proceed to show the prevalence of the rule forbidding marriage within the tribe or group of kindred, and the concurrence of this ban with the fact, or pretence of capturing wives.

Here, still more than in our former investigation, we are made to feel how imperfect and unconnected is the record from which our facts have to be drawn; and farther, how difficult it is to bring together such facts as have been observed, owing to the wide field over which they lie sparsely scattered. In many cases, the authorities are silent just on the points on which we are most eager for information; while on matters of no moment they enlarge *ad nauseam*. But, too often, they have nothing to tell. Skirting a coast-line the traveller sees natives at points here and there, and can describe their dress and personal appearance; of their habits he is as ignorant as a child of the free life of the beasts he sees in a caravan. Where the opportunities of observation are better, the observer often does not know what to look for. Of the *jus connubii* among the Kalmucks not one word is said by Clarke or Pallas or Strahlenberg, and but for some remarks of Bergman's we should be entirely in the dark on the subject.

We begin with the Khonds. This people presents us with capture *as a form*. Major-General Campbell says that the Khonds marry women from remote places, the reason of which he takes to be, that they have to buy their wives, and can get them at lower prices at a distance. "They pretend, moreover," he adds,[1] "to regard it as degrading to bestow their daughters in marriage on men of their own tribe; and consider it more manly to seek their wives in a distant country." Major M'Pherson—a more intelligent witness—gives us the distinct statement, that among the Khonds intermarriage between persons of the same tribe, however large or scattered, is considered incestuous, and punishable by death;[2] a view more consistent with other known facts than that of General Campbell. "Marriage," Major M'Pherson tells us, "can take place only betwixt members of different tribes, and not *even with strangers who have been long adopted into or domesticated with a tribe*, and a state of war or peace appears to make little difference as to the practice of inter-

[1] *Ut supra*, p. 141.
[2] *An Account of the Religion of the Khonds in Orissa*, p. 57; and see M'Pherson's Report on the Khonds, already referred to.

marriage between tribes. The people of Bara Mootah and of Burra Des, in Goomsur, have been at war time out of mind, and annually engage in fierce conflicts, but they intermarry every day. The women of each tribe, after a fight, visit each other to condole on the loss of their nearest common relations." No doubt these friendly intermarriages must in time alter the relations of the tribes to one another; no doubt also the time was when the marriages were *not* effected in friendly fashion.

Let us now examine the cases of the Kalmucks and Circassians. To understand that of the former, we must attend a little to their political system. The Kalmucks are divided into four great nations or tribes under hereditary chiefs or khans;—the Khoskots, the Dzungars, the Derbets, and the Torgots. Each of these, according to Pallas,[1] is under the command of many little and nearly independent princes, called Noïons. The horde commanded by a Noïon is called an Oulouss, and is subdivided into several Aïmaks, each of which again is commanded by a noble called Saïssang. The Aïmaks again are subdivided into many companies or khatoun, consisting of from ten to twelve tents, for convenience in pasturing; and each khatoun has its chief; but whether of the noble class we are not informed. It will thus be seen that there is among the Kalmucks a very large governing or princely class. Now, it appears that they have two systems of marriage

---

[1] *Voyages dans plusieurs Provinces de l'Empire de Russie, &c.*, Paris (no date), vol. ii. p. 191. Nouvelle Edition.

law; one for the common people, and one for the nobles, or princely class. The common people, we are told by Bergman,[1] enter into no unions in which the parties are not distant from one another by three or four degrees: but how the degrees are counted we are not informed. We are told that they have great abhorrence for the marriages of near relatives, and have a proverb—"The great folk and dogs know no relationship,"—which Bergman says is due to members of the princely class sometimes marrying sisters-in-law. We find, however, that these sisters-in-law are uniformly women of an entirely different stock from their husbands—different, or what is taken for different. For no man of the princely class (and it is in the marriages of the Kalmucks of this class, according to De Hell, that the form of capture is chiefly observed [2]), in any of the tribes, can marry a woman of his own tribe or nation. Not only must his wife be a noble, but she must be a noble of a different stock. For princely marriages, says Bergman, "the bride is chosen from another people's stock—among the Derbets from the Torgot stock; and among the Torgots from the Derbet stock; and so on." Here, then, we have the principle of exogamy in full force in regard to the marriages of the governing classes—a large body in each nation, as we have seen, and, which is most to our present purpose, the body in whose marriages the form of capture is said to be observed. Whether or not the

[1] Bergman's *Streifereien*, Riga, 1804, vol. iii. p. 145, *et seq.*
[2] See *ante*, p. 15.

commonalty, with whom the nobles have no intermarriage—the people of black birth, as they are called—were originally of an alien, inferior, and conquered race; and whether or not the governing classes were originally independent exogamous tribes, we have the prohibition against marriage within the stock here concurrent with the form of capture in the weddings of the nobility. How far the commonalty observe the form we have no information, but it is not unlikely that they mimic, after a fashion, the marriage ceremonies of their superiors.

The case of the Circassians is simple, and quickly told:—" The Circassian word for their societies or fraternities," says Bell,[1] "is 'tleûsh,' which signifies also 'seeds.' The tradition with regard to them is, that the members of each all sprang from the same stock or ancestry; and thus they may be considered as so many septs or clans, with this peculiarity, that, like seeds, all are considered equal. These cousins-german or members of the same fraternity, are not only themselves interdicted from intermarrying, but their serfs, too, must wed with the serfs of another fraternity; and where, as is generally the case, many fraternities enter into one general bond, this law in regard to marriage must be observed by all. The confidential dependent, or steward, of our host here is a Tokao who fled to his protection from Notwhatsh, because, having fallen in

---

[1] James Stanislaus Bell, *Journal of a Residence in Circassia*, 1840, vol. i. p. 347.

love with and married a woman of his own fraternity, he had become liable to punishment for this infraction of Circassian law. Yet his fraternity contained perhaps several thousand members. Formerly, such a marriage was looked upon as incest, and punished by drowning; now a fine of two hundred oxen, and the restitution of the wife to her parents, only are exacted." Elsewhere,[1] Bell observes that these fraternities sometimes embrace thousands of persons, between whom marriage is by this ancient law totally prohibited. Here, too, as in Khondistan, and among the Kalmucks, we find the form of capture as well as the principle of exogamy.

Our next case is that of the Yurak Samoyeds (Siberia), among whom no man can take a wife from the tribe to which he belongs.[2] These Samoyeds hold kinsmanship to be coextensive with the tribe. All the members of the tribe, however large or small, consider themselves relations, even where the common ancestor is unknown and the evidence of consanguinity is wholly wanting. They fall into three divisions; the members of any of which may take wives from either of the other two, but not from their own; and as these divisions occupy sites far removed from one another, the Samoyeds have to go great distances for their wives.

We find the same state of things among the Kafirs, the Sodhas of northern India, the Beduanda Kallung

---

[1] *Ut supra*, vol. ii. p. 110.
[2] Latham, *Descriptive Ethnology*, vol. ii. p. 455.

(Singapore) and many others, including the Kirghiz and the Nogais.[1]

The Warali (India) tribes fall into divisions, and no man may marry a woman of his own division; he must go for a wife to one of the others. The Magar tribes fall into thums, all the members of each of which are supposed to be descended from a common ancestor; the Magar husband and wife must belong to different thums; within one and the same thum there is no marriage. Latham, in noticing the Magars, says—"This is the first time[2] I have found occasion to mention this practice. It will not be the last; on the contrary, the principle it suggests is so common as to be almost universal. We find it in Australia, in North and South America, in Africa, in Europe; we shall suspect and infer it in many places where the actual evidence of its existence is incomplete." This is a sweeping statement; but before we conclude we hope to show that it may fairly be accepted as correct.

In the Institutes of Menu it is laid down that a twice-born man might elect for nuptials " a woman not descended from his paternal or maternal ancestors within the sixth degree, and who is not known *by her*

---

[1] It must not be thought that the form of capture occurs wherever exogamy prevails—that exogamy and the practice of capturing wives, which at a certain stage must be the resource of exogamous tribes, will in every case leave the form of capture behind them. We shall see the explanation of this hereafter. We have no information whether or not the Samoyeds practise the form of capture.

[2] Vol. i. p. 80, *Descriptive Ethnology*.

family name to be of the same primitive stock with his father."[1] This passage might be taken as a text for the discussion of the whole question of prohibited marriages, and we must dwell upon it somewhat, as it has an important bearing on the present investigation. The object of the rule is to prevent marriages between members of the same primitive stock; and it points out the family name as the test whether persons are of the same stock or not. It is as if a Fraser might not marry a Fraser, nor a M'Intosh a M'Intosh. By comparing the former state of the Highlands of Scotland with their present condition, especially with the condition of the town populations, we may clear our ideas regarding the origin, meaning, and effect of this institution. Of old, each clan inhabited its particular strath or glen, and had its own well-defined hill-ranges. In the Aird district there were none but Frasers; about Moy were none but M'Intoshes. The members of the clans are now interfused even in the country districts, and in towns like Inverness or Dingwall may be found members of all the clans. Now, suppose that originally a

[1] *Institutes of Menu*, cap. iii. sec. 5. The words "or mother" occur in the gloss of Calluca. The rule fixing the stock by the father is, as we hope to show, far from being archaic. The twice-born classes are the sacerdotal, military, and commercial (Menu, x. 4). Nearly all the Indian castes are now divided into nations that do not intermarry; the nations into sects, some of which do not intermarry. All the nations are divided into certain families, called *gotrams;* a man cannot marry a woman of his own *gotram*. Buchanan's *Journey from Madras*, 1807, vol. i. pp. 273, 300, 354, 396, 419, 421, 423; Muir's *Sanskrit Texts*, Part II., 1859, pp. 378, 387; *Vivada Chintamani*, Calcutta, 1863, Preface, p. 45.

man was not allowed to marry a woman of his own clan, and that, subsequent to the interfusion of the clans, that ancient prejudice remained; the rule for enforcing it—the question of degrees of affinity apart—would just be the rule of Menu. So, in considering the origin of that rule, are we not remanded from the social state in which it was fixed in a code, to an earlier state, in which the population consisted of distinct clans or tribes organised on the principle of exogamy, and living apart from one another, as all tribes do in early times, until they are brought, by conquest or otherwise, under a common government? We have already had examples of tribes with this rule, so that, in this conception of the early state of the Indian population, we are making no improbable supposition. On the contrary, it is not only probable in itself, but it is the only supposition that will explain the fact; and if we accept it as indicating the origin of the rule of Menu, it gives us such an idea of the prevalence of this law of incest as we could never reach by the contemplation of the individual tribes among which it is the law. It will be recollected that the form of capture is found among the Hindus.[1]

We believe it may still be possible, in the case of some communities in which marriage between persons of the same family name is prohibited, to analyse the population into its constituent (stock) tribes, and to prove that the tribes had this law of incest. In one case, in particular, investigation seems to be courted.

[1] *Ante*, p. 13.

The Munnieporees, and the following tribes inhabiting the hills round Munniepore—the Koupooees, the Mows, the Murams, and the Murring—are each and all divided into four families—Koomul, Looang, Angom, and Ningthajà. A member of any of these families may marry a member of any other, but the intermarriage of members of the same family is strictly prohibited. In explanation, so far, of these family divisions,[1] we have the fact, well authenticated in the history of Munniepore, that the Koomul and Looang formerly existed as distinct and powerful tribes, and that the Koomul, in particular, at one time preponderated in the valley. Presuming that these tribes held intermarriages of their members to be incestuous, the origin of two of the family divisions, and of the marriage law, is plain enough, at least so far as the hill tribes are concerned; and it is in the hills alone that the law is strictly enforced. Most of the members of the tribes would remain in the valley and mix with the Meithei, by whose prowess they were vanquished; but we can conceive that bands of the Koomul and Looang might escape to the hills, and mix with each other and with the tribes of the Angom and Ningthajà, whose existence in former times we must postulate, in explanation of the family divisions of the same names. Is it beyond hope that the further examination of local traditions, or exploration of the wilds to the south and north-east of Munniepore, may yet furnish us with information

[1] *Account of the Valley of Munniepore and of the Hill Tribes.* M'Culloch, 1859, pp. 49—69.

regarding the Angom and Ningthajà, or with data from which their existence in former times may be legitimately inferred, apart from the present speculation?

The conclusion at which we have arrived as to the origin of the rule of Menu, will also explain the case of the native populations of Australia, North and South America, and the islands in the Pacific. In these quarters we obtain light regarding the causes which lead to the break-up of the primitive exogamous groups, and to the intermixture in local tribes of people recognised as being of different bloods. Let us first attend to the Australians, whom we find divided into small tribes named after the districts which they inhabit; for though they are nomads, their wanderings, like those of the nomadic agriculturists of the Indian hills, are circumscribed within well-defined bounds. It appears that the tribe inhabiting a particular district regards itself as the owner thereof, and the intrusion of any other tribe upon that district as an invasion to be resented and punished; and that within the district individuals have portions of land appropriated to them.[1] Thus the tribal system is in force, with an apparent perfect separation and independence of the tribes. But, on close examination, the tribes are found to be fused and welded together by blood-ties in the most extraordinary manner. According to credible accounts,[2] the natives of different tribes extending over a great

---

[1] Letter, Dr. Laing to Dr. Hodgkin, 1840. *Reports of the Aboriginal Protection Society.*

[2] *Grey's Journals, &c.,* vol. ii. chap. xi.

portion of the continent, are divided into a few families, and all the members of a family, in whatever local tribes they may be, bear the same name as a second or family name. These family names and divisions are perpetuated and spread throughout the country by the operation of two laws: first, that the children of either sex always take the name of the mother; and second, that a man cannot marry a woman of his own family name.

The members of these families, though scattered over the country, are yet to some intents as much united as if they formed separate and independent tribes; in particular, the members of each family are bound to unite for the purposes of defence and vengeance, the consequence being that every quarrel which arises between the tribes is a signal for so many young men to leave the tribes in which they were born, and occupy new hunting-grounds, or ally themselves with tribes in which the families of their mothers may happen to be strong, or which contain their own and their mothers' nearest relatives. This *secession*, if we may so call it, is not always possible, but it is of frequent occurrence notwithstanding; where it is impossible, the presence of so many *of the enemy* within the camp affords ready means of satisfying the call for vengeance; it being immaterial, according to the native code, by whose blood the blood-feud is satisfied, provided it be blood of the offender's kindred. Thus, as the Australians are polygamists, and a man often has wives belonging to different families, it is not in quarrels uncommon to find children of the same father arranged against one another; or, indeed, against their father himself, for by their peculiar law the father can never be a relative of his children.[1]

[1] Mr. Maine has been unable to conceive how human beings could be grouped on any principle more primitive than that of the patriarchal system, or be bound together by any ruder blood-ties than those of agnation derived from the patria potestas. We think his mistake has arisen from a too exclusive attention, in his researches, to those systems of ancient law which, like the Hindoo, Roman, and Jewish, belonged to races which were far advanced at the earliest dates to which their history goes back. Had he examined the primitive races now extant, he certainly would not have written the following passage:[1] "It is obvious that the organisation of primitive societies would have been confounded if men had called themselves relatives of their mothers' relatives. The inference would have been that a person might be subject to two distinct *patriæ potestates;* but distinct *patriæ potestates* implied distinct jurisdictions, so that anybody amenable to two of them at the same time would have lived under two dispensations. As long as the family was an *imperium in imperio*, a community within the commonwealth, governed by its own institutions, of which the parent was the source, the limitation of relationship to the agnates was a necessary security against a conflict of laws in the domestic forum." Here we see the ingenious thinker trammelled by notions derived from Roman jurisprudence. Among the Australian Blacks—to confine ourselves to a single instance—we have seen that men are relatives of their mothers' relatives, and of none other; and that their societies are *aliunde* held together, notwithstanding the conflict of laws in the domestic forum engendered by polygyny, exogamy, and female kinship. Kinship depends, in fact, not at all on convenience. The first kinship is the first possible—that through mothers, about whose parental relation to children there can be no mistake. And the system of kinship through mothers only, operates to throw difficulties in the way of the rise of the patria potestas, and of the system of agnation. But of this hereafter.

[1] *Ancient Law*, 1861, p. 149.

Among the Kamilaroi, a numerous tribe residing to the north-west of Sidney, the rules in force are very complex and peculiar. These tribesmen fall into divisions resembling castes, and at the same time observe the rule against marriages between members of the same family.[1]

Our information is so imperfect that we do not know whether there exist anywhere in Australia tribes whose distinctive names are those of the families into which the population is divided. But we should not expect to find such tribes. The constant tendency of groups to fall to pieces, and of the parts to separation and independence of one another, and the practice of naming groups from their lands, would tend to obliterate the traces of the original stock-groups, except so far as they have been preserved in the names of families to keep the blood pure by avoidance of marriage between members of the same stock. But we cannot doubt but that such stock-groups at one time existed, organised on the principle of exogamy, and were the germs of the native population. Whencesoever they were derived, it was inevitable that the law which recognised blood relationship as existing only through females, conspiring with the primitive instinct[2] of the race against marriage between members of the same stock, should tend in process

---

[1] Mr. Ridley's account, quoted p. 491, vol. ii., Pritchard's *Natural History of Man*, Norris's edition.

[The marriage-law of the Kamilaroi will be fully considered in a second series of *Studies in Ancient History*.]

[2] [This phrase, it will be found, was only a slip of the pen.]

of time to transfuse the blood of each stock through all the tribal divisions. The men of the group A marrying women of the group B; and the men of the group B marrying women of the group A; and all the children of the women of B being counted of the stock of B; and all the children of the women of A being counted of the stock of A; we at once have so many B's within A, and so many A's within B. And so on, until in time A's from the northmost point appear in the homes of Z at the southmost; and Z's in the homes of A. Each local tribe would thus contain within itself members between whom there was connubium; the original tribal divisions would be lost sight of, and nothing would remain of the stock-groups but the family names to which they gave birth. Should the process of transfusion go far enough, the state of matters which would lead to the practice of capturing wives would be modified, but not extinct. The system of polygamy of itself, and any want of balance between the sexes of different families within a tribe, would long tend to maintain this practice; which, moreover, like every other practice connected with marriage or religion, must be credited with a special tenacity of existence. As we have seen, there prevails among the Australians a system of betrothals—always between persons of different stocks—along with an extensive practice of capturing wives. This is just what might be expected if our theory of the origin of capture be a sound one. Since the tribes of Australians, while exogamous in principle, contain persons who regard each other as of different descent and free to intermarry, marriage can be, and is, made the subject of bargain. Again, habits formed in previous times of necessity—and no doubt occasional necessity still existing—keep up the practice of capture.

We now take the case of the American Indians—North and South. They have political and district divisions;[1] but besides these the nations among them have had from time immemorial divisions into families or clans. "At present, or till very lately"—we quote from the *Archæologia Americana*—" every nation was divided into a number of clans, varying in the several nations from three to eight or ten, the members of which respectively were dispersed indiscriminately throughout the whole nation. It has been fully ascertained that the inviolable regulations by which these clans were perpetuated amongst the southern nations were, first, that no man could marry in his own clan; secondly, that every child should belong to his or her mother's clan. Among the Choctaws there are two great divisions, each of which is subdivided into four clans, and no man can marry in any of the four clans belonging to his division. The restriction among the Cherookees, the Creeks, and the Natches does not extend beyond the clan to which the man belongs. There are sufficient proofs that the same division into clans, commonly called tribes, exists among almost all the other primitive nations. But it is not so clear that they are subject to the same regulations which prevail

[1] *Archæologia Americana*, vol. ii. p. 109.

amongst the southern Indians." At the root of these divisions and prohibitions we find here, as in Australia, the feeling that marriage between persons of the same blood is incestuous. "They profess to consider it highly criminal for a man to marry a woman whose *totem* (family name) is the same as his own, and they relate instances when young men, for a violation of this rule, have been put to death by their own relatives."[1] The

[1] From a circular letter by Mr. L. H. Morgan, of Rochester, New York, issued by the United States Government to its diplomatic agents and consuls in foreign countries, and which contains much interesting information regarding the laws of primitive relationship, we quote the following passage as the most recent and authoritative statement regarding the tribal divisions of the Red Men :—

"Nearly all, if not all, of the Indian nations upon this continent were anciently subdivided into *Tribes* or *Families*. These tribes, with a few exceptions, were named after animals. Many of them are now thus subdivided. It is so with the Iroquois, Delawares, Iowas, Creeks, Mohaves, Wyandottes, Winnebagoes, Otoes, Kaws, Shawnees, Choctaws, Otawas, Ojibewas, Potowottomies, &c.

"The following tribes are known to exist, or to have existed, in the several Indian nations—the number ranging from three to eighteen in each: The Wolf, Bear, Beaver, Turtle, Deer, Snipe, Heron, Hawk, Crane, Duck, Loon, Turkey, Musk-rat, Sable, Pike, Cat-fish, Sturgeon, Carp, Buffalo, Elk, Rein-deer, Eagle, Hare, Rabbit, and Snake; also the Reedgrass, Sand, Water, Rock, and Tobacco-plant.

"Among the Iroquois—and the rule is the same to the present day in most of the nations enumerated—no man is allowed to marry a woman of his own tribe, all the members of which are *consanguinii*. This was unquestionably the ancient law. It follows that husband and wife were always of different tribes. The children are of the tribe of the *mother*, in a majority of the nations; but the rule, if anciently universal, is not so at the present day. Where descent

Indian nations, they say, were divided into tribes, just lest any one might, through temptation or accident, marry a near relation, which "at present is scarcely possible, for whoever intends to marry must take a person of a different tribe;"[1] and the same feeling has been remarked by Dobrizhoffer in South America.[2]

What we have said of the Australians may be assumed to have been true, at one time at least, of the New Zealanders. In "The Curse of Manaia"[3] and several other of the New Zealand legends we have evidence

in the female line prevailed, it was followed by several important results, of which the most remarkable was the perpetual disinheritance of the male line. Since all titles as well as property descended in the female line, and were hereditary, in strictness, in the tribe itself, a son could never succeed to his father's title of Sachem, nor inherit even his medal or his tomahawk. If the Sachem, for example, was of the Wolf tribe, the title must remain in that tribe, and his son, who was necessarily of the tribe of his mother, would be out of the line of succession; but the brothers of the deceased Sachem would be of the Wolf tribe, being of the same mother, and so would the sons of his sisters: hence we find that the succession fell either upon a brother of the deceased ruler or upon a nephew. Between a brother of the deceased, and the son of a sister there was no law establishing a preference: neither as between several brothers on one side, or several sisters on the other, was there any law of primogeniture. They were all equally eligible, and the law of election came in to decide between them."—*Cambrian Journal*, vol. iii., second series, p. 149.

[1] Tanner's *Narrative*, p. 313, quoted in *Arch. Amer.*, and by Grey, *ut supra*.

[2] *Account of the Abipones*, vol. i. p. 69.

[3] *Polynesian Mythology, ut supra*, p. 162. In "The Curse of Manaia" the reader will find an instance of children fleeing from the tribe of birth to that of the mother's kindred.

that the wife never belonged to the tribe of her husband, and that the children belonged to the family of their mother. So among the Feejees, who appear to count blood relationship through the mother only. In the system of vasu-ing, which determines the claims of children upon the tribe of their mother, we have evidence that the mother always belongs to a different tribe from the father, and that the children are held to be of the family or tribe of their mother.[1] At any rate, vasu-ing is a relic of a stage in the development of the Feejees wherein that was the rule.

Curiously enough, there is reason for believing that exogamy prevailed among the Picts; in other words, according to the most approved doctrine, among the Gael or Highlanders; which fact bears at once on the rapes of the Cruithnians, the old Welsh and French customs, and the plebeian marriage-ceremonies of Rome, for the Celtic element was strong in Rome. That the Celts were anciently lax in their morals, and recognised relationship through mothers only, are facts well vouched;[2] and of such facts it is the usual concomitant, that the children should be named after the mother. The facts brought out by the distinguished antiquary, Mr. Skene, from a study of the list of Pictish kings down to 731, when Bede says that the law of succession through females was still in force, may to some extent be explained by the sons taking the names

---

[1] Erskine's *Pacific, ut supra*, pp. 153—215.
[2] Cæsar, *De Bello Gallico*, lib. v. sec. 14. Xiphiline, *Monum. Histor.*, lxi. Solinus, idem. Irish Nennius, liv.

of their mothers; but they point to something beyond this. By favour of Mr. Skene, we are at liberty to give here the results at which he has arrived, and which have not hitherto been published.

1st, That brothers always succeeded each other.

2nd, That in no case does a son succeed a father; after the brothers have reigned a new family comes in.

3rd, That the names of the fathers and of the sons are quite different. In no case does the name borne by any of the sons appear among the names of the fathers, nor conversely is there an instance of a father's name appearing among the sons.

4th, The names of the sons consist of a few Pictish names borne by sons of different fathers. These are— 6 Drusts, 5 Talorgs, 3 Nectans, 2 Galans, 6 Gartnaidhs, 4 Brudes. In no case does the name of a father occur twice in the list of fathers.

5th, In the list there are two cases of sons bearing Pictish names, whose fathers are known to have been strangers, and *these are the only fathers of whom we have any account.* They are—1. Talorg Macainfrit. His father was undoubtedly Ainfrit, son of Aethelfrith, King of Northumbria, who took refuge among the Picts, and afterwards became King of Northumbria; 2. Brude Mac Bile. His father was a Welshman, King of the Strath-Clyde Britons. In an old poem Brude Mac Bile is called son of the King of Ailcluaide, *i.e.* Dumbarton; and when, by the battle of Drunichen, he became King of the Picts, another old poem says, "to-day Brude fights a battle about the land of his grandfather."

The fact that the only fathers of whom we have any account are known to have been strangers—especially when taken along with the other facts which we possess about the Picts—raises a strong presumption that all the fathers were men of other tribes. At any rate there remains the fact, after every deduction has been made, that the fathers and mothers were in no case of the same family name.

We have now, by an irresistible array of instances, established the fact of exogamy being a most widely prevailing principle of marriage law among primitive races. We have found the areas to be, for the chief part, conterminous within which exogamy and the practice of capturing wives *de facto* prevails. Farther, in all the modern instances in which the symbol of capture is most marked, we have found that marriage within the tribe is prohibited as incest, as among the Khonds, the Fuegeans, the Kalmucks, and Circassians; also that in several cases where traces of the symbol appear, as among the Nogais and the Kirghiz, exogamy is more or less perfectly observed. We have seen good reason for thinking that exogamy and the practice of capture *de facto*, co-existed among the old Celts; and that in that co-existence lies the explanation of the symbol among the French, the Welsh, and the plebeians of Rome. Of the *jus connubii* of the Muscovites and Livonians in former times we have no direct information. Magnus is silent on the subject. But it is implied in his narrative that husband and wife invariably belonged to different kinships and village communities. We have found exogamy and the symbol co-existing in ancient India. Not to dwell on the slighter and more doubtful instances, we think it must now be admitted that we have sufficiently proved both the existence of exogamous tribes, and that among such tribes there prevails, or has prevailed, a system of capturing women for wives.

CHAPTER VI.

ON THE STATE OF HOSTILITY.

THE state of hostility is a theme which requires no research to illustrate it. It is a fact too familiar to require demonstration. If war is a lamentable feature of human life, it is not quite so ugly among savages as when waged by civilised men. In proportion to their masses and the weight of the interests at stake, the advanced nations are perhaps quite as frequently embroiled as the most barbarous; also in their case the natural beneficence—if we may so call it—of the impulse to feud is not always apparent. In the lower stages of society we recognise war as a condition of the rise of governments, and of the subordination of classes—its agonies as the growing pains of civil society; in the higher it appears too often as a mere scourge of mankind, deforming and impairing, if not destroying, the precious results and accumulations of long periods of peace and industry.

If the wars of savages are petty, they are habitual. While the domestic affections are little pronounced, the social are confined to the smallest fraction of humanity.

Whoever is foreign to a group is hostile to it. Even in comparatively advanced stages of savagery, groups rarely combine for common purposes; when they do—the object of the combination being accomplished—they return to their isolated independence. And when tribes have combined in nations, and the nations have become polite, it is yet some time before a distinction is drawn between strangers and enemies. No wonder if the distinction be not made by savages. Whoever is not with them is against them—a rival in the competition for food, a possible plunderer of their camp and ravisher of their women. Lay out the map of the world, and wherever you find populations unrestrained by the strong hand of government, there you will find perpetual feud, tribe against tribe, and family against family.

It would be superfluous to select particular districts from which to illustrate this truth, exemplifications of which we have already, in so many instances, had occasion to see. The state of hostility is the normal state of the race in early times. It is incidental to the separation and independence of men in small communities; and, while the arts are as yet in their infancy, small communities are a necessary result of the conditions of subsistence. Thus Lot separates from Abraham. Jacob goes one way and Esau another. And with separation comes estrangement—differences of language and habits—hostility. Till in a short time blood relations are as much apart—as foreign to one another—as people of different races and states.

CHAPTER VII.

EXOGAMY : ITS ORIGIN—COMPARATIVE ARCHAISM OF EXOGAMY AND ENDOGAMY.

AT the outset of our argument it was seen that if it could be shown that exogamous tribes existed, and that the usual relations of savage tribes to each other were those of hostility, we should have found a social condition in which it was inevitable that wives should systematically be procured by capture. It also appeared that if the existence of exogamous tribes either actually capturing their wives, or observing the symbol of capture in their marriage ceremonies, should be established in a reasonable number of cases, it would be a legitimate inference that exogamy has prevailed wherever we find a system of capture, or the form of capture, existing. We now confidently submit that the conditions requisite for this inference have been amply established in the three preceding chapters ; so that we may conclude that wherever capture, or the form of capture, prevails, or has prevailed, there prevails, or has prevailed, exogamy. Conversely, we may say that, wherever exogamy can be found, we may confidently expect to find, after due investigation, at least traces of a system of capture. We have traced the law and the corresponding practice among tribes scattered over a large portion of the globe. What farther knowledge of rude tribes now existing may show to us it would be idle to conjecture; but it might be plausibly maintained, upon the facts already known to us, that the principle of exogamy has in fact prevailed, and the system of capturing wives in fact been practised at a certain stage among every race of mankind.

Perhaps there is no question leading deeper into the foundations of civil society than that which regards the origin of exogamy, unless it be the cognate question of the origin of caste, which admits, however, more readily of ingenious surmises, and what mathematicians call singular solutions. We believe this restriction on marriage to be connected with the practice in early times of female infanticide which, rendering women scarce, led at once to polyandry within the tribe, and the capturing of women from without. Female infanticide—common among savages everywhere—prevails as a system, and has been customary from time immemorial amongst many of the races that exhibit the symbol of capture.[1] With some of the exogamous races it appears to be the

---

[1] The Circassians have not the practice. But there is reason to believe that they only commenced sparing their daughters when they found a profitable market for them. For an explanation of the effect of the law of blood-feud on the practice of infanticide, see the end of Chap. VIII.

[A short essay on the origin of exogamy will be included in a second series of *Studies in Ancient History*.]

rule to kill all female children, except the first-born when a female. To tribes surrounded by enemies, and, unaided by art, contending with the difficulties of subsistence, sons were a source of strength, both for defence and in the quest for food, daughters a source of weakness. Hence the cruel custom which, leaving the primitive human hordes with very few young women of their own—occasionally with none [1]—and, in any case, seriously disturbing the balance of the sexes within the hordes, forced them to prey upon one another for wives. Usage, induced by necessity, would in time establish a prejudice among the tribes observing it—a prejudice strong as a principle of religion, as every prejudice relating to marriage is apt to be—against marrying women of their own stock. A survey of the facts of primitive life, and the breakdown of exogamy in advancing communities, exclude the notion that the law originated in any innate or primary feeling against marriage with kinsfolk. Indeed, we shall hereafter see that it is probable that necessity may have established the prejudice against marrying women of the group even before the facts of blood-relationship had made any deep impression on the human mind. At present it may be observed that the existence of infanticide, so widespread, in itself indicates how slight the strength of blood-ties was in primitive times. To form an adequate notion, on the other hand, of the

[1] In one village of the Phweelongmai, on the eastern frontier of India, Colonel Macculloch found in 1849 that there was not a single female child.

extent to which tribes might, by means of infanticide, deprive themselves of their women, we have only to bear in mind the multitude of facts which testify to the thoughtlessness and improvidence of men during the childish stage of the human mind.

To show that the analysis by which the true solution of the questions respecting endogamy and exogamy is to be obtained, is the analysis of a series of phenomena which appears to form a progression, we notice the following as the divisions into which the less advanced portions of mankind fall when ranked according to their rules as to connubium:—

EXOGAMY PURE.—1. Tribal (or family) system.—Tribes separate. All the members of each tribe of the same blood, or feigning themselves to be so. Marriage prohibited between the members of the tribe.

2. Tribal system.—Tribe a congeries of family groups, falling into divisions, clans, thums, etc. No connubium between members of same division: connubium between all the divisions.

3. Tribal system.—Tribe a congeries of family groups embracing several village communities or nomadic hordes: members of families (or primitive stock groups) somewhat interfused. No connubium between persons whose family name points them out as being of the same stock.

4 Tribal system.—Tribe in divisions. No connubium between members of the same division: connubium between some of the divisions; only partial connubium between others—*e.g.*, a man of one may

marry a woman of another, but a woman of the former may not marry a man of the latter. Approach to caste.

5. Tribal system.—Tribe in divisions. No connubium between persons of the same stock: connubium between each division and some other. No connubium between some of the divisions. Caste.

ENDOGAMY PURE.—6. Tribal (or family) system.—Tribes separate. All the members of each tribe of the same blood, or feigning themselves to be so. Connubium between members of the tribe: marriage without the tribe forbidden and punished.

7. Tribal system indistinct.—Members of primitive (stock) groups interfused. (1.) Marriage forbidden except between persons whose family name points them out as being of the same stock. (2.) Marriage forbidden except between the members of particular families. Persons having connubium marked as a caste, old tribal divisions being lost sight of.

Although these tribal systems may be arranged as above so as to *seem* to form a progression, of which the extremes are pure exogamy on the one hand, and endogamy—transmuted into caste of the Mantchu and Hindu types—on the other, we have at present no right to say that these systems were developed in anything like this order in tribal history. They may represent a progression from exogamy to endogamy, or from endogamy to exogamy; or the middle terms, so to speak, may have been produced by the combination of groups severally organized on the one and the other of these principles. The two types of organization may be equally archaic. Men must originally have been free of any prejudice against marriage between relations—not necessarily endogamous, *i.e.* forbidding marriage except between kindred, but still more given to such unions than to unions with strangers. From this primitive indifference they may have advanced, some to endogamy, some to exogamy.[1]

The separate endogamous tribes are nearly as numerous, and they are in some respects as rude, as the separate exogamous tribes. It may be noted, however, that endogamy appears in populations formed by the fusion of many tribes, as the almost uniform characteristic of the dominant race. Hereafter we shall see how a tribe organized on the principle of endogamy might be developed from one organized on the principle of exogamy, in perfect consistency with the law against the intermarriage of relations. And while the existence of tribes like those of the Mantchu Tartars, who prohibit marriages between persons *whose family names are different*, is of great weight in favour of endogamy as a primitive type of organization; on the other hand, castes like those of India, embracing members of several different families, and with a marriage law like that of Menu, strongly suggest that many endogamous tribes have been developed from tribes organized on the oppo-

---

[1] [As this sentence has been misunderstood by a distinguished author, it seems necessary to suggest that it be read in connection with the first sentence of this paragraph and the concluding paragraph of this Chapter.]

site principle. Since, moreover, the reconversion of a caste or of an endogamous tribe into an exogamous tribe is inconceivable—we have no experience of caste disappearing except in advanced communities, and then only on a revolution of sentiment being produced by political influences—the choice seems to be between regarding the two classes of tribes as organized *ab initio* on distinct principles, or holding the exogamous to be the more archaic.

We may notice as strange, that frequently tribes thus oppositely organized are found inhabiting the same area. On the sub-Himalayan ranges, for example, are the Sodhas, who intermarry with the Rajputs, not with each other; the Magars, who prohibit marriages between members of the same thum; and, again, the Kocch, Bodo, Ho, and Dhumal, who are forbidden to marry except to members of their own tribes or kiels. And, in some districts—as in the hills on the north-eastern frontier of India, in the Caucasus, and the hill-ranges of Syria—we find a variety of tribes, proved, by physical characteristics and the affinities of language, of one and the same original stock, yet in this particular differing *toto coelo* from one another—some forbidding marriage within the tribe, and some prescribing marriage without it.

What has been said is enough to show that the question of the comparative archaism of exogamy and endogamy is as difficult as it is interesting. We shall in the next chapter lead up to a fuller discussion of that question, while investigating more minutely than we have hitherto done the conditions of the form of capture being evolved. We shall there endeavour to establish the following propositions :—1. That the most ancient system in which the idea of blood-relationship was embodied was the system of kinship through females only. 2. That the primitive groups were, or were assumed to be, homogeneous. 3. That the system of kinship through females only tended to render the exogamous groups heterogeneous, and thus to supersede the system of capturing wives. 4. That in the advance from savagery the system of kinship through females only was succeeded by a system which acknowledged kinship through males also ; and which, in most cases, passed into a system which acknowledged kinship through males only. 5. That the system of kinship through males tended to rear up homogeneous groups, and thus to restore the original condition of affairs—where the exogamous prejudice survived—as regards both the practice of capturing wives and the evolution of the form of capture. 6. That a local tribe, under the combined influence of exogamy and the system of female kinship, might attain a balance of persons of different sexes regarded as being of different descent, and that thus its members might be able to intermarry with one another, and wholly within the tribe, consistently with the principle of exogamy. 7. That a local tribe, having reached this stage and grown proud through success in war, might decline intermarriage with other local tribes and become a caste. 8. That on kinship becoming agnatic, the members of such a tribe might yield to the universal tendency of rude races to eponomy, and feign themselves to be all derived from a common ancestor, and so become endogamous. And 9. That there is reason to think that some endogamous tribes became endogamous in this manner.

CHAPTER VIII.

ANCIENT SYSTEMS OF KINSHIP AND THEIR INFLUENCE ON THE STRUCTURE OF PRIMITIVE GROUPS.

The earliest human groups can have had no idea of kinship. We do not mean to say that there ever was a time when men were not bound together by a feeling of kindred. The filial and fraternal affections may be instinctive. They are obviously independent of any theory of kinship, its origin or consequences; they are distinct from the perception of the unity of blood upon which kinship depends; and they may have existed long before kinship became an object of thought. What we would say is, that ideas of kinship must be regarded as growths—must have *grown* like all other ideas related to matters primarily cognisable only by the senses; and that the fact of consanguinity must have long remained unperceived as other facts, quite as obvious, have done. In other words, at the root of kinship is a physical fact, which could be discerned only through observation and reflection,—a fact, therefore, which must for a time have been overlooked. No advocate of innate ideas, we should imagine, will maintain their existence on a subject so concrete as relationship by blood.

A group of kindred in that stage of ignorance is the rudest that can be imagined. Though they were chiefly held together by the feeling of kindred, the *apparent* bond of fellowship between the members of such a group would be that they and theirs had always been companions in war or the chase—joint-tenants of the same cave or grove. To one another they would simply be as comrades. As distinguished from men of other groups, they would be of the group, and named after it.

Hence, most naturally, on the idea of blood-relationship arising, would be formed the conception of *Stocks*. Previously individuals had been affiliated not to persons, but to some group. The new idea of blood-relationship would more readily demonstrate the group to be composed of kindred than it would evolve a special system of blood-ties between certain of the individuals in the group. The members of a group would now have become brethren. As distinguished from men of other groups, they would be of the group-stock, and named after the group.[1]

The development of the idea of blood-relationship into a system of kinship must have been a work of

---

[1] It is a question for philologists how far the earliest words which denote a human group involve the idea of blood. In one case they seem not to have done so. Grant, in his *Origin and Descent of the Gael*, says that teadhloch and cuediche or coediche, Gaelic names for family, mean, the first, having a common residence; the second, those who eat together. The Gael had, however, the more general terms finne and cinne—the former meaning born of the same stock, and the latter denoting the tribe.

time—at least the establishment over any great area of any such system as an institution of customary law must have been slowly effected. It is most improbable that that idea, when first formed, was anywhere at once embodied in a well-defined system of kinship.

We shall endeavour to show—

I. *That the most ancient system in which the idea of blood-relationship was embodied, was a system of kinship through females only.*

Once a man has perceived the fact of consanguinity in the simplest case—namely, that he has his mother's blood in his veins, he may quickly see that he is of the same blood with her other children. A little more reflection will enable him to see that he is of one blood with the brothers and sisters of his mother. On further thought he will perceive that he is of the same blood with the children of his mother's sister. And, in process of time, following the ties of blood through his mother, and females of the same blood, he must arrive at a system of kinship through females. The blood-ties through females being obvious and indisputable, the idea of blood-relationship, as soon as it was formed, must have begun to develop, however slowly, into a system embracing them. What further development this idea might have—whether it would simultaneously have a development in the direction of kinship through males —must have depended on the circumstances connected with paternity. If the paternity of a child were usually as indisputable as the maternity, we might expect to find kinship through males acknowledged soon after kinship through females.[1] But however natural it might be that men should think of blood-ties as possible to be propagated through fathers, blood-ties through fathers could not find a place in a system of kinship, unless circumstances usually allowed of some degree of certainty as to who the father of a child was, or of certainty as to the father's blood.[2] A system of relationship through fathers could only be formed—as we have seen that a system of relationship through mothers would be formed —after a good deal of reflection upon the fact of paternity. And fathers must usually be known before men will think of relationship through fathers—indeed, before the idea of a father can be formed. There could be no *system* of kinship through males if paternity was usually, or in a great proportion of cases, uncertain. The requisite degree of certainty can be had only when the mother is appropriated to a particular man as his wife, or to men of one blood as wife, and when women thus appropriated are usually found faithful to their lords.

[1] It has been doubted whether the blood-tie through the father is entitled to rank with that through the mother. It may be that the connection between father and child is less intimate than that between mother and child as regards the transmission of characteristics, mental or physical. And the former tie is unquestionably less obvious than the latter. It is, however, an undoubted blood-tie, and must have been thought of soon after that through mothers. All that it concerns us to show in the text is, that when the idea of it was formed it could only receive development into a system of kinship on certain conditions, which were not easily satisfied.

[2] It will be seen that there may be certainty as to the father's blood (as where all the possible fathers are brothers) without there being certainty as to the father.

Considering that the history of all the races of men, so far as we know it, is the history of a progress from the savage state; considering the social condition of rude tribes still upon the earth,—remembering that the races which can be traced in history had all a previous history, which remains unwritten,—it cannot seem a very strange proposition that there has been a stage in the development of human races when there was no such appropriation of women to particular men—when, in short, marriage, as it exists among civilised nations, was not practised. We believe we shall show, to a sufficient degree of probability, that there have been times when marriage, in this sense, was yet undreamt of. Wherever this has been the case, the paternity of children must have been uncertain; the conditions essential to a system of kinship through males being formed would therefore be wanting; no such system would be formed; there would be—there could be—kinship through females only.

Not to assume that the progress of the various races of men from savagery has been a uniform process, that all the stages which any of them has gone through have been passed in their order by all, we shall be justified in believing that more or less of promiscuity in the connection of the sexes, and a system of kinship through females only, have subsisted among races of men among whom no traces of them remain, when we have shown their existence in a considerable number of cases—if in these there appear nothing exceptional. After what has been said above, it must be plain that kinship through females only, if it exist at all, must be a more archaic system of relationship than kinship through males—the product of an earlier and ruder stage in human development than the latter—somewhat more than a step farther back in the direction of savagery. To prove its existence on such a scale as to entitle it to rank among the normal phenomena of human development, is, we may now say, to prove it the most ancient system of kinship. As customs tend to perpetuate themselves and die hard, it will not in any degree make against our explanation of the origin of kinship through females only, that it should be found in some cases along with marriage relations which allow of certainty as to fathers. It is inconceivable that anything but the want of certainty on that point could have long prevented the acknowledgment of kinship through males; and in such cases we shall be able to conclude that such certainty has formerly been wanting—that more or less promiscuous intercourse between the sexes has formerly prevailed. The connection between these two things—uncertain paternity and kinship through females only, seems so necessary—that of cause and effect—that we may confidently infer the one where we find the other.

Let us see, then, what can be said for the proposition that there has been a stage in the progress of men in which a woman was not usually appropriated to a particular man as his wife.

All the evidence we have goes to show that men were from the beginning gregarious. The geological record distinctly exhibits them in groups—naked hunters or feeders upon shell-fish, leading a precarious life of squalid misery. This testimony is confirmed by all history. We hear nothing in the most ancient times of individuals except as being members of groups. The history of property is the history of the development of proprietary rights *inside* groups, which were at first the only owners;[1] and of all other personal rights—even including the right in offspring—it may be said that their history is that of the gradual assertion of the claims of individuals against the traditional rights of groups.

We, of course, know nothing about the co-ordination of the sexes in the earliest groups. The reader knows already what must be our conjecture as to what it was. We can trace the line of human progress far back towards brutishness; finding as we go back the noble faculties peculiar to man weaker and weaker in their manifestations, producing less and less effect, — at last scarcely any effect at all—upon his position and habits. As we go back, we find more and more in men the traits of gregarious animals, slighter and slighter indications of operative intellect. As among other gregarious animals, the unions of the sexes were probably, in the earliest times, loose, transitory, and in some degree promiscuous.

Before the invention of the arts, and the formation of provident habits, the struggle for existence must often have become very serious. The instincts of self-preservation, therefore, must have frequently predominated and shaped

---

[1] *Ancient Law, ut supra*, p. 268.

the features of society freely, as if the unselfish affections had no place in human nature. None of the races of mankind can have been spared the cruel experience of this initiatory stage; or can have escaped the effects of that experience on its character and customs. Even those most favourably situated must have had long periods of trial, and have suffered from the incessant hostility of neighbours. So, without supposing the course of human events to have been uniform, we must conceive of early human society as having been throughout affected by influences of the same general, unfriendly character, and as having been determined, though perhaps by unequal pressure, towards one uniform type in all its parts.

Foremost among the results of this early struggle for food and security, must have been an effect upon the balance of the sexes. As braves and hunters were required and valued, it would be the interest of every horde to rear, when possible, its healthy male children. It would be less its interest to rear females, as they would be less capable of self-support, and of contributing, by their exertions, to the common good. In this lies the only explanation which can be accepted of the origin of those systems of female infanticide still existing, the discovery of which from time to time, in out-of-the-way places, so shocks our humanity. It is of no consequence by what theories the races who practise infanticide now defend the practice.[1] There can be no doubt that its

---

[1] Often, as among the Khonds, it is found to be an institution of religion.

origin is everywhere referable to that early time of struggle and necessity which we have been contemplating.

What is now true in varying degrees of all the rudest races may be assumed to have been true of all the earliest groups. We may predicate of the primitive groups that they were all or nearly all marked by a want of balance between the sexes—the males being in the majority. The reader will have little difficulty in granting that we may do so when he reflects on the prevalence of exogamy, the origin of which must be referred to that want of balance. And we think he will be still more ready to make the concession when we shall have surveyed the facts connected with polyandry—the origin of which must be referred to the same cause.

What diminished the number of the female sex would increase the importance of women. The first result of the balance of the sexes being against the females, must have been to give every woman more than one, it might be several wooers. Apart from any disproportion of the sexes, we might expect the more engaging females of a horde to be surrounded by suitors. Savages are unrestrained by any sense of delicacy from a copartnery in sexual enjoyments; and, indeed, in the civilised state, the sin of great cities shows that there are no natural restraints sufficient to hold men back from grosser copartneries. But within a horde possessing few women, such copartneries would be a necessity. And as savages assert for themselves a high degree of independence, it is obvious that grave difficulties must have surrounded the constitution and regulation of such copartneries. And to the consideration of these difficulties we are led the instant we conceive of the primitive groups as containing fewer women than men.

The men of a group must either have quarrelled about their women and separated, splitting the horde into hostile sections; or, in the spirit of indifference, indulged in savage promiscuity. That quarrels and divisions were of frequent occurrence cannot be doubted. These were the first wars for women, and they went to form the habits which established exogamy. And whether quarrels arose or not, we are led to contemplate groups—the horde or its sections—indulging in a promiscuity more or less general. The quarrels must have been between sections of the hordes rather than between individuals. No individual at that stage could well carry off a woman, isolate himself, and found a family. However brave and strong, he could scarcely maintain his independence for any time against numerous assailants. Unless these quarrels went the length of completely disintegrating the groups—a result which the gregarious nature of men tended to prevent—we must arrive at last at groups within which harmony was maintained through indifference and promiscuity.

These groups would hold their women, like their other goods, in common. And the children, while attached to mothers, would belong to the horde.[1] We

---

[1] The tie between mother and child, which exists as a matter of necessity during infancy, is not unfrequently found to be lost sight

find traces of the former existence of groups of this description; and it is probable that before the rise of kinship, all the human groups were of that model.

On the rise of kinship, the difficulty due to the scarcity of women would more easily be overcome. The first advance from a general promiscuity—assuming its existence—would naturally be to a promiscuity less general—to arrangements between small sets of men to attach themselves to a particular woman. Previous to the establishment of a system of kinship—when men were bound to each other only by the tribal tie—it is obvious that there would constantly be difficulties in the way of their forming such combinations. When, however, the system of kinship through females only had been firmly established, every group stood resolved into a number of small brotherhoods, each composed of sons of the same mother. And within these, the feeling of close kinship would simplify the constitution of the polyandrous arrangement.

Now, here, at length, we are upon the firm ground of fact. We have examples of general promiscuity; and examples of modified promiscuity, in which, with a pretence of marriage, the woman may bestow her favours upon any one, under certain restrictions as to rank and family. We have numerous examples of polyandry, and they are such as to show that polyandry

---

of among savages on the age of independence being reached. The liability of mothers to be carried off would, among exogamous races, simplify the general filiation of children to the group, rather than to mothers.

must be regarded as a modification of and advance from promiscuity. We have examples of polyandry in which the wife has several husbands, who are not necessarily relatives; and very many examples of polyandry in which the husbands are all brothers. We often find these two forms of polyandry in the same district, in different sections of the population: here, the husbands as a rule, are no relations; there, the husbands as a rule, are brothers. Further, where the husbands are not brothers, we find the system of relationship through females only; and, so enduring is custom, we very often find that system where marriage has long been so regulated as to permit of kinship through males. In many cases we find traces of the system of kinship through females only lingering about the laws of marriage and succession to estates and titles, even where male kinship has been long established. Moreover, in nearly all the cases in which traces are to be found of kinship through females only, traces of polyandry also remain. Thus, what we find is just what was to be expected, if the account we have offered of the origin of polyandry were correct.

We repeat, that in showing the prevalence of polyandry, we shall be showing the prevalence of a modification of promiscuity. This is manifest as regards the ruder species of polyandry, in which the husbands are not relations. It is equally, though less obviously, true of the less rude polyandry in which the husbands are brothers. From the way in which polyandry is presented to us, we shall have a proof that the less rude polyandry was developed from the ruder by the help of the system of kinship through females only—was superinduced, that is, upon a promiscuity less qualified than itself. Promiscuity, producing uncertainty of fatherhood, led to the system of kinship through mothers only. This kinship paved the way for polyandry such as we commonly find it; and this form of polyandry introduced male kinship.[1] That, along with the ruder polyandry, we always find the system of kinship through females only, and that where the less rude form prevails we can generally trace that system, is moreover a proof *a posteriori* of what we have shown must be the case, that the origin of kinship through females only is referable to uncertainty of male parentage.

We shall not concern ourselves with the direct evidence which might be adduced to show that there once prevailed among men a promiscuity less qualified than polyandry. We may however recall the fact, that tradition is found everywhere pointing to a time when marriage was unknown, and to some legislator to whom it owed its institution: among the Egyptians to Menes; the Chinese to Fohi; the Greeks to Cecrops; the Hindus to Svetaketu.[2] And we shall proceed to show how much evidence remains to give verisimilitude to these tradi-

---

[1] We shall see farther on how numerous the known cases are in which the progress to male kinship and the patriarchal system was a progress having this kind of polyandry for one of its stages. The other main highway of progress must have lain through the system of confining women—a system probably established by exogamy and the practice of capturing wives.

[2] See Muir's *Sanskrit Texts*, 1860. Part ii. p. 336.

tions. Passing over communities in which, according to ancient historians, something like a general promiscuity prevailed—such as the Massagetæ, Agathyrsi, and the ancient Spartans; passing over also the numerous races now existing, which, according to modern travellers, have no conception of conjugal fidelity [1]—we shall now

[1] It may be as well to append some modern examples of promiscuity, and of practices which have the same effect in rendering uncertain male parentage. The Ansarians have their wives in common; the people of Martawan, of the tribe of Ansarians, let out their wives and daughters (Volney, *Travels*, chap. xxvii.). The Keiaz (Paropamisans) lend their wives to their guests (Latham, *Des. Ethn.*, vol. ii. p. 246); so do the Eimauk (Caubul),—Elphinstone, 1815, p. 483; so, we are informed, do the Kandyans. The Mpongme (Africa) lend wives (Reade, *Sav. Afr.*, p. 259); so do the Koryaks and Chukchi, who lend out daughters as well (N.E. Siberia), —Erkman, vol. ii. p. 531, and see Cochrane's *Journey*, 1825, vol. i. p. 336. The Koryaks are also polyandrous. The same disregard of conjugal fidelity appeared in Caindu, Casca (Turkistan Tartary), and in Cumana (Gaya, p. 104; Marco Polo, *ut infra*, p. 258). We find it now among the Aimaks (*Des. Ethno.*, vol. i. p. 333. It was customary in Kamul (Marco Polo, Bohn's edition, p. 110). Montesquieu, b. 16, c. viii., remarks on the licentious wantonness of the women of Patan, against which the men had to adopt measures of self-protection. Mr. Wilson of Mussoorie, in an admirable report on the Puharies of Gurwahl (*A Summer Ramble in the Himalayas*, q. v. p. 182, says of the Gungarees and Perbuttees: "Their immorality is something incredible—chastity being little appreciated even where it does exist." In various other quarters we find practices fatal to certainty of male parentage; such as frequent divorces, *e.g.* among the Bedouins (Burckhardt, *Notes*, i. 111); and marriages for an agreed-upon term of endurance, usually short. Such marriages were usual in Sounan, Arabia Felix (Hamilton's *New Account of the East Indies*, vol. i. p. 51); in Siam (*Ibid.*, vol. ii. p. 279). In China such marriages are said to be still customary. In a recent report of the proceedings of the Society of Sainte-Enfance in China,

go on to consider the regulated promiscuity known as polyandry, and see to what extent it exists, and what traces of its former existence still remain.

Let us first see what is the area over which polyandry now prevails. It prevails universally in Tibet, and is common in the Himalayan and sub-Himalayan regions adjoining Tibet; in the valley of Kashmir; among the Spiti, in Ladak; in Kistewar and Sirmor. It occurs among the Telingese; in the Sivalik mountains, and in Kasia. There are unmistakable traces of its existence till recently in Gurwhal, Sylhet, and Cachar. Farther south in India we find polyandry among the Tudas of the Nilgherry Hills, the Coorgs of Mysore, and the Nairs, the Maleres, and Poleres

in the *Esperance* of Nancy, it is said that, in many parts, Chinamen may repudiate their wives, and marry again, every year. As a result, the children belong to the mother, who has over them the power of life or death. The same must have been the case in Turkistan (Marco Polo, *ut supra*, p. 99). According to Livingstone (*Travels*, p. 394), marriage in Loando is almost unknown—an unsettled concubinage. And see *Ibid*, p. 496, for an example of savage indifference as to marital purity. In the Polynesian Mythology, we have an excellent casual proof of the uncertainty of male parentage, even where there is marriage (polygamous). A young man distinguishes himself, and turns out to be the chief's son. He was "a young man, the name of whose father had never been told by his mother." The lady was one of the chief's wives! And see Turner's *Tibet*, p. 10, and M'Culloch's *Munniepore*, for examples of a system of pawning wives. See also, for similar or worse customs, Buchanan's *Journey from Madras*, 1807, vol. ii. pp. 129, 492, and vol. iii. p. 66; Krusenstern's *Voyage*, 1813, vol. ii. p. 245 (Kamschatka); La Perouse's *Voyage*, 1798, vol. ii. p. 195 (Island of Maouna); Maundeville, chap. xxiii. (Chatay); and Huc's *Travels*, vol. ii. p. 142, Nat. Illus. Lib.

of Malabar. We find it off the Indian coast in Ceylon; and going eastward strike on it as an ancient though now almost superseded custom in New Zealand, and in one or two of the Pacific islands. Going northward we meet it again in the Aleutian islands; and taking the continent to the west and north of the Aleutians, we find it among the Koryaks to the north of the Okhotsk Sea. Crossing the Russian Empire to the west side, we find polyandry among the Saporogian Cossacks: we thus have traced it at points half round the globe. This is not all, however. Polyandry is found in several parts of Africa and of America. We have the authority of Humboldt for its prevalence among the tribes on the Orinoco, and he also vouches for its former prevalence in Lanzerota, one of the Canary Islands.[1]

From ancient history we learn that polyandry at one time existed over even a greater area. Traces of it

---

[1] Turner's *Tibet*, 1800, p. 348. Vigne's *Kashmir*, 1842, vol. i. p. 37. Cunningham's *Ladak*, 1854, p. 306. Buchanan's *Journey, &c.*, 1807, vol. ii. pp. 408—412. Archer's *Upper India*, 1833, vol. i. p. 185. Latham's *Descriptive Ethnology*, 1859, vol. i. pp. 24—28; vol. ii. pp. 398, 496, and 462. Humboldt's *Personal Narrative* (Williams's Translation), 1819, vol. i. chap. i. p. 84; and vol. v. part ii. p. 549. Hamilton's *New Account of the East Indies*, 1727, vol. i. pp. 274 and 308. Reade's *Savage Africa*, p. 43. Erkman's *Travels in Siberia*, vol. ii. p. 531. *Marriage Ceremonies*, by Seignior Gaya, 1698, pp. 70 and 96. Tennent's *Ceylon*, 1859, vol. ii. p. 429. "Legend of Rupe," Grey's *Polynesian Mythology*, 1854, p. 81. *A Summer Ramble in the Himalayas*, 1860, p. 202. Fisher's *Memoir of Sylhet, &c.*, in *Journal of Asiatic Soc. Bengal*, vol. ix. p. 834. *Asiat. Res.*, vol. v. p. 13. Our information regarding the Saporogian Cossacks has been obtained from Sir John M'Neil.

remained in the time of Tacitus among the Germans.[1] And while in certain cantons of Media, according to Strabo,[2] polygyny was authorised by express law, which ordained every inhabitant to maintain at least seven wives; in other cantons the opposite rule was in force: a woman was allowed to have many husbands, and they looked with contempt on those who had less than five. Cæsar informs us that in his time polyandry prevailed among 'the Britons.[3] We find direct evidence of its existence among the Picts in the Irish Nennius,[4] not to mention traces of it in the Pictish Laws of Succession. Further we find traditions of it among the Hindus[5]— especially among the Rajputs. And we find it among the Getes of Transoxiana (the Yuti or Yuechi of the Chinese historians).[6] To see where else it prevailed we must go back upon our authorities and examine the various phases of polyandry which they present, and obtain a test for detecting its presence where historical evidence of its existence is wanting.

The ruder form of polyandry, as we have said, is that in which the husbands are *not* brothers; the less rude is that in which they *are* brothers. The polyandry of the Kasias, the Nairs, and the Saporogian Cossacks,

---

[1] *German*, xx., Latham's edn., p. 67, *et seq.*
[2] Lib. xi. Casaub, 526; and see Goguet, vol. iii. book vi. c. i.
[3] *De Bello Gallico*, lib. v. c. xiv.
[4] Appendix LI.
[5] Tod's *Annals, &c. of Rajasthan*, 1829, vol. i. p. 48; and see Max Müller's *Hist. of Sans. Anc. Lit.*, pp. 45, *et seq.*; Tod's *Travels*, 1839, p. 464.
[6] Tod's *Travels, ut supra.*

appears to be purely of the ruder sort, and is attended by the system of kinship through females only. It is left doubtful what is the form of the institution in some instances, as in the Aleutian Islands, and among the Koryaks. But in all the other cases in which polyandry occurs, the authorities show that the ruder form occurs among the lower classes wherever the less rude occurs, except in Tibet, where polyandry is universal and the husbands are always brothers; except in Malabar, where polyandry is universally practised by all classes, saving the Brahmans only, but is of the ruder species among the high caste Nairs, and of the less rude among the lower castes, the Teers, Maleres, and Poleres. It is in the nature of the case that all the possible forms of polyandry must lie in between, or be embraced in, the Nair and the Tibetan forms.

Let us attend then to the accounts we have of these two forms. Of the Nair polyandry we have three accounts. The account in the *Asiatic Researches*,[1] is that among the Nairs it is the custom for one woman "to have attached to her two males, or four, or perhaps more, and they cohabit according to rules." With this account that of Hamilton agrees,[2] excepting that he states that a Nair woman could have no more than twelve husbands, and had to select these under certain restrictions as to rank and caste. On the other hand, Buchanan states[3] that the women after

[1] Vol. v. p. 13.
[2] *Account of the East Indies, ut supra*, vol. i. p. 308.
[3] Buchanan's *Journey*, vol. ii. p. 411.

marriage [1] are free to cohabit with any number of men, under certain restrictions as to tribe and caste. It is consistent with the three accounts, and is directly stated by Hamilton, that a Nair may be one in several combinations of husbands; that is, he may have any number of wives. The accounts, however, differ in regard to one important particular. Buchanan represents the wife as living in family with her mother or brother, while Hamilton represents her as having "an house built for her own conveniency" on being married to the first of her husbands. In the *Asiatic Researches* the wife is represented as living with her mother or brother. The probability is that both arrangements are occasionally adopted, the more usual course being for the wife to remain in the family of her mother and brothers. In Ceylon, where the higher and lower polyandry co-exist, marriage is of two sorts—Deega or Beena—according as the wife goes to live in the house and village of her husbands, or as the husband or husbands come to live with her in or near the house of her birth.[2] And among the Kandyans the rights of inheritance of a

[1] In the *Asiatic Researches*, it is said, "The Nairs practise not marriage, except so far as may be implied from their tying a thread round the neck of the woman on the first occasion."

[2] See Forbes's *Ceylon*, 1840, vol. i. p. 333. Mr. Starke, late Chief-Justice of Ceylon, says that "sometimes a deega married girl returned to her parents' house and was there provided with a beena husband who lived with her in family" (private letter). The beena husband's tenure of office seems to have been very insecure. See Forbes, *ut supra*. The Kandyans are now under British rule, and their marriages regulated by a special ordinance.

woman and her children are found to depend on whether the woman is a beena or a deega wife.

The three accounts which we have of the Nair polyandry are agreed that the Nair husbands are usually not brothers—usually not relatives—and that the institution leaves male parentage and the father's blood quite uncertain. "In consequence of this strange manner of propagating the species," says Buchanan,[1] "no Nair knows his father, and every man looks upon his sister's children as his heirs. He indeed looks upon them with the same fondness that fathers in other parts of the world have for their own children, and he would be considered as an unnatural monster were he to show such signs of grief at the death of a child, which, from long cohabitation with and love for its mother, he might suppose to be his own, as he did at the death of a child of his sister. A man's mother manages his family; and after her death his eldest sister assumes the direction. *Brothers almost always live under the same roof;* but if one of the family separates from the rest, he is always accompanied by his favourite sister. A man's movable property, after his death, is divided among the sons and daughters of all his sisters; and if there are lands, their management falls *to the eldest male of the family.*"[2]

Now here, derived from the ruder polyandry, is an exceedingly rude, *the rudest,* form of family system with which we are acquainted. And it is a sort of

---

[1] *Ut supra,* vol. ii. p. 412.   [2] See Buchanan, vol. ii. p. 594.

family system which is found, more or less modified in some of its features, in several cases, where marriage is now either monogamous or polygamous. Its chief features are the absence of a paternal head, and the system of female succession. Among the Kocch, with whom marriage is now monogamous, we find the same system, excepting that the family circle includes the daughter's husband, as a subordinate member of the family. A Kocch man goes, on his marriage, like the beena husband of Ceylon, to live in family with his wife and her mother; on his marriage all his property is made over to his wife; and on her death her heirs are her daughters.[1] Here we conclude that the advance from the ruder polyandry to monogamy took place in some way consistent with the preservation of the main features of the family system peculiar to the ruder polyandry—consistent with the mother's maintaining her position as the head of the family, and with an increase of the influence of women as connecting links in the social and proprietary systems. We shall presently see that the advance in this direction must be counted exceptional; at the same time it cannot well be doubted that such a family system as we find among the Kocch had its origin in the ruder species of polyandry.

What, then, was the normal line of progress? We think that we shall be able to show what it was—that it lay between the lower and higher polyandry. In the accounts we have, we can detect stages of preparation

[1] *Des. Ethn.*, vol. i. p. 96.

for the change from the former species of polyandry to the latter. We must regard as the rudest cases those in which the wife lives not with her husbands, but with her mother or brothers. In these cases a woman's children are born in and belong to *her* mother's house. In the cases next in order of rudeness, the wife passes into cohabitation, according to fixed rules, with the husbands, in a house of her own—becoming thus detached from her family, though still connected with it through the right of her children to become heirs to the family estate. Her children would still belong to her mother's family—the want of a community of blood and interests among the husbands preventing the appropriation of the children to them. Such cases, however—detaching the woman from her family—would prepare the way for a species of marriage still less rude, in which the woman passed from her family, not into a house of her own, but into the family of her husbands, in which her children would be born, and to which they would belong. This could only happen when the husbands were all of one blood, and had common rights of property—in short, when they were brothers.

This last was a most important step in advance. The girl of a house no longer remained at home with her mother and brothers—aiding in and succeeding to the management; she passed into another family, associating with the sons thereof as wife; while her place at home was assumed by a stranger—as wife to her brothers. There being now a community of blood and interests in the husbands, there was nothing to prevent the appropriation to them of her children—an appropriation which would disqualify the children for being heirs to the property of her mother and brothers. To give effect now to the old law of succession, would be, not to keep property in families, but to introduce a system of exchanges of family estates. Moreover, when this form of marriage became general, and when conjugal fidelity was secured by penalties, we should expect to find that the system of kinship through males would appear—this species of marriage allowing of certainty as to the father's blood, though not of certainty as to fathers. A woman's children would become the heirs of the husband's family in which they would be born, and to which they would belong.

Now it is this highest development of polyandry, and of the family system which polyandry admitted of, which we find in Tibet.

"Here," says Turner, speaking of Tibet,[1] "we find a practice—that of polyandry—universally prevailing; and see one female associating her fate and fortune with all the brothers of a family without any restriction of age or of numbers. The choice of a wife is the privilege of the elder brother. . . . The number of husbands is not, as far as I could learn, defined or restricted within any limits; it sometimes happens that in a small family there is but one male; and the number, perhaps, may seldom exceed that which a native of rank, during my residence at Teshoo Loomboo,

[1] Turner's *Tibet*, 1800, p. 348.

pointed out to me in a family resident in the neighbourhood, in which five brothers were then living very happily with one female, under the same connubial compact. Nor is this sort of league confined to the lower ranks of people alone: it is found also frequently in the most opulent families."

Let us now see to what extent polyandry of the Tibetan type can be traced elsewhere than in Tibet; and what evidence there is of its being an advance from the Nair species of polyandry. The authorities already cited [1] exhibit the Tibetan as the prevailing species of polyandry in nearly the whole of the Himalayan and sub-Himalayan regions: Kashmir, Ladak, Kinawer, Kistewar, and Sirmor. It is the general form of polyandry in Ceylon. It is the form which Humboldt found among the red-men. "Among the Avaroes and the Maypures," he says, "brothers have often but one wife." It is the form which Cæsar found among the Britons. "Uxores habent deni duodenique inter se communes, *et maxime* fratres cum fratribus, et parentes cum liberis; sed si qui sunt ex his nati, eorum habentur liberi a quibus primum virgines quæque ductæ sunt." [2] And to show that the two forms of polyandry are stages in a progress, we repeat that almost everywhere, outside Tibet, we find the lower form accompanying the higher. In some quarters the lower only is known—as in Kasia and among the Nairs. In others—Kooloo, for example—

---

[1] *Ante*, p. 98.
[2] *De Bello Gallico*, v. xiv.

the lower form is prevalent; the higher [1] also is known, but is exceptional. Again, in numerous quarters the higher is the general form, and the lower the exceptional—as in Ceylon; and lastly, in some quarters, as in Tibet, we lose sight of the lower form altogether. The higher polyandry has become a national institution.

And finding the higher polyandry a national institution, we observe that we are in a position to show that most probably polyandry formerly prevailed over a still vaster area than that within which we have hitherto found it. We have seen that with polyandry, of the Tibetan type, wherever it was long and generally established, kinship through males must have been introduced; the father's blood, though not the father, being certain, where the wife was faithful. We have also seen, in the case of the Britons, that the children of the woman were accounted to belong to the husband who first espoused her; and that in Tibet, the right of choosing the wife belongs to the eldest brother, to whom, also, the children of the marriage are held to belong. We must now, to obtain what we have been in search of—a test of the former presence of polyandry —look at the Tibetan form of polyandry in a state of decadence. We find it in such a state in Ladak. "In

---

[1] Archer, in his *Upper India* (1833), vol. i. pp. 235–6, says of the Grooah (Kooloo): "Here one woman cohabits with two, three, and four men, *and they may even be all brothers;* this practice is universal. I was informed of the rules and modes of intercourse, all evincing a state of society least beholden to civilisation, or less sophisticated than any yet known."

Ladak," says Moorcroft,[1] "when an eldest son marries, the property of his father (more properly the family estate) descends to him, and he is charged with the maintenance of his parents. The parents may continue to live with him, if he and his wife please; if not, a separate dwelling is provided for them.[2] A younger son is usually made a Lama. Should there be more brothers, *and they agree to the arrangement*, the juniors become inferior husbands to the wife; all the children, however, are considered as belonging to the head of the family. The younger brothers have no authority; they wait upon the elder as his servants, and can be turned out of doors at his pleasure, without it being incumbent upon him to provide for them. *On the death of the eldest brother, his property, authority, and widow, devolve upon his next brother.*" And that whether the younger brother has agreed to the polyandrous arrangement or not. He has a customary right of succession to his brother's property, and to his widow, and he cannot take the one without taking the other.

Here we are brought to consider the meaning and origin of the legal obligation which we find laid on younger brothers, among certain peoples, to marry in their turn the widow of their deceased elder brother. There can be no doubt that that obligation was in its origin the counterpart of a legal right of succession. It is so with the Kirghiz, Aenezes, and Mongols —

[1] Moorcroft and Trebeck's *Travels*, 1841, vol. i. p. 320.
[2] See M'Culloch's *Munniepore*, pp. 8 and 67, for a similar custom among the Loohoopas.

the next brother being heir even where the elder leaves issue.

When history begins, the Hebrew law preferred the issue to the next brother; but when he or the next of kin succeeded, it was on the old footing. This is clear from the book of Ruth.[1] The *hereditatis emptor* of the deceased took to wife at the same time his widow, "to raise up the name of the dead upon his inheritance." The obligation to marry the widow was the counterpart of the right of succession. And we can see the connection between the obligation and heirship dropping slowly out of view. In Deuteronomy [2] it is provided that the husband's brother shall "perform the duty of an husband's brother" to the widow, only when the brethren dwell together, and one of them dies childless. The obligation is here presented pure—as *a duty* falling on the brother, which it was disgraceful to neglect.[3]

[1] Chap. iv. ver. 6.
[2] Chap. xxv. ver. 5—10.
[[3] In a subsequent essay ("The Levirate and Polyandry," *Fortnightly Review*, 1877), portions of which will be included in the second series of *Studies in Ancient History*, the author pointed out two errors into which he has fallen in the argument upon the Levirate now being stated. Misled by the case of Boaz and Ruth (which he took, wrongly, to be an example of the Levirate), he has concluded that he has found the Levirate to be the counterpart of a right of succession; and then, owing to this error, he has connected the Levirate and the law of inheritance noticed on page 108—as if the two must have had something more in common than their being both of them remainders of polyandry. Now (as is shown in the essay referred to) the Levirate occurs only where the succession of son to father has been established, and that so firmly that even a fictitious son is preferred to a real brother—so

In India, by the time when the Institutes of Menu were compiled, the obligation was laid on the brother only in case the deceased left no son. Grave doubts that it belongs to a different stage of the history of the Family from the law of inheritance which preferred brothers to sons, and gave a surviving brother right to his deceased brother's widow. And, instead of being the counterpart of a right of succession, it cut out the Levir from an inheritance. It imposed upon a surviving brother an obligation, that of "raising up seed" to his childless brother deceased; and the Levirate child was counted the child of the deceased, and was his heir—excluding the Levir.

[These errors make some modifications necessary at this point. It remains, nevertheless, that the same conception of marriage and of fatherhood appears in the Levirate and in Tibetan Polyandry. In the latter, a wife had all the brothers of a family for husbands. With the former, on the husband's death without children, his brother filled his place—generally without a marriage, as among the Hindoos (among whom this might happen in the husband's lifetime also if he were childless). And the widow could claim this of him—so that she had in a husband's brother, as it were, a husband in reserve. Moreover, custom held the deceased to be so effectually replaced by his brother that her child by the brother was counted the child of the deceased; the one brother being taken as equivalent to the other, as if it were an indifferent thing which of them was father, it was assigned to the brother to whom she had been given in marriage. And, with Tibetan Polyandry, her children, by whichsoever brother begotten, would have been the children of the man who had taken her in marriage, the eldest brother, the head of the family (see page 107).

[In either case, the brothers were, in relation to the wife, interchangeable with, and equivalent to, each other, her child being counted the child of that brother who had taken her in marriage. Can this, in the case of the Levirate, be accounted for consistently with an original general practice of monandry? If not, we are, it would seem, forced to regard the Levirate as a relic of polyandrous practice which held its ground for a certain contingency after polyandry had disappeared, and monandry had become general. The Hindoos, it had arisen as to the extent and propriety of the obligation, the number of sons to be begotten on the widow,[1] and the terms on which the brother should live with her. "The first object of the appointment being obtained, according to law, both the brother and the widow must live together like a father and daughter by affinity." Again, it is doubted whether the obligation extends to the twice-born classes. "Such a commission to a brother or other near kinsman is nowhere mentioned in the nuptial texts of the Veda. . . . This practice, fit only for cattle, is reprehended by learned Brahmans; yet it is declared to have been the practice even of men while Vena had sovereign power."[2] Yet elsewhere in the code the obligation is contemplated as legal, and provision is made for the rights of succession of the issue of the Levirate union. "Should a younger

may be said, justified the *niyoga* on the ground that a bride was given to the family of the bridegroom and not to the bridegroom only—which, of course, is the theory of Tibetan polyandry (Apastamba II., 10, 27, 2—7. *Sacred Books of the East*, vol. ii. p. 164).

[The relation of the Levirate to Tibetan polyandry, however, cannot be adequately discussed in a note. A fuller consideration of it will be found in the forthcoming work above-mentioned; and meanwhile reference may be made to the *Patriarchal Theory* (London, 1885), ch. 16 & 17.

[The case of Boaz and Ruth, as has been said above, is not an example of the Levirate. Boaz came in, not as Levir, but as Goël or redeemer of the inheritance of the dead. The Goël was not required by law to marry the widow as a condition of the redemption, though no doubt he generally did so.]

[1] Chap. ix. ver. 61, 62.
[2] Chap. ix. ver. 66.

brother have begotten a son on the wife of his deceased elder brother, the division (of the estate) must then be made equally between that son, who represents the deceased, and his natural father: thus is the law settled." We repeat, that in Menu's time the obligation had not only been, to some extent, dissociated from the corresponding right of inheritance but was falling into disrepute. We see it also falling into desuetude among the Hebrews. In the earliest age the Levir had no alternative but to take the widow; *indeed she was his wife without any form of marriage.*[1] By the Mosaic Law, however, he might get quit of her if he chose by submitting to the ceremony of "loosing the shoe."

It is impossible not to believe that we have here presented to us successive stages of decay of one and the same original institution; impossible not to connect the obligation, in its several phases, with what we have seen prevailing in Ladak; impossible not to regard it as having originally been a right of succession, or the counterpart of such a right, derived from the practice of polyandry. Regarded as in its origin a right of succession, it exhibits the next younger brother as succeeding to the *universitas* of the elder—taking up all his rights and obligations—*inter alia*, his widow. But how came the right of succession to open, as in the ruder cases, to the brother in preference to the son of the deceased? We repeat, that the only explanation that can be given of this is, that the law of succession

[1] Lewis's *Hebrew Republic*, 1725, vol. iii. p. 268.

was derived from polyandry. The succession of brothers to one another, in order of age, is a feature of the law of succession under both forms of polyandry. Under the ruder, brothers succeed one another; and failing brothers, the sister's children come in: under the less rude, brothers succeed one another; and failing brothers, comes in the eldest son of the brotherhood. And nowhere, excepting where there is or has been polyandry, have we such a system of succession—brothers succeeding in preference to sons.

The same conclusion is forced upon us from another point of view. In the lowest cases of polyandry the children belong to the mother; in the more advanced to the eldest brother (an approach towards agnation). Now the peculiarity of the obligation is, in all cases, that it was an obligation "to raise up seed" to the elder brother. The children begotten by the younger brother were accounted the children of the elder deceased. It is obvious that it could more easily be feigned that the children belonged to the brother deceased, if already, at a prior stage, the children of the brotherhood had been accounted the children of the eldest brother, *i.e.*, if we suppose the obligation to be a relic of polyandry.

Curiously enough, Dr. Latham would invert the order of development by deducing the ruder fact — polyandry — from the less rude obligation. But, clearly, this is an inversion of the order of nature — which is progressive — in which the ruder gives birth to the less rude, not the less rude to the ruder.¹

Assuming the correctness of this view of the origin of that obligation, we must hold that polyandry in the Tibetan form prevailed at one time throughout India;² among the race from which the ancient Hebrews were descended and among the Moabites and the ancient Persians;³ among the Druses and all the Arab tribes in Syria;⁴ the Mongols, Ostiaks, Kirghiz Turks, and tribes of the Caucasus;⁵ among the Makololo, and, we may believe, many other peoples in Africa.⁶ It is needless to repeat that we must also conclude that among the peoples just enumerated the Tibetan form of polyandry was preceded by the Nair, and, at a still earlier date, by utter promiscuity.

We have found polyandry in so many lands, among so many races, and in such phases of progressive development, that we are surely justified in classing it among the phenomena most distinctive of—the most

---

¹ The subject of polyandry has been most carelessly, it seems to us, handled by Dr. Latham. It is enough to refer to *Des. Ethn.* vol. ii. p. 463, *et seq.*, where he recklessly lays it down that the *descensus per umbilicum* is part and parcel of polyandry.

² *Institutes of Menu*, c. iii. § 173, and c. ix. § 57, 58, and § 182; *As. Res.*, vol. iii. p. 35.

³ Deut. xxv. 5—11; Ruth i. 11—13; Klenker, *Zendavesta*, iii. p. 226.

⁴ Volney's *Travels*, vol. ii. p. 807; Burckhardt's *Notes*, vol. i. p. 112.

⁵ *Des. Ethn.* vol. i. pp. 312, 346, and 455; Haxthausen, *Trans-Caucasia*, p. 403.

⁶ Livingstone, p. 185.

likely to occur at—the earlier stages of the progress of any race of men. Its origin can only be ascribed to a scarcity of women as compared to men. And the vast area over which it anciently prevailed, can leave no doubt in the mind that in former times the balance of the sexes must have been seriously disturbed (artificially), and that we were right in predicating of the primitive groups that they usually contained fewer women than men. When the phenomena of exogamy—also due to a scarcity of women—are contemplated along with the phenomena of polyandry, the impression this fact produces on the mind is almost as strong as the feeling produced by demonstration. To whatever extent a want of balance between the sexes prevailed, to that extent certainty as to male parentage was in the earlier stages of progress excluded. With polyandry itself there is uncertainty upon this point. In the lower cases the uncertainty is absolute. And regarding, as we must do, the higher as an advance from the lower, we are forced to conclude that wherever we have found polyandry, or traces of it, there must anciently have prevailed the system of kinship through females only.

In a preceding chapter we found the system of kinship through females only, universally prevailing among th Australian Blacks;[1] prevailing among the majority of the nations of the American Red-men;[2] and among

---

[1] *Ante,* p. 60. [This statement, however, requires qualification. It is now known that there are Australian tribes in which kinship is counted through males.]

[2] *Ante,* p. 65–7.

the South-Sea Islanders.[1] That is, we found it among peoples now practising polygyny, and which have advanced far towards the patriarchal system. We infer that with these peoples the unions of the sexes were originally promiscuous or polyandrous. With regard to the Red-men, indeed, there is little room for doubting that they formerly all practised polyandry. It is now occasionally to be found among them, and their system of relationship—their names for kinsmen and kinswomen—point to its having been their universal custom.

Mr. Morgan of Rochester, New York, whose account of the Indian nations we have already had occasion to refer to, gives the following as radical features of the system of relationship prevailing among them: 1. "All the brothers of a father are equally fathers to his children (this where there is now no polyandry). 2. All the children of several brothers are brothers and sisters to each other; all the grandsons of a man's brothers are his grandsons."[2] These features of the system bear the stamp of a polyandrous origin;[3] they

[1] *Ante*, p. 67.
[2] *Camb. Journ.*, 1860, pp. 144, 145.
[3] It may be asked why the Red-men should not now have kinship through males if they have passed, as they appear to have done, through the stage of polyandry of the Tibetan type. Our answer is, that in some cases *they have* male kinship, and that probably in Australia, and among the majority of the nations of the Red-men the earlier species of kinship has been perpetuated by the system of capturing wives. We shall hereafter see that the system of capture introduces uncertainty as to male parentage, independently of the causes of such uncertainty which we have been considering. We shall also see that all polyandrous peoples may not have been exogamous, while all exogamous peoples *must* have been polyandrous.

are features of the system of relationship which might be expected to accompany the higher polyandry. The schedules returned to Mr. Morgan show that among the Tamul and Telugu, peoples of Southern India, numbering about twenty-four millions, "all the brothers of a father are usually called fathers, but in strictness, those who are older than the father are called *great fathers*, and those who are younger, *little fathers.*" And both the Tamul and Telugu are still, as we have seen, to some extent polyandrous. The same system of relationship is found among the Puharies, a people on the skirts of the Tibetan region, and that manifestly practised polyandry till a late date. With the Puharies, all the brothers of a father are equally fathers to his children.[1]

We have seen that the Kasias, the Nairs, and the Saporogian Cossacks, have the system of kinship through females only. We find that system in Tulava, in the neighbourhood of the Nairs. "Among the Buntar"— the highest rank of Sudras in Tulava—"a man's children," says Buchanan, "are not his heirs. During his lifetime he may give them money; but all of which he dies possessed goes to his sisters and to their children." The cause must be the same in either case, though marriage in Tulava has shifted from polyandry to polygyny.[2] Among the Rajputs we have traces of

---

[1] Report of Mr. Wilson, *ut supra*.
[2] Buchanan, *ut supra*, vol. iii. p. 16.

the system of female kinship.¹ The Kocch have kinship and succession through females only; and so have the *But* (Bodo).² Farther we find that system among the Banyai,³ in Ashanti, Aquapim, and Congo, and are assured that traces of it are to be found all over Africa.⁴

We have already had occasion to notice its occurrence among the Chinese.⁵

Let us now see what evidence there is of the former existence of the system of kinship through females only. We recall the fact that, in an earlier chapter, we saw reason to believe that it anciently prevailed among the Celts.⁶ We infer that among the Celts there was anciently no certainty of male parentage. We now notice that we find traces of such a system in India in the Sutras of Gautama. In these, marriage with the daughter of a maternal uncle—a cousin on the mother's side—is emphatically prohibited as being clearly against the principles of the sacred writings.⁷ Such a prohibition, found with an exogamous race—and almost all the Indian races were and are, as we have seen, exogamous—can be referred only to the system of kinship through females only. And it is impossible to avoid connecting with this the tradition that the five Pandava princes—brothers so called—were husbands of one wife. "How is it," asks Max Müller,⁸

---

[1] Tod's *Annals, &c., ut supra*, p. 48.
[2] *Des. Ethn.*, vol. i. pp. 96, 109.
[3] Livingstone's *Travels*, pp. 617—622.
[4] Reade's *Savage Africa*, p. 43.
[5] *Ante*, p. 96-7.   [6] *Ante*, p. 68.
[7] Max Müller's *Hist. of Anc. Sans. Liter.*, 1859, p. 53.
[8] *Hist. of Anc. Sans. Liter.*, 1859, p. 46.

in discussing the character of the Mahabharata, "that the five Pandava princes who are at first represented as receiving so strictly Brahmanic an education, could afterwards have been married to *one* wife? This is in plain opposition to Brahmanic law, where it is said, 'they are many wives of one man; not many husbands of one wife.' Such a contradiction can only be accounted for by the admission that in this case epic tradition in the mouth of the people was too strong to allow this essential and curious feature in the life of its heroes to be changed." In other words, we have here the tradition "that the races among whom the five principal heroes of the Mahabharata were born and fostered," practised polyandry. This is confirmed by all that is related of the Pandava princes. They were the reputed sons of Pandu,—but, in fact, three of them were sons of one of his wives by three different gods, and the other two were sons of another wife by the Aswini-Kumaras.[1]

[1] Williams's *Indian Epic Poetry*, 1863, p. 17. It is worthy of notice that in a passage of the Mahabharata, book i., vv. 4719–22, which has been translated by Dr. Muir (*Sanscrit Texts*, part ii. p. 336), we have the following account of the freedom of women in the early world. "Women were formerly unconfined, and roved about at their pleasure, independent (within their respective castes). Though in their youthful innocence they abandoned their husbands, they were guilty of no offence; for such was the rule in early times. This ancient custom is even now the law for creatures born as brutes, which are free from lust and anger. This custom is supported by authority, and is observed by great Rishis, and *it is still practised among the Northern Kurus.*" In a note, Dr. Muir adds that the practice of promiscuous intercourse was, according to the legend, abolished by Svetaketu, son of the Rishi Uddalaka, who was incensed at seeing his mother led away by a strange Brahman. Svetaketu established conjugal fidelity.

Pandu himself was the son of a marriage with a brother's widow. When the five princes married one wife, the eldest was first married to her by the family priest, and then the other four in their order, according to priority of birth. The princes are represented as living in family with Kauli, their mother—the head of their house. In the poem, Bishma, their granduncle—grandfather's brother—is often styled *their grandfather;* and though Bishma was really the uncle—father's brother—of Pandu, he is sometimes styled *his father.*[1] All these circumstances point to a system of polyandry of the Tibetan type. The very terminology is that of polyandry, and which polyandry has left behind it among the Tamul, the Telugu, the Puharies, and the Red-men of America. In short, though the original tradition has obviously been tampered with, enough of it remains to oblige us to acknowledge it as a genuine tradition of a stage of Aryan civilisation, when the marriage system was polyandrous as it is now in Tibet. It is almost needless to point out that we have, in this tradition, a confirmation of our view of the origin of the obligation which, in the code of Menu, is recognised as imposed on brothers in turn to marry the widow of a brother deceased. We shall find a further confirmation of that view in the case of the Hebrews.

We are not without evidence of the existence in early times of the system of female kinship among the Semitic races. It would appear that while Abraham still lived, his tribesmen as yet recognised only that

[1] See Williams's *Indian Epic Poetry*, 1863, pp. 93, 99, and 114.

primitive kinship in some important relations in life—
e.g., as affecting the right of intermarriage. Between
the times of Abraham and the promulgation of the
Levitical law, a complete revolution took place in
Jewish custom. The patriarch himself married his
sister-german, or by the same father; and his brother
Nahor married his niece,[1] the daughter of a brother.
So Amram, the father of Moses and Aaron, married his
father's sister (Exod. vi. 20). These women were not
relatives, in a full legal sense, of their husbands. They
were connected with them through males only, and
through males in those times there was not, as yet,
a perfect kinship. We have similar evidence of the
existence of the system of kinship, through females
only, among the Phœnicians.[2]

Among the Greeks, traces of this early law remained
in historic times. To pass over the tradition that in
Greece before Cecrops children always bore the names
of their mothers,[3] we have the fact that at Athens a
brother might marry a sister-german (or by the same
father only), but not a sister-uterine or consanguineous.
Here again we have a relic of the doctrine that a child
had no paternal relatives. A sister-uterine was a near
kinswoman, but a sister-german was no kinswoman at
all. Montesquieu[4] ascribes this Athenian rule to a

---

[1] Genesis xi. 26—29; and see xx. 12.
[2] *Achilles Tatius*, lib. i.
[3] *Varro, apud August. de Civ. Dei*, l. 18, c. 9. *Suidas*, voce προμηθ. t. iii. p. 189; and vide *Goguet*, vol. ii. book i. art. i.
[4] Book v. c. 5.

device of the legislature for regulating successions; but he belongs to the class of philosophers who make more of enactments than of popular usages. As Bunsen[1] has pointed out, there can be no doubt that the true meaning and origin of the rule were what we have indicated.

There is one case which might be cited to throw doubt upon some of the conclusions at which we have arrived in this chapter. This is the report of Philo, that the Spartans allowed a man to marry his sister-uterine, but not his sister-german, or by the same father.[2] This may have been circulated for the sake of the contrast which it presented to Athenian custom; at any rate, we hold it to be incredible—as discordant with old law as with the habits of the Lacedæmonians. It is beyond belief that there was this superior regard for the father's blood in ancient Sparta, where the marriage tie was so loose that men lent their wives to one another, and cared little by whom children were begotten, provided they turned out strong and healthy. It is incredible, that in a community where any sort of importance was attached to blood, the unquestionable blood-tie between children of the same mother should be so disregarded. If we are to credit the report at all, it must be on the supposition that the Spartans were

---

[1] *De Jure Hered. Athen.*, p. 148; Göttingen, 1813.

[2] The reader may suspect that this is a relic of strict agnatic law. But for the reasons stated in the text, we hold that view to be excluded. The system of relationship through males only has never, in any well-authenticated case, been developed into such a rule as this.

exceptional in their development, like the ancient Persians (from whom the Druses derived their customs). And we do not regard the case of the Persians as of weight against our reasoning, but the contrary. The Persian customs were just those of hordes who consecrated an incestuous promiscuity into a system. If they allowed the marriage of brothers and sisters consanguineous, they also sanctioned the unions of sons and mothers, and of fathers and daughters, and in some cases required them for the purposes of religion.[1]

At the outset of our argument we saw that if the system of kinship through females only could be shown to exist, or to have existed, it must be accounted a more archaic system of kinship than the system of relationship through males,—the product of an earlier and ruder stage in human development; and that to prove its existence on such a scale as to entitle it to rank among the normal phenomena of human development would be to prove it the most ancient system of kinship. We now submit that we have amply established our proposition. We have collected abundant evidence of the non-existence in many places of the conditions necessary for the rise of kinship through males; in many of these cases—some of them cases of great populations—we have been able to adduce evidence of the existence of the system of kinship through females only. We have seen that polyandry must be accepted as a stage in the progress towards marriage proper and the patriarchal

[1] See a full account of the Persian customs in Selden's *Jus Naturale, ut supra*, chap. xi.

system. The lower forms of polyandry we have found to be accompanied by the system of kinship through females only. We have seen polyandry change its form till it allowed of kinship through males, and then die away into an obligation on the younger brothers in turn to espouse the widow of the eldest brother; and in some cases, Indo-European as well as Semitic, in which we found that relic of polyandry, we have found, or found traces of, the system of kinship through females only. Had the facts bearing on our inquiry ever been systematically observed, noted, and collected, it is probable our case might be made to appear stronger than it does. But as it is, we submit that we have done quite enough to establish the truth of our proposition.

Before leaving this subject we would observe that, whether the system of kinship through females only prevailed universally at the first or not, it must have prevailed wherever exogamy prevailed—exogamy and the consequent practice of capturing wives. Certainty as to fathers is impossible where mothers are stolen from their first lords, and liable to be re-stolen before the birth of children. And as exogamy and polyandry are referable to one and the same cause—a want of balance between the sexes—we are forced to regard all the exogamous races as having originally been polyandrous. While polyandry supplied a method whereby the want of balance might be the less felt, and may thus have retarded, and in some cases prevented, the establishment of exogamy, wherever exogamy took root polyandry must have been practised. Therefore we must hold it to be beyond dispute that among exogamous races the first system of kinship was that which recognised blood-ties through mothers only.

We may be pardoned for here adverting to the views of ancient kinship advanced by Mr. Maine. We have already pointed out[1] that Mr. Maine seems not to have been able to conceive of any social order more primitive than the patriarchal. And as he found agnation—or kinship exclusively through males—to be a common concomitant of the patriarchal system, he has committed himself to the opinion that that was the only kinship known to primitive times. He argues, indeed, against the possibility of kinship through females in early times as being inconsistent with social order and stability. The learned and ingenious writer must be held to have taken up the threads of legal history, where they began to unwind themselves, anew, after the completion of a social revolution. It is quite undoubted, as he says, that few indigenous bodies of law belonging to communities of the Indo-European stock do not exhibit peculiarities which are referable to agnation. With the advance of society—the growth of marriage laws—the superiority of the male sex must have everywhere tended to establish that system. But, before that result could be reached, many stages of progress had to be traversed. And while traces of

[1] *Ante*, p. 62.

agnation are to be found in the early customs of most of the Indo-European races, we have seen that the indigenous customs of most early communities exhibit peculiarities intelligible only on the supposition that kinship and succession through females were the rule before the rise of agnation. Farther, we have seen that wherever non-advancing communities are to be found—isolated in islands or maintaining their savage liberties in mountain fastnesses—there to this day exists the system of kinship through females only. The State of old, says Mr. Maine, recognised as its units, not individuals, but families. True. But at a yet older date we must conclude that neither the State, nor the family, properly speaking, existed. And at that earlier time the unnamed species of kinship—the counterpart and complement of agnation—was the chief determinant of social phenomena.[1]

[1] [In this passage the author, while maintaining that agnation, the system of kinship through males only, was preceded by a system of kinship through females only, does not question the prevalence of agnation; and it will appear immediately that, when this work was written, he thought agnation in most cases supervened where kinship through males had come to be acknowledged. It will be found, however, on reference to *The Patriarchal Theory* (London, 1885), that he afterwards saw reason for concluding that, while with male kinship there was a tendency to agnation, agnation was actually arrived at in exceptional cases only. His theory of the origin of agnation will be found in that work. One of the reasons for regarding agnation as an exceptional form of kinship is that, excepting in Rome, there is scarcely any example of it anywhere to be found—and no example of it to be found among the ancient nations.]

We now go on to show

II.—*That the primitive groups were, or were assumed to be, homogeneous.*

It appeared at the outset that individuals must have been primarily affiliated not to persons but to groups, and that the first effect of the rise of the idea of kinship must have been to give birth to the conception of stocks: farther, that the establishment over any great area of the system of kinship through females only must have occupied a considerable period of time. Until that system was firmly established, there could be no such interference with the homogeneity of the groups as to be worth consideration. An amount of heterogeneity short of that which would introduce at least the *germ* of a system of betrothals may fairly be overlooked. While as yet there was no system of kinship, the presence of captive women in a horde, in whatever numbers, could not introduce a system of betrothals. Heterogeneity as a statical force can only have come into play when a system of kinship led the hordes to look on the children of their foreign women as belonging to the stocks of their mothers; that is, when the sentiments which grew up with the system of kinship became so strong as to overmaster the old filiation to the group (and its stock) of the children born within it. We may depend upon it that this was a stage of progress which it took long to reach, and thus that it was long before the original homogeneity of the groups was substantially impaired.

That in the stage of progress we are contemplating, adoption was practised (the adoption of one group by another to which some writers ascribe such great effects), is altogether unlikely. If it was, it would most probably — as in later times — proceed on the fiction that the uniting groups were of the same original stock. But looking to the state of hostility between groups at the stage we are considering, and the degree of advancement implied in the conception of adoption, we cannot believe that the groups then tended to amalgamate, however they may have tended to divide. We conclude that we must regard the primitive groups as having been, or having been assumed to be, homogeneous up to that stage when, through the joint operation of exogamy and the system of kinship through females only, foreigners recognised as such began to be systematically born within them.

III.—*The system of kinship through females only tended to render the exogamous groups heterogeneous, and thus to supersede the system of capturing wives.*

We may here be very brief. We have already seen[1] the effects of the joint operation of exogamy and this system of kinship among the Australians. Indeed, what their effects must have been is exceedingly obvious. Owing to exogamy, the mothers in each horde were foreigners, and, owing to the system

---

[1] *Ante*, p. 60.

of kinship, the children born to them were esteemed foreigners also. Thus, so far as the system of infanticide allowed, the hordes contained young men and women accounted of different stocks, who might intermarry consistently with exogamy. Hence grew up a system of betrothals, and of marriage by sale and purchase. In Australia and America we saw that in spite of the law of blood-feud, the heterogeneity is now such that the system of betrothals is well established, and that of the original stock-groups the names alone appear to remain.

IV.—*As civilization advanced, the system of kinship through females only was succeeded by a system which acknowledged kinship through males also; and which in most cases passed into a system which acknowledged kinship through males only.*[1]

It is obviously needless to say anything in support of the first branch of this proposition. The difficulty was to show, as we have done in our first proposition in this chapter, that there was a more archaic system which did not acknowledge kinship through males. With the fact of kinship through males in advanced communities, every reader is familiar. Farther as to the second branch of the proposition, it is unnecessary to adduce evidence, or to do more than give some explanations. Those who are acquainted with Mr. Maine's (in many respects admirable) chapter on primitive society and ancient law, will see from the terms of our

[1] [See note on p. 126.]

proposition, that we have not altogether adopted his view that agnation at one time or other prevailed everywhere in the advancing communities; but it is beyond dispute that its prevalence was most general. As it will be convenient hereafter to speak of agnation as a familiar system, we must here say something of its nature. This system, as it long prevailed in Rome, may be best explained by using the terminology of Roman Jurisprudence, to which indeed its name belongs. Its general description is that it embraced only the ties of blood through males. But it will be well to see who were thus included in the kindred. Those united by ties of blood through descent from the same married pair being called cognates, the agnates were those cognates who traced their connection exclusively through males. By a fiction, adopted persons and their descendants through males were within the agnatic bond. All the children of a married pair were agnates, as well as all the grandchildren through sons, but the grandchildren through daughters were not in the number of agnates. The children of the same father by different mothers were kindred, but the children of the same mother by different fathers were not relations to any legal effect. The sons of brothers were kinsmen, but the sons of sisters, or of brother and sister, were no relations; for a woman's children were held to be not of the kin of their mother but of their father. And in no case was there a tie of kinship between a woman's children and her natural relatives unless there was an affinity between her and her husband. If the one system involved anomalies so did also the other. Where female kinship prevails, a Rajah's son may become a hodman—taking the state of his mother—while the son of the Rajah's sister mounts the throne. The nephew—a sister's child—is a relation of the Rajah, but his son is none at all. No more is his brother's son; for through a male under that system there is no blood-tie.

Under each system, while it prevailed, the effects of kinship were confined to those who according to it were relations. And often it is in the laws of succession that we find the best evidence of the former existence among a race of either system. The rule preserved in the Customs of Normandy, which prohibited uterine brothers from succeeding to one another's lands, attests the former prevalence there of agnation;[1] and, in some quarters, as in Congo, the descent of the crown from the uncle to the sister's son is nearly all that remains to witness to the former prevalence of the system of kinship through females. It will be a curious chapter in history which successfully narrates the progress of the revolution by which the passage from the earlier to the later of these systems was effected; exhibiting the stages in the development of the family system, as

[1] [After what has been said as to the prevalence of agnation (Note, p. 126) it seems necessary to say that there is an error here. The Customs of Normandy did exclude uterine brothers from succeeding each other in property derived from their respective fathers; but did not exclude them from succeeding each other in property derived from their mother. There was, therefore, the fullest admission of the relationship of uterine brothers—and nothing to attest the former prevalence of agnation.]

based upon the patria potestas and agnatic kinship as deduced therefrom.[1]

Let us see whether we cannot in a few sentences suggest some of the steps in that progress. The reader must suppose the progress to commence as soon as, through the joint operation of exogamy and the system of female kinship, the groups have been rendered so far heterogeneous as to permit of marriage within the group.

Children having been affiliated to mothers instead of to groups, the first approach to a family system would be through a separation of residences—all of a group having no longer a common haunt or dwelling, but at first all of the same stock within a group associating as a gens or house; and next, mothers and their children occupying separate homes. With this separation of residences would come a closer knitting together of the

[1] [The author has here been influenced by the well-known theory of *Ancient Law*, which derives relationships from the patria potestas, and holds them, as determined by the patria potestas, to have been at first agnatic; it is implied here that a family system based upon patria potestas was common, and that agnatic kinship was deduced from patria potestas. Of course, his own theory of the origin of relationship, as stated in this work, is entirely different from that. And it seems proper to note that he afterwards became convinced that agnation was not derived from, nor founded upon, patria potestas, and that he formed a new theory of the origin of agnation (*The Patriarchal Theory*, London, 1885, chs. xii. and xiii.). On this theory agnation might be expected to occur more rarely than a high paternal power such as might grow into patria potestas or some similar institution. But, in fact, patria potestas seems not to have been found anywhere in the ancient world except in Rome. Gaius declared it to be distinctively a Roman institution.]

kindred first in the gens, and next of mothers and children in the family—rude proprietary rights distinct from the tribal, distinct from the gentile — in the common home, weapons, and garnered food. There would be introduced such a species of family system as we find among the Nairs — the rudest that can be imagined. And from this to the family system, peculiar to polyandry of the Tibetan type, we have seen the stages of development.

In the Nair stage, kinship would be of importance chiefly in two respects—(1), as determining the right of intermarriage ; (2), as determining the right of succession. It might be expected that the system of kinship through females only would first lose importance in regard to successions.

While the Nair family system lasted, we may assume that the common home of the brothers and mother would not often be such as to permit (conveniently) of a general succession—failing the brothers—of all the sisters' children, where there was more than one sister ; and that the first advance to a restricted system of succession would be through the limitation of the right of succession, *primo loco*, to the children of the eldest sister. We have seen the practice [1] growing of fathers making gifts *inter vivos*, to women's children whom they had reason to think their own ; and as this practice grew with the number of cases in which there was a degree of certainty of male parentage, there would be a farther practical restriction of the right of succession

[1] *Ante*, p. 117.

through females. And with the practice of gifts *inter vivos*, to putative children, would grow a feeling against allowing estates to pass from the house of the brothers to that of, or to the putative children of, the polyandrous husbands of the sister, and a corresponding disposition towards a system of marriage which would allow of the property passing to the brother's own children. The system which would suggest itself would be the Tibetan system—to have a wife in common in the house of their mother. This system would produce certainty of the children being of their own blood; they would be born in the house, and would become its heirs.

The next step in advance is obvious. The succession of the younger brother to the elder was a feature of the earlier law—sisters' sons only succeeded failing their uncles. Now, everything conspired to invest the eldest brother, when he came into the succession, with some of the attributes of a paterfamilias. This he did only on the death of all the polyandrous fathers. But—in his relation to his younger brothers—in respect of his being the first to marry, reaching puberty first, and choosing the future wife of himself and brothers—in respect of the first-born, and frequently more than one of the children of his marriage, being unquestionably his offspring—it was natural that the fiction should be formed that *his* were all the children. Women had already, and in the recourse to Tibetan polyandry, been deposed from the sovereignty and management of families; and now, with additional guarantees for the wife's fidelity, parentage was either become certain, or feigned to be so; the elder brother was a sort of paterfamilias, the right to succeed him being in his younger brothers in their order; after them, in their eldest son. Thus, the idea of fatherhood—formed under the system of Nair polyandry—attained something like maturity under the Tibetan, and took its place in customary law. And so far as it was a step towards, or accompanied by, kinship through males, it was a step away from kinship through females, and especially as regards rights of succession.

Apart from such certainty of fatherhood as was incidental to the marriage of eldest sons, the earliest examples of such married life as would give certainty of male parentage would probably be furnished by the chiefs of tribes, who might have the power to secure to themselves one, or perhaps several wives. In Kandya, Ceylon, where polyandry is universal among the lower and middle classes, the chiefs are strictly monogamists, apparently regarding polyandry as a low practice, unworthy of men in their position. As settled habits arose, as property accumulated, and the sexes became more evenly balanced, the example of the chiefs would find more and more imitators, and their cases would furnish a model for an improved system of succession. Thus would arise a practice of monogamy or of polygyny. Brothers would not now always be co-husbands; the Tibetan form of polyandry would die out, and the marriage of a brother to his elder brother's widow would become first an act of succession necessary for the assumption of the brother's place as head of the family; next, as the succession of sons was introduced as in right prior to the brother of a father—chiefly through the brothers leaving the house and contracting separate marriages—it would become an obligation founded on usage, and which, being unproductive of material advantages, would not unfrequently, from men's other marriages, be found irksome and inconvenient. Finally, the obligation itself would die out under the influence of ideas of propriety, which grew up with the improved marriage system. In the Institutes of Menu the obligation is seen in a state of decadence under the influence of such ideas.[1]

Paternity having become certain, a system of kinship through males would arise with the growth of property, and a practice of sons succeeding, as heirs direct, to the estates of fathers; and as the system of kinship through males arose, that through females would—and chiefly under the influence of property—die away. The cases of Abraham and Nahor, however, show that it would be long before that system ceased to be influential as regards intermarriages; that it might, as regards them, linger to some effect even after men had reached the patriarchal state. From the patriarchal state, with such a customary law as prevailed in Abraham's time, to the system of agnation as it prevailed in Rome, is still a long progress. Every step in it, we may be sure, was affected by considerations derived from property. While wives were captured, if there was any sense of property at all, wives would be regarded as property. When at a later stage they came to pass from the houses of their

[1] [See note 3, p. 109.]

birth into alien houses—by purchase—they would still be property. And with the wives considered as property, it is easy to conceive how there would have arisen a sense of property in children. Hence, additional features of the patria potestas. And when a woman had been *sold* to her husband by her father, and had thus come to be considered the husband's property, it is easy to see how neither her original family, nor that into which she had married, should be able to inherit any property through her. But the right of inheritance, as property became abundant, tended to become, and did become, the test of kinship. And in course of time, the notion of kinship derived through females would disappear among a people who cared nothing for a kinship barren as regarded patrimonial advantages. The result would be the system of agnation.[1]

It is not necessary for us here to do more than repeat that we have, in numerous cases, found agnation, or at least kinship through males, preceded by the system of kinship through females only. It was so in the cases of the Hebrews, Hindus, Celts, and Greeks; it was presumably so in all those cases in which we find kinship through males accompanied by that relic of polyandry—the obligation laid on younger brothers in turn to marry the widow of the elder brother deceased. And since we have shown special cause for believing that all the exogamous races had originally the system

[1] [For the theory of the origin of agnation subsequently formed by the author, see *The Patriarchal Theory*, ch. xiii., London, 1885. As already stated (note, p. 126), it is maintained in that work that agnation was an exceptional form of kinship.]

of kinship through females only, we are entitled to assume that it was so among those exogamous peoples with which, as with the Khonds, the Circassians, and the Kalmucks, we find relationship to be agnatic.[1]

V.—*The system of kinship through males tended to rear up homogeneous groups, and thus to restore the original condition of affairs among exogamous races, as regards both the practice of capturing wives and the evolution of the form of capture.*

The first effect of kinship through males must have been to arrest the progress of heterogeneity. The introduction of foreign women into a tribe no longer brought into it children accounted foreigners; for either the children were no longer of the mother's stock, but of the father's, or if of the mother's, they were yet of the father's also. Where, then, in a tribe, a balance of persons of different stocks had not been reached, it was henceforth unattainable. Farther, with kinship through males would arise the habit of feigning a common descent from some distinguished man—a fiction which would lead in many cases to the denial or neglect of

---

[1] [The word agnatic has here (and occasionally in subsequent passages) been used incautiously—owing to the author having at the time the impression that agnation commonly supervened upon the acknowledgment of kinship through males. But the Khonds may really have had agnatic relationship. Succession to land and agricultural stock was among them strictly limited to males and the sons of males—the village succeeding to land on the failure of heirs male. The father's position was high; but it is clear that they had not patria potestas. See Macpherson, *Memorials of Service in India*, p. 62, 1865.]

'such heterogeneity as existed. Of the new groups that were formed, the homogeneity was perfectly secured. The family now tended to grow into the tribe of kinsfolk. The children born to a polygynous husband were all kinsfolk, of whatever stocks their mothers were. The children of brothers, though they married women of different stocks, were kinsfolk. And however the family increased by the addition of generations, its members were all within the kindred. And that as well where the exogamous prejudice survived as where it perished. Where it survived, the women of a family could find no mates within its bounds, and marrying into other groups would follow, and their children with them, the kindred of their husbands. They would be out of the group. Thus, within such exogamous groups as were remodelled, and within such new exogamous groups as were formed, under this species of kinship, there could be no marriage within the group. There would be no place for a system of betrothals; and except where friendly relations subsisted between the groups to allow of marriage by purchase, their members would once more be able to get wives only by capturing them. Thus, even if, in the first stage, the system of capture had—as we see in Australia that it partially has —been superseded, the exogamous races, in entering on a new phase of advancement, had reserved for them a farther experience of that system, to confirm or reestablish the old association between marriage and the act of rapine. And we cannot doubt that many exogamous peoples have had this twofold experience. We know of several exogamous races which, after having had kinship through females, had kinship through males; and we cannot doubt that the same was the case with the other exogamous races that have had the form of capture and agnatic relationship. And indeed, as in the later stage, the experience must have been more uniform and continuous, there being nothing, in the absence of friendliness between the groups, to interfere with the system of capture, so it is observable that the form of capture is now most distinctly marked and impressive just among those races which have male kinship. It might be doubted, but for the case of the Fuegians and traces of the symbol, as if of a thing decayed, occurring in America, whether the experience of the earlier stage could generate the form. There is no doubt it can, and has frequently done so; but the question whether it could have done so, might, on mere general reasoning have been decided in the negative.

VI.—*Under the combined influence of exogamy and the system of female kinship, a local tribe might attain a balance of persons regarded as being of different descent, and its members might thus be able to intermarry with one another, and wholly within the tribe, in consistency with the principle of exogamy.*

This sufficiently appears from what has preceded; and it farther appears from what has preceded, that such a balance of the sexes as would render a group independent of other groups in the matter of marriage would more speedily be reached in respect of the practice of polyandry.

VII.—*A local tribe having reached the stage contemplated in the last proposition, and having grown proud through successes in war, might become a caste.*

It is obvious that the feeling of superiority to other tribes, concurring with independence of them as regards marriage, might lead a tribe first to avoid, and then to decline and prohibit, intermarriage with the tribes which it esteemed inferior. And a tribe with a marriage-law restricted by such a prohibition is a caste, or has made an approach towards being a caste. That castes have, in fact, been produced in this way, is rendered certain by the fact already referred to—that nearly all the Indian castes, from the highest to the lowest, are divided into gotrams or families, and that marriage is prohibited between persons of the same gotram, who, according to the rule of Menu, are shown by their common name to be of the same original stock. We hold that this at once shows the caste to have been composed of members of different original stocks, and the stocks themselves to have been originally exogamous. There can, we think, be little doubt that all castes of this description were formed by the processes which we have been explaining. The Kamilaroi among the Australians appear to be such a caste.[1] And were the natives of Australia to be left to themselves, their system

---

[1] [See note on p. 63.]

of kinship remaining what it is, we might expect hereafter to find among them numerous caste tribes of this description.[1]

It is a rider on what has preceded that caste may appear at that stage of a people's progress while they are yet polyandrous. And of caste among people at that stage we have several instances.

VIII.—*On kinship becoming agnatic, the members of a caste, formed as above explained, might—yielding to a common tendency of rude races—feign themselves to be all descended from a common ancestor, and thus become endogamous.*

On the appearance of kinship through males, much confusion must for a time have prevailed in the application of the principle of exogamy. Some marriages that were formerly allowable would become illegal: as, for instance, the marriage of brother and sister-german, or of the children of brothers; on the other hand, some marriages that were before illegal would become allowable, as for instance the marriages of sisters' children.

[1] It is worth mentioning that many of the rude caste tribes in the hills of India,—such as the Kocch,—have the blood-tie through mothers only. Whether marriage is subject to any, or what, restrictions within these caste tribes, we have no information. The reader will understand that, in speaking of castes, we distinguish between castes proper—the divisions of a people as determined by the right of intermarriage—and the classical subdivisions of castes proper, which are often met with, and which are also frequently called castes. We believe with Dr. Roth that the division into classes resulted from the growth and establishment of professions, and was of later date than the division into castes proper.

At least the marriages last mentioned would be consistent with exogamy where relationship became agnatic. And as the old rules thus became inapplicable new rules would be formed, which in some cases might ignore the principle upon which the old proceeded. At any rate it is manifest that, while the application of the principle in the new circumstances was *in dubio*, the fiction of a common descent from an illustrious ancestor, should it be put forward, would come in aid of the confusion to destroy or render obsolete the principle of exogamy. The members of the caste already restricted to marriages among themselves, and now feigning themselves all to be kindred, would become endogamous.

Indeed, all that is necessary for the production of an endogamous tribe is, that a caste tribe composed of members of different stocks should, anyhow, at any time, yield to the tendency to eponomy. We see, however, that in the stage of transition from the system of female kinship to agnation, or to a system of male kinship, there must have been a time highly favourable for the introduction of the fiction of a common descent, and of the destruction thereby of exogamy. Of the tendency of rude races to employ that fiction, it is unnecessary that we should say anything; it is familiar to all students of early history. Nothing is more common than to find the belief in a common descent among peoples obviously heterogeneous; sometimes the belief is found even in communities which are not only heterogeneous, but the composition of which is known to be entirely artificial.[1]

[1] *Ancient Law*, p. 263, 1861.

And if we anywhere find the form of capture among an endogamous race, as we do among the Bedouin Arabs, and appear to do among the Hebrews, it is not, we think, too much to say that the presence of the form is confirmatory of the supposition that the race became endogamous through employing this fiction, and by the processes which we have been explaining. At least this is the only explanation which we can offer of the appearance among an endogamous people of the form of capture.[1]

We have now gone over the ground laid out at the close of the last chapter. It will be seen that some of the propositions mutually support one another. For example, the observed heterogeneity of certain castes which are subject to the rule of exogamy, goes to show that their ancestors must have had the system of kinship through females only; for exogamy, by itself, will not explain the welding together, in a group, of persons of different original stocks. And to those who, from the earlier chapters, have formed the opinion that we are

[1] As to the unity of physical characteristics observed in most castes, we notice that even in the stage when exogamy is yet observed, they were, owing to their intermarriages and the close connections permitted by a system of kinship which ignored half of the natural blood-ties, steadily advancing to one type, as consanguinii. Where the caste became properly endogamous the circumstances were only just more favourable to the production of that type. There is nothing in the observed unity discordant with the assumption of original heterogeneity; nothing, especially when we consider the periods of time at our disposal, to allow for the production of a uniform type among a people strictly limited to marriages among themselves.

right in our theory of the origin of the form of capture the appearance of the form among an endogamous race will strengthen the supposition that many endogamous races, which have not—or which we do not know to have—the form, may originally have been exogamous.

We may fitly close this chapter with some surmises —thrown out for what they are worth—as to some of the effects on early society of the law of blood-feud, which exists everywhere, so far as we know, among rude races, and which of course grew up with, and out of, kinship. So far as the law of blood-feud retarded the production of heterogeneity within the groups in any district, it was unfriendly to progress. From another point of view it appears that it must have favoured progress, especially among exogamous races, at that stage when kinship was through females only. It bound all the kindred to avenge the death of any one, and the obligation was a point of religion. At first, probably, the protection to the person which this law afforded may have extended only to adults, but in time it came to be extended even to infants. This extension indeed was a logical necessity. And when infants came within the benefit of the law, their lives must often have been spared to avoid the blood-feud with their mother's kindred—a body of protectors, as we have seen, usually living outside and foreign to the gens or house of birth. Thus the law of blood-feud must be credited with a mitigation, perhaps in some cases with the suppression, of infanticide, male as well as female, in exogamous societies, at that stage when kinship is through mothers

L

only. And by checking this practice it tended to restore the balance of the sexes, to allow of the rise of polygyny and the decay of polyandry. It is a curious fact that nowhere now, that we are aware of, is infanticide *a system* where exogamy and the earliest form of kinship co-exist.[1]

When, however, with agnation, groups became homogeneous, containing none but kindred, and containing in fact all *the* kindred, this beneficial action of the blood-feud must have ceased. Where necessity or convenience prompted to infanticide among agnatic groups, the law of blood-feud opposed no impediment to the practice. If the children perished it was at the hands of their kindred. Accordingly the most impressive *systems* of infanticide—chiefly systems of female infanticide — now existing, occur among exogamous races which have male kinship.

On the one hand, then, the law of blood-feud would seem to have played an important part in introducing monogamy, polygyny, and the patriarchal system; on the other hand, it would seem at a later stage to have favoured the perpetuation of exogamy, and of systems of infanticide.

---

[1] [Since this reasoning, as to the tendency of the blood-feud with female kinship, as time went on, to put a check upon infanticide was first published (1865), two proofs of its soundness have appeared—one from New Zealand, the other from Australia. See *Old New Zealand*, London, 1876, p. 85 ; and the *Journal of the Anthropological Institute*, Feb. 1878, p. 250.]

CHAPTER IX.

THE DECAY OF EXOGAMY IN ADVANCING COMMUNITIES.

It will complete the view of early society, to which we have been led by our investigation of the origin of the form of capture, if we point out the principal causes of the breakdown of exogamy in advancing communities. We have seen the liability of the principle to decay in the confusion incident to the growth of the system of kinship through males; and have found reason to think that it gave place to endogamy in many tribes which had, previous to the revolution in kinship, nearly attained a balance—sufficient for the purposes of marriage—of persons accounted of different stocks. It remains, then, that we should consider the causes of the neglect of the principle where it perished gradually, and without the people becoming endogamous.

To indicate the causes in any case will be sufficient for our purpose. We select the cases of Greece and Rome as being those which, to the generality of readers, are most familiar. That the Greeks and the Romans were originally exogamous may be inferred from three distinct grounds, separately, and in combination. (1), They present us with the form of capture in marriage ceremonies. (2), Many of their mythic traditions are incapable of a rational explanation, except on the hypothesis that they anciently had the system of capturing women for wives. (3), The composition and organization of their tribes and commonwealths cannot well be explained, except on the hypothesis that they resulted from the joint operation, in early times, of exogamy and the system of kinship through females only. The two first grounds we have already noticed; on the third we must now dwell somewhat. It not only affords new evidence of the prevalence of exogamy, but introduces us to the chief causes of its decay in advancing communities.

The old theory of the composition of States was based upon the tendency of families to multiply round a central family, whose head represented the original progenitor of them all. The family, under the government of a father, was assumed to be the primary group —the elementary social unit; in it were found at once the germs of the State, and of sovereign authority. Many circumstances recommended this theory, and none more than its apparent simplicity. It was easy to find abundant analogies for the prolongation of the family into the State. A family tends to multiply families around it, till it becomes the centre of a tribe, just as the banyan tends to surround itself with a forest of its own offshoots. And it is obvious to follow up this figure, by remarking that the feelings of kindred, which hold families together in tribes, tend to bind together, in nations, tribes which, like the Greek races, trace back their descent to kinsmen.

The origin of the State on this view is so simple, that a child may comprehend it. But it is very easily shown that the theory cannot be supported. In the first place, it is not borne out by history. The tribes are numerous whose members claim to be descended from a common progenitor. Inquiry, however, everywhere discloses the fact, that the common progenitor is a fiction—a hero or god, called into being to explain the tribe—from whom the tribe did not derive its being. In many cases, not only the fact that the genealogy is fictitious, but even the time when it was invented, can be shown;[1] and nowhere can tribes or nations be traced back to individuals. Also, the theory turns on a fundamental error as to the primitive state. It postulates that human history opens with perfect marriage, conjugal fidelity, and certainty of male parentage; that, from the first, all the necessary conditions of the rise of a perfect family system were satisfied. Demonstrably, history did not so begin; and hence, demonstrably, the family—the social unit of the theory—is not the primary unit it is assumed to be. Farther, and apart from these objections, the theory is wanting in this essential quality of a good theory, viz., that it should explain, or be capable of being made to appear to explain, the facts. The more acute thinkers who

---

[1] This can be done in regard to the Greek races which traced their descent to the sons of Hellen.

have adopted it, and who at the same time have rejected, as they felt constrained to do, the principle of contiguity, as a principle on which groups in early times united,[1] have discerned serious difficulties in the way of entertaining the theory. Mr. Maine especially seems to have been impressed with these difficulties, and to have been unable to find any proper solution of them.

"In most of the Greek States, and in Rome," says Mr. Maine,[2] "there long remained vestiges of an ascending series of groups, out of which the State was at first constituted. The family, house, and tribe of the Romans, may be taken as the type of them; and they are so described to us, that we can scarcely help conceiving them as a system of concentric circles, which have gradually expanded from the same point. The elementary group is the family connected by common subjection to the highest male ascendant. The aggregation of families [which elsewhere[3] he calls the fictitious extension of the family] forms the gens or house. The aggregation of houses makes the tribe. The aggregation of tribes forms the commonwealth."

Obviously, this is not an explanation of the growth of the commonwealth. It does not show how, consistently with the assumption of the family as the elementary unit, the various aggregations spoken of

---

[1] Aristotle kept clear of many of the difficulties which surround the theory of the derivation of the State from the family, by making the combination of families of different stocks depend on contiguity of residence, and on convenience.

[2] *Ancient Law*, p. 128.   [3] *Ibid.* p. 200.

were effected. The gens, clan, or house, which occurs in early tribes wherever we look, was in India, Greece, and Rome, as elsewhere, composed of all the persons in the tribe (included in families, of course), bearing the same name, and accounted of the same stock. Were the gentes really of different stocks, as their names would imply, and as the people believed? If so, how came clans of different stocks to be united in the same tribe? The production of a tribe of one stock—of a homogeneous agnatic group—is readily conceivable on the family hypothesis. But how came a variety of such groups—of different stocks—to coalesce in a local tribe? On the other hand, how came a tribe of descent to be divided into clans situated in different local tribes; how came such a tribe to be at all divided into clans or houses?

To these questions no proper answer has, so far as we know, been given. The common supposition is, that the heterogeneity of the local tribes was somehow brought about by the fiction of adoption. It is supposed that the agnatic groups must have united through this fiction, the one adopting the other on the pretence of kinship; although, after their union, they preserved their distinctive names. Mr. Maine does not expressly say that the observed combination of heterogeneous elements in tribes, and hence in the commonwealth—often assumed to be composed wholly of kindred—was due to the employment of the fiction of adoption; but he leaves that conclusion to be drawn by his readers. "If," he says, "adoption had never existed, I do not see how any one of the primitive groups [*i.e.* the agnatic brotherhoods, for he contemplates none other], whatever were their nature, could have absorbed one another; or, on what terms any two of them could have combined, except those of absolute superiority on the one side, and absolute subjection on the other." Here the difficulty is distinctly perceived; but, is it overcome? What is the evidence that the fiction of adoption was ever employed on so grand a scale as we must suppose to explain the heterogeneity of such groups as the tribes of Rome, Greece, or India? We say that there is none. It is a case of error, induced by the maxim "causa æquat effectum." As the fiction of adoption was the only cause conceived of that might have produced the observed phenomena, it has been assumed to have been employed on the scale required by its supposed effects. But, we repeat, there is no evidence that it was so employed. And there is no likelihood that it was so employed. Our belief is, that adoption has been much more extensively employed by philosophers to explain, than it was by rude races to produce, heterogeneity. It is of no consequence how families and gentes were adulterated by the practice of adoption. The difficulty to be got over does not lie so much in any want of purity of the so-called stocks, as in the union of different stocks—admittedly different—in the same tribe.

The phenomena we have been contemplating offer no difficulty when regarded from the point of view to which we have been led by our investigation. To satisfy the reader of this, we must to some extent recapitulate.

We started in the last chapter from the conception of populations, the units of which were homogeneous groups or tribes, which, on the introduction of kinship, became the stock groups of each particular district or country, and gave their names to the variety of stocks subsequently known to the district or country. And we saw how, into the groups, and into their sections, if they divided, exogamy conjointly with the system of kinship through females only, while it endured, systematically imported strangers, and thus in time rendered the groups heterogeneous, and the general population to the same extent[1] homogeneous. We saw how thus every local tribe came to consist of persons of different stocks; also how all of the same stock, in each, were bound together by rights and obligations springing out of kinship; and how they were also united—though to less practical effect—to all others of the same stock in whatever local tribes residing. Farther, we saw that, when kinship became agnatic, the character of the local tribes became stereotyped, the causes of heterogeneity ceasing to operate.

In each local tribe all the men of the same stock and name were bound by kinship to common action, in certain cases, against the men of other stocks, both in the tribe and elsewhere. Here we have the gentes in the local tribe. And gentes of the same stock and name would exist in different neighbouring local tribes. We shall learn from this how the causes which led to

[1] That is, to the same *recognized* extent, but really to a much greater, half the blood-ties being overlooked.

the diffusion of the stocks throughout the population, favoured the union of the population in the commonwealth. Most probably contiguous tribes would be composed of precisely the same stocks—would contain gentes of precisely the same names, and thus be in the strictest sense akin—kindred. There is no difficulty in conceiving equal unions taking place between such tribes under the influence of kinship, similarity of elements and structure, contiguity and convenience. And on the union of several local tribes under a common government, the gentes of each stock in the combination would be recognized as forming together a *tribe of descent*, as in reality they would do. Thus, the tribes of descent in the commonwealth would each embrace several gentes which had taken shape, and acquired special rights and property in the local tribes in which they respectively were, before the union in the State. As the gens (or the germ thereof) would arise under the influence of female kinship, it would precede—probably long precede—agnatic kinship and the family system as they existed in Rome. And we have already seen something of the processes by which the gentes would be resolved into rude family groups, and the family system gradually advanced into the patriarchal, till the gentes would be resolved into a series of families of the Roman type.[1] The order of social development, in our view, is then,

[1] [It may be well to give a reminder here that the author was afterwards led to regard the family of the Roman type—the father's power patria potestas, and the system of kinship agnation—as not normal but as altogether exceptional. That form of the family seems to be discoverable nowhere except in Rome.]

that the tribe stands first; the gens or house next; and last of all, the family. We are satisfied that the more the reader studies the phenomena of early tribal composition—the phratries and such-like unions of persons in different tribes—the more he will be convinced that this was the order of the genesis of tribes, gentes, and families; and that in no other way can the phenomena of the composition of early states be satisfactorily explained.[1]

Assuming that we have given the true account of the origin of clans of different names and stocks in local tribes, and of the appearance of distinct houses of the same name in tribes of descent, in ancient commonwealths, we might greatly extend the area of exogamy. But to do so is not our present purpose. We observe that the breakdown of exogamy in advancing communities must have been most intimately connected with this evolution of clans and families, and of clan and family estates within the tribe. As we have already

[1] We rcommend to the reader a perusal of the Translators' Preface to the Oxford translation (1830) of C. O. Müller's *History and Antiquities of the Doric Race*,—the translators being Henry Tufnell and Sir George Cornewall Lewis. If the reader keeps in view that we have good evidence of the existence at one time of the system of kinship through females only among the Dorians, we believe he will not be able to peruse the passage of Dicœarchus translated in that preface, and the Editors' comments thereon, without being strongly impressed that our views are the only views on which the phenomena of early Doric communities can be made intelligible. And if he farther study chap. x., part ii., of Mr. Grote's *History of Greece*, we believe his impression of the correctness of our views will be deepened.

had occasion to point out, the only species of property known anywhere originally appears to have been property in common. Everywhere it would appear that the groups were at the first the only owners. And the history of the right of property, as we have it, is just that of the growth *inside* groups of proprietary rights distinct from the tribal. It was an advance when clan estates were recognized as distinct from the tribal; it was a farther advance when family estates were recognized as distinct from those of the clan. Barbarism was already far in the rear when individual property made its appearance.

Now, when the authentic history of Rome begins, marriage laws had not only become stringent, but modern in character, conjugal fidelity had become common, and, as the consequence, relationship had become agnatic. The tribal system, moreover, had been stripped of several of its leading features. Property had long been localized in families as distinct from gentes; and this localization had cut the families off from one another, and to a large extent from the gentes. Families were still associated in gentes, the gentes in tribes, for political purposes; and there remained to the gentiles the right and *spes successionis* to family estates, failing legitimate heirs. But already the laws of succession which had sprung up with family property—which were springing up with individual property—were training the people to consider a few persons only as their kinsmen in any special sense. And the course of decadence of the recognition of extended kinships in

Greece followed much the same path. However strongly implanted the principle of exogamy may have originally been, it must have succumbed to the influences which thus disintegrated the old bonds of kinship. So complete was the disintegration, that in Rome, while the right of succession still remained in the gentiles as evidence of kinship, and its rights and obligations, having been originally co-extensive with the gens, we find this so far lost sight of in the nebulosities of legal terminology, that the lawyers declared that all consanguinity ended with their names for its seven degrees —names invented with a view to the regulation of successions; ended there, "quia ulterius per rerum naturam nec nomina inveniri nec vita succedentibus prorogari potest."[1] A maxim, by the way, which proved very convenient to those pontiffs who maintained that the Levitical rule prohibited marriage between all blood relations, and which is probably found very convenient now in Russia, where the Greek Church still asserts that view of the Levitical rule. For the rest, it must be enough to say that exogamy died out with the blood-ties on which its existence depended, and that the process of destruction of those ties which the laws of succession inaugurated, was carried on and completed by the law of Testaments. If to this general view anything should be added, perhaps it is that the earliest violations of the rule of exogamy would appear to have been called for in the case of female heiresses. Such ladies, if they made proper marriages according to old law—

[1] Paulus, *Senten. Recept.*, lib. iv.

at that stage of progress when a wife was usually what they call in Ceylon a deega wife, *i.e.* passed from her own family into the family and village of her husband —must have carried their estates into other tribes or gentes, and so have cut off their own gentiles from the prospect of succeeding them. Numbers xxxvi. contains an account of the origin among the Israelites of the rule prohibiting a female heiress from marrying out of the tribe of the family of her father. And the prohibition is not uncommon.

CHAPTER X.

CONCLUSION.

HERE our argument ends. Apparently simple as was the problem to be solved, it has now received a solution for the first time. That solution opens a new series of problems for the consideration of the philosopher; of some of which, indeed, we have offered solutions, which, in the fervour of the first conception, may have been put forward in too sanguine a spirit. It will be something, however, if, in proposing and trying to solve such problems, we have at least succeeded in showing their importance, by displaying them on the level of the foundations of civil society. The chief of these questions respect the origin of exogamy and of endogamy. As to the origin of the former, it will be remarked that we have not spent time on the consideration of the question, whether it may not have been due to a natural feeling against the union of near kinsfolk. Its general description might dispose one to think that it might have been due to such a feeling. But, owing to the nature of ancient kinship, as we have seen it, exogamy afforded no proper security against the intermixture of persons near of kin. It permitted, in reality, many marriages which we now disallow. Ties of blood that were not recognized—though that they were ties of blood must have been vaguely perceived—were practically non-existent. And, in the first stages of human development, it was agreeable to exogamy that brothers and sisters of the half-blood should marry, while uncles might marry nieces, and nephews aunts. Afterwards, unions equally incestuous, as we should say, were allowable in consequence of the limitation in blood-ties derived from agnation. One thing is very clear, that in ancient times such questions as have been raised by modern science, as to the propriety of the marriages of near relatives, were never considered. On the whole, the account which we have given of the origin of exogamy appears the only one which will bear examination. The scarcity of women within the group led to a practice of stealing the women of other groups, and in time it came to be considered improper, because it was unusual, for a man to marry a woman of his own group. Another important question respects the universality of kinship through females only. The strong *a priori* presumptions in favour of that, as the most archaic system of kinship, backed by so much evidence as we have been able to adduce, seem to us satisfactorily to establish the position which we have taken up. On the other hand, much labour and investigation will yet be needed to show clearly that that kinship was not merely a concomitant of exogamy and polyandry, should cases occur in which it must be held that neither polyandry nor exogamy was primitive custom. Assuming the universality of that kinship, the question remains: What were the stages of development of the family system, founded on the principle of agnation, as at Rome? Some of those questions we have grappled with; at others we have done little more than glance. Are we too sanguine if we venture to predict that their solution will yet be reached, and will exhibit early human history in a very different light from that in which it has hitherto been regarded, by what Dugald Stewart calls "that indolent philosophy which refers to a miracle whatever appearance both in the natural and moral worlds it is unable to explain"?

APPENDIX.

APPENDIX.

NOTE A.

THE FORM OF CAPTURE.

[NEARLY all the examples of the form of capture here collected, and, indeed, all the clearest and best of them, have been taken from works published before this symbol had been made the subject of serious speculation. In general they were noted by the writers who observed them simply because of their singularity, without knowledge of the frequency of similar customs in connection with marriage; and, one or two excepted, without any attempt to account for the appearance at the initiation of marriage of a pretence of violence and capture. Being described to us as curiosities of custom merely, they can readily be taken as trustworthy. No doubt the description is often briefer and more imperfect than it would have been had the writer known that what he was describing could help to throw light upon the condition of early men.

Probably all the best-known examples of the form have been brought together in this Appendix; and it may suffice to show that, in one shape or another, this symbol has been very widely spread. But there has been no attempt to make a full collection of examples, though that, no doubt, would be of much value.

In relation to the significance of this symbol—in case this should be taken to be still matter of controversy—it may be pointed out that those cases of the form of capture in which there was a pretence of conflict between the bride's relatives and the bridegroom's, whether in the shape of a sham battle or of a siege of the bride's house, are cases in which the modest shrinking from marriage, which has been attributed to early women, can have had nothing to do with what took place, and which, moreover, disclose very clearly the real origin of the symbol. For the bride was passive, or nearly so, in those cases; nothing, or at any rate very little, was expected from her; it was assumed that she could not defend herself, and that she ought to be defended. Her relatives went through the form of resisting her being carried away; and the result of the pretence of conflict was that she was taken from them as if by superior force, and borne off like a captive by the bridegroom and his friends. Such cases show us peoples among whom (while what was done had meaning for them) a woman's relatives, after they had agreed to part with her to a husband, did not deliver her up to him, but made believe that she was taken from them in fight by an enemy. And they disclose nothing beyond the semblance of a fight in which the forcible carrying away of the woman by strangers was vainly resisted by her kindred. It will be found, with actual capture and the form appearing side by side, that the effect of a friendly arrangement, where there is one, is to make capture easy—the woman's friends do not give her up; they make a defence, though they let her be taken, and we even find them afterwards pretending to resent the capture. And while wives are commonly got by capture, peaceful delivery of the bride is a thing unknown in these cases—perhaps a thing not to be thought of.

But the other varieties of this symbol all indicate the same origin for it. In cases of bride-catching there was actual capture; the woman's friends, when they had been arranged with, did not give her up—they let the bridegroom take her when he could. And when the woman had notice, and might hide herself (and the hiding had not become a mere form), if she could elude her pursuer she got off the marriage. In brideracing, the bridegroom had to prove successful in a purely conventional ordeal; but the prevalence of capture and the cases already noticed considered, it cannot be doubted that this embodied the idea that capture should precede marriage—that a woman should not go out of her tribe except by capture. If the bridegroom did not catch the bride he did not have her for a wife. The woman seems to have usually had so good a chance of escaping that her acquiescence in the lot proposed for her might be inferred from her being overtaken.]

In the cases of the form of capture first to be presented, the leading idea symbolised is the capture of the bride after a conflict with her kinsmen. There appears in some of the earlier cases of the series a pretence of besieging the bride's house, or invading it and carrying her off.

1. The people of Berry, in France, observe in their marriages several complex ceremonials. Among them is the form of capture, of which we have a lucid description from the pen of George Sand.

The marriage-day having arrived, the bride and her friends shut themselves up in the home of the bride, barricade the doors, bar the windows, and otherwise prepare as if for a siege. In due course the bridegroom and his friends arrive and seek admittance. They try, at first, to obtain it by a variety of ruses, made in course of a long conversation, after a prescribed traditionary pattern, which is carried on between spokesmen of the parties. They are weary pilgrims wanting rest; they are robbers fleeing from the police and seeking an asylum; and so forth. Admittance being refused, they assail and batter at the doors; they try, as it were, to take the place by storm. Those within the house, on the other hand, become active in its defence. Pistols are fired on both sides, and the barking of dogs, the shouts of the men and the outcries of the women, swell the uproar. When they are wearied there is a parley and another conversation, which, like the preceding, is after a traditionary pattern. The bridegroom's party are at last admitted on stating that they have brought a husband and presents for the bride. Then a struggle commences for the possession of the hearth. The incidents of attack and defence are again simulated, but with such an appearance of reality that broken ribs and heads are not unfrequently the result. The issue, of course, is that the assailants are victorious. The bridegroom obtains his bride, and the more peaceful ceremonies of the marriage are proceeded with.—*Le Mare au Diable*, by George Sand. App. p. 151 et seq. Paris, 1863.

2. Several varieties of the form of capture appear among the South Slavonians.

On the seaboard of Croatia marriages always take place on Sunday, but the marriage festivities begin on Saturday afternoon. When night comes (on Saturday), the bride and her friends being assembled, all the doors of the bride's house are closed to prevent a surprise by the bridegroom's party. The assembled guests are on the alert, and as soon as they hear the sound of singing at a distance (the expected visitors sing as they come) all the lights are put out, and all keep silence. The visitors, having come up, knock repeatedly without getting any answer; but at length a conversation (in this case also on a traditional pattern) begins, in which the people outside try, on various pretexts, to get admission. They are poor travellers seeking for a ewe that has strayed; the weather is bad, the snow up to their knees, the water up to their shoulders; and this kind of colloquy is kept up for a long time. At length the door is opened; the first man who steps over the threshold serves wine all round; and, when every one has had to drink, the girls of the house pass in file before the visitors that they may look out their "lost ewe." The bride comes last; the bridegroom embraces her; and then singing and dancing begin.

What happens among the Croats is evidently a disintegrated form of what happens among the Berricors. There is less show of resistance. There is less still in some other South Slavonian districts where the same sort of thing appears.

At Gradiska and at Brod, on the night before a wedding, the bridegroom's brother and some of his friends go to the bride's house. The doors are closed against them; but the resistance offered, we are told, is not so great, nor kept up so long, as on the coasts of Croatia. After a time the visitors pay something, and the door is opened to them. The door is similarly closed against the bridegroom's party, and admission bought by them, among the Bulgars and among the Dalmatians.

Wherever the use of arms continues among the South Slavonians, all the men go armed to a wedding. At Konavlje, two armed parties, one from the bridegroom's house, the other from the bride's, start at the same time for the church, meeting midway. The one party claims delivery of the bride, the other refuses; and a long dispute takes place which always ends in a compromise—the bride's party promising the other that they will deliver up the bride to it, but only at the church-door.

In many South Slavonian districts the bride goes through the form of hiding herself. In Bulgaria, when she arrives at her new home, she refuses to cross the threshold, and an attempt is made to drag her over it. She resists; and at last her compliance is purchased by the promise of some present.—*Le Droit Coutumier des Slaves meridionaux d'après les Recherches de M. V. Bogisic. Par* Fedor Demelic. P. 89, *et seq.* Paris, 1877.

Such are the South Slavonian wedding customs of to-day. Going some way back, one learns without surprise from Dobrowsky (*Gesch. der Böhmisch. Sprache,* p. 56) that, among the Morlaken in Dalmatia, "a courtship always ends, when both parties are agreed, in carrying off the bride, as among the Cossacks;" and, further (p. 117), that a dance in use among the Krainers might be taken " to be the allegorical representation of Slavonic maiden-stealing."

The symbol of a siege is described to us in an indistinct form in Transylvania, but the indistinctness may in part be due to the brevity of the description. "When the bridegroom and his friends arrive at the bride's house, they find the door locked. The bridegroom must, as best he can, climb over into the court, open the door from within, and admit his companions."— Boner's *Transylvania*. P. 492. London, 1866.

3. Among the Mussulmans of India, in their weddings, when the bridegroom, attended by his friends in procession, arrives at the house of the bride, he finds the gate shut and guarded. He attempts to get in by a ruse. "Who are you that dare obstruct the king's cavalcade?" The answer is, "Why, at night, so many thieves rove about, it is very possible you are some of them." A long jocular conversation follows, ending in a struggle. "At times, out of frolic, there is such pushing and shoving, that frequently many a one falls down and is hurt." The party are at last admitted on paying a sum of money. Then follows a sham fight within the gates; after which, and other ceremonials, the bridegroom carries off his bride.— Herklot's *Customs of the Mussulmans of India*. P. 126. London, 1832.

4. It is the form of a siege which Lord Kames has described as occurring among negroes of Central Africa (see text, page 19). In this case, the bridegroom is the midnight invader of the hamlet, temporarily deserted by its guardians. The braves feign absence; the women unprotectedness. The house is easily mastered, and the bride carried off in triumph.— Kames's *Sketches of the History of Man*. Vol. I., p. 449. Edinburgh, 1807.

5. At Dungally (Straits of Macassar), a marriage having been arranged between the daughter of Tooa, late Rajah of Dungally—who had resigned in favour of his son Arvo—and the son of a Rajah, who had visited the town with a piratical prow, on the day appointed for the marriage all the warriors of the place were armed; and, about one in the afternoon, the young man with his father and all the men belonging to the prow, armed as if for an engagement, came on shore. They were received by the Rajah Arvo and others, and, after some preliminaries, about twenty of the crew were picked out to walk before the bridegroom, all armed with spears and

shields. "They then proceeded from the beach to the town ... At the same time about thirty men, armed with spears and shields, came from the town as if to oppose them, when a sham fight was entered into, which they performed very well, gradually retreating towards the town as the bridegroom and his party advanced thereto. A *patempore*, or piece of chintz, was extended across the gateway as if to prevent their entrance, till the Rajah's son had made a present to the men of Dungally; he therefore gave them some betel-nut and some serric, which they chew with the betel, on which they withdrew the *patempore*. He then advanced some two rods farther, when the *patempore* was again put across. At the same time his people and those of the opposite party appeared to show the greatest anger towards each other by darting spears over each other's heads, until another present was made. The *patempore* was again removed, and replaced as before at short distances, till he reached the house where the bride was. He then went up, ascended the steps to go into the house, at the door of which the *patempore* was again placed, where he was required to make a larger present. He took out of his pocket a handful of betel-nut and serric to give them, and as they were reaching for it, they let the *patempore* slip, when he went past without giving them any, which caused considerable laughter. ... The bridegroom was then conducted to a large room where the bride was waiting to receive him. ... After supper the couple were conveyed to their apartment, which was richly hung with *patempores*."—Theophilus Moore, *Marriage Customs and Modes of Courtship of the Various Nations of the Universe.* Second Edition. P. 196, et seq. London, 1820. [Quoted by Moore from a "respectable author"—not named.]

In this case we have first a sham fight outside the town, then a feint of resistance at the gateway, and thereafter a show of disputing from point to point the advance of the bridegroom and his party until they had made their way into the bride's house.

6. Of the form of capture among the Circassians (described at page 18) all that need here be said is that in this case—as also in the plebeian marriage at Rome—it takes the shape of an invasion of the house, and forcible carrying off of the bride.

7. "Dr. Krapf thinks that marriage is checked [among the Wa Kamba, Africa] by the large amount required to be paid for a wife, and by a singular custom among the Kambas, according to which the bridegroom is required to carry off his bride by

force after the preliminaries are completed. This is attempted by the help of all the friends and relatives that the man can muster, and resisted by the friends and relatives of the woman, and the conflict now and then terminates in the discomfiture of the unlucky husband, who is reduced to the necessity of waylaying his wife when she may be alone in the fields or fetching water from the well. When the lady is brought home, the price is paid, and all contest is ended."—Pritchard's *Natural History of Man*. Vol. II. p. 402. London, 1855.

The statement in Krapf's *Travels*, &c., is less detailed, but is substantially the same.

8. The Kookies, of whom there are several tribes on the north-east frontier of India, are fair representatives of the whole population, from Cape Negrais northwards, through Chittagong and Tipperah, to the Naga settlements above Munniepore. The Kookies, according to Colonel McCulloch [long political agent at Munniepore, author of the *Account of the Valley of Munnipore* referred to at p. 59; private letter], "have no marriage ceremony. When they go to bring away the bride, after having paid for her, they usually receive more kicks than halfpence from the village; that is, they usually get well beaten. But, after the fight is over, the woman is quietly brought from her home and given to the party that came for her, outside the village gate."

In this as in the preceding case there is so much of an appearance of earnest in the fight for the bride that the bridegroom's party might be beaten—and this seems to have been the usual thing among the Kookies. Both, nevertheless, are clearly examples of the simulated conflict. Among the Wa Kamba the bridegroom was, in general, allowed to get his bride; while if he failed to get her in the fight he had to take her in some other way. Among the Kookies, honour being satisfied —the proper form having been complied with—she was sent to him.

As may be seen at page 13, the simulated conflict occurs in a disintegrated form among the Khonds of Orissa.

9. The country of the Kolams extends all along the Kandi Kondá or Pindi Hills on the south of the Wurda River, and along the table-land stretching east and north of Manikgad, and thence south to Dantanpalli, running parallel to the western bank of the Panhitá. "In the celebration of their marriages they follow a custom which prevails also among the Khonds, as it does among the tribes of the Caucasus, and did among not a few of

the ancient European nations, I mean the practice of carrying off a bride by force. When a young man desires to enter on the connubial state, two or three friends of the family, having heard of a suitable partner in the neighbourhood, and most probably having come to a good understanding with her relations, proceed thither on their errand of abduction. The men in the village, who see what is going on, do not interfere, and the opposition of the matrons is easily overcome. The nuptials are celebrated in the bridegroom's house, after which he and his bride pay a visit to the family of the latter, and the friendship, which had been seemingly interrupted, is formally re-established."
—*Papers relating to the Aboriginal Tribes of the Central Provinces.* By the Rev. S. Hislop. Edited by R. Temple. 1866.

The description given here can only apply to cases in which marriage has been arranged for. There is no serious opposition. The men hold aloof. It is the women who resent the capture, but their resistance is meant to be of no avail. The Kolams, however, appear to have capture and the form of capture side by side.

10. The ancient and most general way of obtaining a wife among the Maoris of New Zealand, Mr. Taylor tells us, was for the man to get together a party of his friends and carry off the woman by force. And " even in the case when all were agreeable, it was still customary for the bridegroom to go with a party, and appear to take her away by force, her friends yielding her up after a feigned struggle. A few days afterwards the parents of the lady, with all her relatives, came to the bridegroom for his pretended abduction. After much speaking and apparent anger the bridegroom generally made a handsome present of fine mats, &c., giving the party an abundant feast."—*Te Ika A Maui; or, New Zealand and its Inhabitants*, p. 163. By the Rev. Richard Taylor. London, 1855.

Here we have the form of capture—in the shape of the simulated conflict—and, at the same time, a clear disclosure of its origin.

11. Among the Mongols of the Ortous, M. Huc tells us, marriage is a matter of sale and purchase, which is clearly expressed in such phrases as " I have bought for my son the daughter of so and so ;" " We have sold our daughter to such and such a family." The marriage-day having arrived, " the bridegroom sends early in the morning a deputation to fetch the girl who has been betrothed to him, or rather whom he has bought. When the envoys draw near, the relations and friends

of the bride place themselves in a circle before the door, as if to oppose the departure of the bride; and then begins a feigned fight, which of course terminates in the bride being carried off. She is placed on a horse, and having been led thrice round her paternal home, is taken at full gallop to the tent which has been prepared for her near the dwelling of her father-in-law." Thereafter the relations and friends of both families repair to the wedding feast.—Huc's *Journey through Tartary, Thibet, and China.* Trans. by W. H. Hazlitt. Vol. I., p. 185. London, 1852.

At page 15 will be found de Hell's account of the same ceremony as observed in Kalmuck marriages, especially in those of the noble and princely class.

12. In Abyssinia, Mr. Mansfield Parkyns tells us, on the night before a wedding festivities take place both at the house of the bridegroom and at the house of the bride, during which the "deball," or war-dance (hereafter described) is from time to time performed. On the wedding-day the bridegroom and his friends go to the bride's house, all riding on mules, armed with guns, swords, and lances, and dressed in fine clothes—clothes, arms, and mules being often lent by some great man for the occasion. "When arrived near the bride's house the nearest convenient plain is selected, and the horsemen commence galloping about, the gunners fire off their matchlocks, and the lancers dash here and there, enacting altogether a sort of sham fight. This, I suppose [says Mr. Parkyns] is done to divert the bridegroom's mind." On entering the house the bridegroom's friends and the bride's range themselves on opposite sides of it. The man expresses his willingness to marry the girl; the arrangements with the father are concluded; and then " the bridegroom takes his bride, and *sans cérémonie* turns her out, giving her into the charge of his friends outside the door." He returns to join in the "deball," or war-dance, in which both parties engage. "This dance is performed by men armed with shields and lances, who with bounds, feints and springs attack others armed with guns, so as to approach them, and at the same time avoid their fire, while the gunners make similar demonstrations, and at last fire off their guns either in the air or into the earth, and then, drawing their swords, flourish them about as a finish." By and by the bride is carried off on a mule with one of the bridesmen seated behind her. She appears to be treated on the wedding-night by the bridegroom and his bridesmen as a woman who had fallen into the hands of a war-

party might have been.—*Life in Abyssinia*, by Mansfield Parkyns. Vol. II. pp. 51-56. London, 1853.

13. In the kingdom of Foutah, in the west of Africa, marriage was by purchase, the terms being arranged beforehand, and the agreement of the parties proclaimed at the priest's house. "There remains," we are told, "only one difficulty, which consists in withdrawing the wife from her paternal home. All her cousins assemble in front of the door to oppose the bridegroom's entrance, but he always finds means to conciliate them with presents. He then puts forward one of his relatives well mounted, commissioned to bring him his wife on horseback. But hardly has she mounted behind him when the women take to lamentations and endeavour to stop him. Nevertheless, the rights of the husband carry the day."—Walckenaer's *Collection des Relations des Voyages*. Vol. IV. pp. 20, 21. Paris, 1842.

Another account says that, after the marriage has been arranged, "the husband, accompanied by some friends of his own age, comes in the evening, by moonlight, to the house of his wife, and endeavours to carry her off. He is always successful, notwithstanding her resistance and her cries, and although she is seconded by all the young girls of the village or town. The air resounds with their lamentations. As this is but a simple custom, and has nothing more serious in it than the attempts of the young people to oppose the captor, this comedy always ends in the bride falling happily into the arms of her husband."—Walckenaer's *Collection*. Vol. IV. pp. 173, 174.

14. "In their marriages," says Sir Henry Piers, of the Irish, "especially in those countries where cattle abound, the parents and friends on each side meet on the side of a hill, or, if the weather be cold, in some place of shelter, about midway between both dwellings. If agreement ensue, they drink the agreement bottle, as they call it, which is a bottle of good usquebaugh, and this goes merrily round. For payment of the portion—which is generally a determinate number of cows—little care is taken. . . . . On the day of bringing home, the bridegroom and his friends ride out and meet the bride and her friends at the place of meeting. Being come near each other, the custom was of old to cast short darts at the company that attended the bride, but at such distance that seldom any hurt ensued. Yet it is not out of the memory of man that the Lord of Hoath on such an occasion lost an eye. This custom of casting darts is now

obsolete."—Vallency's *Collectanea de Rebus Hibernicis.* Vol. I., p. 122. 1786. No. 1, *Description of Westmeath,* by Sir Henry Piers, written in 1682.

The symbol in this case is disintegrated to a great extent. But, no doubt, at an earlier date there was the perfect semblance of a battle. It is very singular to find, in the simulation of attack by the bridegroom's party, the short darts of old Celtic warfare used down to the seventeenth century.

It is well known that actual abduction was very common among the Irish. Many provisions concerning "abduction without leave" are to be found in the Irish law-books, from which it is to be gathered that an arrangement was usually come to after the event. Abduction with leave, abduction by arrangement, would of course be the form of capture.

An account of the simulated conflict, as it is described to us among the Welsh, will be found at page 18. Besides that this is a good example of the simulated conflict, it is valuable as affording the suggestion that this variety of the form of capture *might* pass into " bride-racing."

Mr. Logan, in his book on the Highland clans, in noticing Sir Henry Piers's account, above cited, gives some facts which go to show that the Scottish Highlanders also had the form of capture. And correspondents of good authority state that, in some parts of the Highlands, and in some districts of Aberdeenshire, it was common for the parties of the bride and bridegroom to go in procession to a point of meeting midway between their dwellings, and on the way to the minister's house, and when they came near each other, to fire volleys at one another from pistols and muskets; while, on the return home, the marriage procession was fired at nearly all the way. After what has been shown of the Irish and Welsh, it can scarcely be doubted that this is a relic of the simulated conflict; and this is made the less doubtful by our finding in the Isle of Skye and in the West Highlands a faint but unmistakable relic of another variety of the form of capture in a ceremony known as " stealing the bride." It occurred in the middle of a reel. The groomsman and bridesmaid slipped into the place in the dance of the bride and bridegroom, while the bridegroom suddenly jerked the bride out of the room.

15. The evidence that the Greeks observed the form of capture otherwise than as " bride-racing " relates to the Dorians only, and is noticed at page 12; but what was true of them was most probably true, anciently, of all the Greek tribes,

for the Dorians differed from the others chiefly through having better preserved the ancient customs. That the Dorians had the form of capture is proved by the story of Demaratus; but neither this nor Plutarch's statement, which proves the form of capture among the Spartans—among whom latterly it sufficed to seize the bride and carry her from one room to another—shows whether the simulated combat occurred among the Greeks or not. That they had it anciently, however, cannot be doubted. In the practice of παιδεραστία the ἄτας was always carried off by force, the intention of the ravisher having been previously communicated to the youth's relations, who made a feigned resistance. Here is the form of capture in the shape of the simulated conflict; and it may safely be concluded that a people who had it in this shape in such a matter, and had it also in their marriages, had it anciently in this shape in their marriages.[1]—Strabo, B. 10, c. 4, s. 21.

The cases which follow are examples of bride-catching—cases in which the bridegroom had to catch and carry away his bride after having come to an understanding with her friends—proceeding, although the marriage was the subject of contract, as if acting without consent. The old Norse word *quân-fang*—wife-catching—was used in the sense of marriage, which proves that bride-catching was a Norse institution. An excellent example of bride-catching, from Tierra del Fuego, is given in

---

[1] [The case of the Garos (India—Dalton's *Descriptive Ethnology of Bengal*) has not been included among the examples here given—for an obvious reason; but it is curious, and should not pass without notice.

Among the Garos proposals of marriage come from the woman's side. The marriage having been arranged, the girl goes off to the hills. The man follows her and finds her, and (having provisions with them) they stay there for some days. On their return the marriage is publicly announced and solemnised. After bathing the bride in a stream, her friends proceed to the house of the bridegroom, "who pretends to be unwilling, and runs away, but is caught and subjected to a similar ablution, and then taken, in spite of the resistance and counterfeited grief and lamentations of his parents, to the bride's house."

Here the bridegroom is the party taken in marriage, and there is, at the last, a form of capturing the bridegroom.

But, first of all, the girl goes off to the hills by herself, and the man follows and finds her. This looks very like a remainder of the form of capture (as will appear immediately); and it suggests that there was a time when, among the Garos, proposals did not come from the woman's side, and that they have had their experience of getting wives by capture. This is made more probable—even if it is not put beyond doubt—by their being exogamous.]

the text at page 20. The case of the Tunguzes and Kamchadales, mentioned at page 17, is also of this class.

1. Among the Tartars, William de Rubriquis tells us, "when any man hath bargained with another man for a maid, the father of the damsel makes him a feast; in the meantime she flies away to some of her kinsfolk to hide herself. Then her father says to the bridegroom, 'My daughter is yours; take her wheresoever you can find her.' Then he and his friends seek her till they find her, and, having found her, he takes her by force and carries her to his own house."—Pinkerton's *Collection*. Vol. VI., p. 183.

2. Among the Wa-teita (Central Africa) marriage is by purchase, but, after the contract is made, the woman has to be captured. "When an M-teita marries he settles the preliminaries with the father in accordance with the usual negro custom—that is to say, he buys her for three or four cows. This important matter settled, the girl runs away and hides among distant relatives until such time as her betrothed finds out her hiding-place and catches her. He then gets some of his friends, who carry her back to her future home, two men holding her by the legs and two by the arms, shoulder high, amidst much singing and dancing. The four men who carry the girl are said to be rewarded in a very peculiar fashion."—*Through Masai Land*, by Joseph Thomson, p. 93. London, 1885.

3. "An instance of the manner in which the young men of that country [the district near Kayaye on the river Gambia] obtain wives also came under our observation. One of the inhabitants of the neighbouring villages, having placed his affections, or rather desires, on a young girl at Kayaye, made the usual present of a few colas to her mother, who, without giving her daughter any intimation of the affair, consented to his obtaining her in any way he could. Accordingly, when the poor girl was employed preparing some rice for supper, she was seized by her intended husband, assisted by three or four of his companions, and carried off by force. She made much resistance by biting, scratching, kicking, and roaring most bitterly. Many, both men and women, some of them her own relations, who witnessed the affair, only laughed at the farce, and consoled her by saying that she would soon be reconciled to her situation."—Gray and Dochard's *Travels in Western Africa*, p. 56. London, 1825.

4. Among the Zulus marriage is by purchase, and the bride is, after much ceremonial, handed over to the bridegroom and

his people by a party of her kinsfolk. But custom requires that she should make three attempts to run back to her old home, and that she should be prevented by the bridegroom's people. The last attempt, made on the second day, and after she has been installed in her position as wife, is the only serious one. "There have been cases where the bride got out of the gate, which was a terrible disgrace to the young man who had been appointed to stop her, to the husband, and all concerned, besides the expense, seeing that the whole ceremony had to be gone through again."—*Among the Zulus and Amatongas*, by David Leslie, pp. 116-118. Second edition. Edinburgh, 1875.

5. The form of capture among the Maoris of New Zealand, in the shape of the simulated combat, as described by Mr. Taylor, has already been mentioned. Another account (Earle's *Residence in New Zealand*) says that the bridegroom, after obtaining consent, had to carry off the girl by force, and that a severe struggle sometimes took place, in which the man was not always successful. If the girl could manage to escape and get into her father's house, the marriage was off. If the man could carry her to his house, she was forthwith his wife.

6. "On the large islands [of the Fijian group] is often found the custom prevalent among many savage tribes of seizing upon a woman, by apparent or actual force, in order to make her a wife. On reaching the home of her abductor, should she not approve of the match, she runs to some one who can protect her; if, however, she is satisfied, the matter is settled forthwith. A feast is given to her friends the next morning, and the couple are henceforth considered as man and wife."—*Fiji and the Fijians*. By Thomas Williams, p. 174. London, 1858.

7. In the Amazon valley the natives have no particular ceremony at their marriages except that of always carrying the girl away by force, or making a show of doing so, even when she and her parents are quite willing. The way in which the capture is made is very singular. "When a young man wishes to have the daughter of another Indian, his father sends a message to say he will come, with his son and relations, to visit him. The girl's father guesses what it is for, and, if he is agreeable, makes preparations for a grand festival. This lasts, perhaps, two or three days, when the bridegroom's party suddenly seize the bride, and hurry her off to their canoes. No attempt is made to prevent them, and she is then considered as married." —Wallace's *Travels on the Amazon*, p. 497. London, 1853.

8. Among the Ahitas [Philippine Islands], when a marriage is in question, the girl's parents send her, before sunrise, into the woods, and the would-be husband follows her an hour after. If he brings her back before sunset there is marriage; if not, the affair is at an end.—Earl's *Native Races of the Indian Archipelago*, p. 183. London, 1853.

In this case there seems to be an approach to bride-racing.

9. Among the Greenlanders, when a young man has resolved to marry, he first proposes the match to his parents, whose consent in general is given readily. Then two old women are sent to negotiate with the parents of the bride. They at first say nothing of a marriage, but speak in praise of the bridegroom and his family; whereupon the girl "directly falls into the greatest apparent consternation, and runs out of doors tearing her bunch of hair; for single women always affect the utmost bashfulness and aversion to any proposal of marriage, lest they should lose their reputation for modesty, though their destined husbands be previously well assured of their acquiescence. . . . During their daughter's bashful fit, the parents tacitly comply with the proposal, without any express approbation. The women then go in search of the refractory maid, and drag her forcibly into her suitor's house, where she sits for several days quite disconsolate, with dishevelled hair, and refuses nourishment. When friendly exhortations are unavailing, she is compelled by force, and even blows, to receive her husband. Should she elope, she is brought back and treated more harshly than before."—Crantz's *History of Greenland*. Vol. I., p. 146. London, 1820.

The same kind of thing occurs among the Esquimaux of Cape York. The bridegroom is required to carry off his bride by main force, and the woman to resist as much as possible "until she is safely landed in the hut of her future lord, when she gives up the combat very cheerfully, and takes possession of her new abode."—Hayes, *The Open Polar Sea*, p. 432. 1867.

10. Among the Indians of Canada, Carver tells us, after the marriage was over, the bridegroom took his wife on his back, and, amid the plaudits of the spectators, carried her to his tent. —Carver's *Travels*, p. 374. 1781.

11. Among the Soligas [India], "when a girl consents to marry, the man runs away with her to some neighbouring village, and they live there until the honeymoon is over. They then return home, and give a feast to the people of their

village."—Buchanan's *Journey from Madras.* Vol. II., p. 178, 1807.

12. "The marriage ceremony is very simple among the Aenezes [Arabs]. . . . The marriage-day being appointed (usually five or six days after the betrothing), the bridegroom comes with a lamb in his arms to the tent of the girl's father, and there cuts the lamb's throat before witnesses. As soon as the blood falls upon the ground the marriage ceremony is regarded as complete. The men and girls amuse themselves with feasting and singing. Soon after sunset the bridegroom retires to a tent pitched for him at a distance from the camp; there he shuts himself up, and awaits the arrival of his bride. The bashful girl meanwhile runs from the tent of one friend to another till she is caught at last, and conducted in triumph by a few women to the bridegroom's tent; he receives her at the entrance, and forces her into it; the women who had accompanied her then depart."—Burckhardt's *Notes.* Vol. I., p. 107.

13. Burckhardt, after noticing that, among the Bedouins of Mount Sinai, marriage is a matter of sale and purchase, in which the inclinations of the bride are not consulted, proceeds:— "Among the Arabs of Sinai the young maid comes home in the evening with the cattle. At a short distance from the camp she is met by the future spouse and a couple of his young friends, and carried off by force to her father's tent. If she entertains any suspicion of their designs, she defends herself with stones, and often inflicts wounds on the young men, even though she does not dislike the lover, for, according to custom, the more she struggles, bites, kicks, cries, and strikes, the more she is applauded ever after by her own companions. She is then taken to her father's tent. There follows the throwing over her of the abba, or man's cloak, and a formal announcement of the name of her future husband. After this she is dressed in bridal apparel, and mounted on a camel, although still continuing to struggle in a most unruly manner, and held by the bridegroom's friends on both sides. She is led in this way two, and three times round, and finally into, the bridegroom's tent. The resistance is continued till the last. The marriage, of course, ends in a feast and presents to the bride."—Burckhardt's *Notes.* Vol. I., p. 263.

14. Among the Mezeyne marriage appears to be a matter of sale and purchase, and to be constituted, as among the Aenezes, through capture as a form. It is attended by a custom which is met with in other cases, but scarcely in so striking

a shape. "A singular custom," says Burckhardt (*Notes*, Vol. I. p. 269), "prevails among the Mezeyne tribe, within the limits of the Sinai peninsula, but not among the other tribes of that province. A girl having been wrapped in the abba at night [*i.e.* after the capture, as in the preceding case], is permitted to escape from her tent and fly into the neighbouring mountains. The bridegroom goes in search of her next day, and remains often many days before he can find her out, while her female friends are apprised of her hiding-place, and furnish her with provisions. If the husband finds her at last (which is sooner or later, according to the impression that he has made upon the girl's heart), he is bound to consummate the marriage in the open country, and to pass the night with her in the mountains. The next morning the bride goes home to her tent that she may have some food, but again runs away in the evening, and repeats these flights several times, till she finally returns to her tent. She does not go to live in her husband's tent till she is far advanced in pregnancy; if she does not become pregnant, she may not join her husband till after a full year from the wedding-day." Burckhardt says the same custom is observed among the Mezeyne Arabs elsewhere.

This custom must have been handed down from a state of the greatest "wildness." The clandestine intercourse of husband and wife at Sparta and in Crete seems to be a tradition of it. Customs suggestive of it occur in other places. In Africa, in some districts, husband and wife for years meet only in the woods. The stealthy communication of husband and wife is required by custom, also, among the Nogais and the Circassians.

Reference may here be made to page 47, where it appears there is authority for believing that, among the Israelites, as well as among the Arabs, "the taking" of the bride was the chief ceremony in the constitution of marriage; which would show that the Israelites, also, had the form of capture.

The cases next given are examples of bride-racing—cases in which, after a woman's friends had agreed to a marriage for her, the man had, as a condition of having her as his wife, to overtake her in a race. The German word *brütloufti*,—bride-racing—is used in the sense of marriage, which proves that bride-racing was a German institution. In the Greek legends there are numerous hints of it having been a Greek institution also. At page 15 it is shown that bride-racing was practised among the Kalmucks (who had the form of capture, also, in the shape of the simulated conflict). The "love-chase" of the Kirghiz, shown in the first example following, is obviously a version of the Kalmuck custom.

1. "There is one race, called the 'Love-chase,' which may be considered a part of the form of marriage among the Kirghis. In this the bride, armed with a formidable whip, mounts a fleet horse, and is pursued by all the young men who make any pretensions to her hand. She will be given as a prize to the one who catches her; but she has the right, besides urging on her horse to the utmost, to use her whip, often with no mean force, to keep off those lovers who are unwelcome to her, and she will probably favour the one whom she has already chosen in her heart. As, however, by the Kirghis' custom a suitor to the hand of a maiden is obliged to give a certain *kalym*, or purchase-money, and an agreement must be made with the father for the amount of dowry which he gives his daughter, the 'Love-chase' is a mere matter of form."—Schuyler's *Turkistan*. Two Vols. Vol. I., p. 43. London. 1876.

What follows shows us that another relic of capture appears in the marriages of the Kirghis. "As mullahs are very rare in the Steppe," says Mr. Schuyler, "a religious ceremony of any kind at a marriage is unusual; but one thing must be strictly performed . . . . the young man must enter the *kibitka* where the bride is seated and take her out, although both entrance and exit are forcibly opposed by all her friends. This is probably a remnant of the old primitive custom when marriage was an act of capture."

"The Kirghiz race," Mr. Schuyler tells us (p. 34), "has almost as much of a Mongol as of a Turkish type. This is especially noticeable," he says, "in the aristocratic class—above all, in their women; and one reason is said to be that the Kirghiz, until recent times, preferred, whenever possible, to marry Kalmuck women, carrying them off from the confines of China or the Astrakhan Steppe."

2. Vámbéry says that this "marriage ceremonial" (bride-racing), no doubt with modifications from case to case, is in use among all the nomads of Central Asia. He describes it in the case of the Turkomans. The young maiden, attired in bridal costume, mounts a high-bred courser, taking on her lap the carcase of a lamb or goat. She sets off at full gallop, followed by the bridegroom and other young men of the party, also on horseback. She has always to strive, by adroit turns, &c., to avoid her pursuers, that no one of them approach near enough

to snatch from her the burden in her lap. The chase ends, it may be believed, in her being caught. "The game" is called Kökbüri.—Vámbéry's *Travels in Central Asia*, p. 323. London. 1864.

3. The natives of Singapore, who are accustomed to boating, have an aquatic variety of bride-racing. They have it, also, in the shape of a foot-race. They hold great jubilees, at the fruit season, near the groves of the tribe, which often lie together, and during these jubilees their marriages take place. "The marriage ceremony," says Mr. Cameron, "is a simple one, and the new acquaintance of the morning is often the bride of the evening. On the part of the suitor it is more a matter of arrangement with the parents than of courtship with the daughter; but there is a form generally observed which reminds one strongly of the old tale of Hippomenes and Atalanta. If the tribe is on the bank of a lake or stream, the damsel is given a canoe and a double-bladed paddle, and allowed a start of some distance; the suitor, similarly equipped, starts off in chase. If he succeeds in overtaking her, she becomes his wife; if not, the match is broken off. . . . It is seldom that objection is offered at the last moment, and the race is generally a short one. The maiden's arms are strong, but her heart is soft, and her nature warm, and she soon becomes a willing captive. If the marriage takes place where no stream is near, a round circle of a certain size is formed, the damsel is stripped of all but a waistband, and given half the circle's start in advance; and if she succeeds in running three times round before her suitor comes up with her, she is entitled to remain 'a virgin; if not, she must consent to the bonds of matrimony. As in the other case, but few outstrip their lovers."—*Our Tropical Possessions in Malayan India*. By J. Cameron, p. 116. London, 1865.

Bowrien, speaking of the Mantrays of the Malay peninsula, describes the foot-race much as it is given above, and adds that at times "a larger field is appointed for the trial, and they pursue one another in the forest."—*Trans. Ethn. Soc.*, Vol. III., p. 81.

4. Bride-racing is found also among the Koraks (North-Eastern Asia). The race takes place within a large tent containing numerous separate compartments, called pologs, arranged in a continuous circle round its inner circumference, and the girl is clear of the marriage if she can run through the series of pologs without being caught. Besides that she has a start, the women of the encampment throw every possible im-

pediment in the man's way, "tripping up his unwary feet, holding down the curtains to prevent his passage, and applying willow and alder switches unmercifully to a very susceptible part of his body" as he stoops to raise them. Hampered as he is, however strong and swift he may be, the man has scarcely any chance of succeeding unless the woman wishes it. In a trial described by Mr. Kennan he was hopelessly distanced, but the bride waited for him in the last polog. The race, in fact, gives the woman a veto upon the marriage.—Kennan's *Tent Life in Siberia.* 1870.

The cases which follow illustrate in one way or another the movement from capture in connection with marriage.

1. At pages 35–38 it is shown that at a period not remote, in Muscovy, Lithuania, Livonia, and other parts of the north of Europe, there prevailed a practice of capturing women for wives by armed force, the capture being followed by a negotiation with the parents, and, on that being completed, by marriage; and it is pointed out that, though there was actual capture, the intervention of sponsalia and the consent of parents before the consummation of the marriage shows this to be a mode of transition from actual capture to marriage by contract with capture as a form. We learn from the Chronicle of Nestor, the oldest of the Russian Chronicles, what were, at an earlier period, the marriage customs of some of the inhabitants of those countries.

The Polians, Nestor tells us—speaking of the neighbourhood of Kieff—had formal marriage. The bridegroom did not go to fetch his bride, but she was carried to him in the evening, and the price agreed to be given for her was sent the next day. But the Polians were singular in that region in having marriage so regularly conducted. Their neighbours, the Dreyvians, Nestor says, had no marriage; they carried away maidens by force, and took them to their beds. So far as appears, they got their wives by capture only, without agreement either before the capture or after. The Radimitschans, the Viatitschans, and the Severians, Nestor says, like the Dreyvians got their wives by capture, without agreement with the parents either before or after the capture; but they had hit upon a method of making wiving by capture easy, so that they had the form of capture in the germ. There was inter-tribal arrangement before the capture, though there was no arrangement with parents. "They arranged noisy, merry games, in which they were brought together; they played, danced, and sang devilish songs; and, at the end, each man carried away a woman, who became his wife." (*Russiche Annalen.* Edited by A. L. Schlözer. Part II., p. 125.)

It is not surprising that reminiscences of the time when wives were got by capture should linger to this day in the marriage customs of the Russians as of the other Slav peoples.

"'To the forcible carrying away of the bride seems to refer,' says Orest Miller, 'a long series of nuptial songs from all parts, not only of Russia, but of the whole Slavonic world.' In them the bridegroom is spoken of as a foreigner and a stranger who has been wafted—Heaven knows whence!—by a black cloud, and who is surrounded by brave companions hostile to the bride. Even among the Czechs, whose ideas have been considerably modified by foreign influences, the arrival of the bridegroom is still announced by the words, 'The enemy is near at hand!' 'The bridegroom, that evil thief, has come,' says a bologda song. In Russia he is often called, after the invaders of the land, the Tartars or the Lithuanians. In order to get at the bride, the bridegroom has to batter down the walls of stone, to 'let fly the arrow of pearl,' to 'shatter the guarding locks.' . . . . One of the many acts in the long drama, as it were, which is performed at every peasant's wedding, consists in a representation of the attack and defence of the bride. Thus, in Little Russia, when the bride's dresses have been unplaited and the cap is being put on her head, she is bound to resist with all her might, and even to fling her cap angrily on the ground. Then the groomsmen, at the cry of 'Boyars, to your swords!' pretend to seize their knives and make a dash at the bride, who is thereupon surrounded by her friends, who come rushing to the rescue."—Ralston's *Songs of the Russian People.* Pp. 284, 285. 1872.

2. "The Mirdites," says Mr. Tozer, "never intermarry, but when any of them, from the highest to the lowest, wants a wife, he carries off a Mohammedan woman from one of the neighbouring tribes, baptises her, and marries her. The parents, we are told, do not usually feel much aggrieved, as it is pretty well understood that a sum of money will be paid in return; and, though the Mirdites themselves are very fanatical in matters of religion, yet their neighbours [the Christian and Mohammedan tribes being alike Slavs] are reputed to allow the sentiment of nationality to prevail over that of creed. . . . Prince Bib himself won his spouse in this way. My reader will naturally inquire . . . . what

becomes of the Mirdite women? The answer is, they are given in marriage to the neighbouring Christian tribes. If any one considers this incredible in so large a population, he is at liberty to adopt the more moderate statement of M. Hecquard, who only speaks of this custom as existing among the chiefs; but I state the facts as they were stated to me, and, since the ground of the custom was distinctly affirmed to be the feeling that marriage within the tribe is incestuous, and, wherever in similar cases this belief has existed, the custom of exogamy, as it is called, together with the capture of wives, has existed also, I feel very little doubt, in my own mind, that the stronger statement is the true one."

Mr. Tozer goes on to observe that "the case of the Mirdites is a peculiarly interesting one, because, while the system of exogamy is perfect, it presents us with the reality of capture on the eve of merging in the form—since a sum of money is paid afterwards, and but little resistance apparently offered—but permanently checked in doing so by the fact that the women carried off are Mohammedans, who cannot, without violence, be married to Christians."—*Researches in the Highlands of Turkey.* Vol. I., pp. 318 *et seq.* By the Rev. H. J. Tozer. London, 1869.

3. We find the following account of the constitution of marriage among the Turkomans:—

"The most singular customs of these people (the Turkomans) relate to marriage. The Turkomans do not shut up their women, and there being no restraint on the social intercourse between the sexes, as in most Mussulman countries, love matches are common. A youth becomes acquainted with a girl; they are mutually attached, and agree to marry: but the young man does not dare to breathe his wishes to the parents of his beloved, for such is not etiquette, and would be resented as an insult. What does he do? He elopes with the girl, and carries her to some neighbouring obah, where, such is the custom, there is no doubt of a kind reception; and there the young couple live as man and wife for some six weeks, when the Reishsuffeeds, or elders of the protecting obah, deem it time to talk over the matter with the parents. Accordingly they represent the wishes of the young couple, and, joined by the elders of the father's obah, endeavour to reconcile him to the union, promising, on the part of the bridegroom, a handsome *bashlogue*, or price, for his wife. In due time the consent is given, on which the bride returns to her father's house, where, strange to say, she is retained for six months or a year, and sometimes two years, according, as it appears, to her caprice or the parents' will, having no communication with her husband unless by stealth. The meaning of this strange separation I never could ascertain. . . . Afterwards the marriage presents and price of the wife are interchanged, and she goes finally to live with her husband."—Fraser's *Journey.* Vol. II., p. 372. 1838.

"Matches are also made up occasionally by the parents themselves, with or without the intervention of the Reish-suffeeds, but the order and ceremonies of the nuptials are the same. There is a regular contract and a stipulated price; the young people are permitted to enjoy each other's society for a month or six weeks; and the bride then returns, as in the former case, to spend a year or more with her parents."—*Ibid.*, vol. II., p. 375.)

The stealthy communications of husband and wife, and postponement for a period of open cohabitation, which appear in this case, have already been noticed as occurring among the Mezeyne after a contract for marriage, and after the form of capture had been observed. In Sparta, too—where also the form of capture was observed—the young wife was not, immediately after the marriage, domiciled in her husband's house, but had communications with him for some time clandestinely, till he brought her, and frequently her mother, to his home.[1] —Xenophon, *Rep. Lac.*, 1-5.

Cases in which the form is greatly disintegrated have already been mentioned as occasion served (some are given in Chapter II.), and it does not seem necessary now to go at

[1] [In other cases we have forcible abduction followed by an arrangement, and thereupon marriage. In this case, circumstances having changed without the contract having come (such, at any rate, is the statement) into the foremost place, abduction has been succeeded by elopement—an arrangement following after the man and woman have lived for some time together away from the woman's relatives. Then, as among the Mezeyne (after a contract and capture made of the woman again and again), the woman returns, or is returned, to her family—to be given up after a proper interval.

It has already appeared, on the authority of Vambéry, that the Turkomans (or some of them) have a tradition of bride-racing.

According to Mr. A. W. Howitt, elopement was extensively practised among an Australian tribe, the Kurnai. The lovers, after they had gone off, were joined by a party of the man's kinsfolk, and thereupon the woman was treated as she would have been by the same people had they taken her in battle. She was, in general, pursued before long by her relatives. When she was recovered, the man usually got her in the end. (*Kamilaroi and Kurnai*, by Lorimer Fison and A. W. Howitt, 1880.)]

length into such cases. The most important class of them, perhaps, is that in which there occurs, either at leaving the bride's house or on arrival at the husband's, some faint symbol of the woman's captivity; the meaning of which is sometimes made more unquestionable by our finding along with it, or close beside it, the form of capture in one of its clearer varieties. With the patricians at Rome it sufficed that the bridegroom should carry the bride over the threshold of his house (" because," Plutarch says, " the Sabine women did not go in voluntarily, but were carried in by violence"); that he should part her hair with a spear (" in memory of the first marriages being brought about in a warlike manner"). At Sparta, latterly, it was enough for the bridegroom to catch up the bride and carry her from one room to another. At an earlier stage, it was a necessary form at Sparta that the bride should be carried off with violence. The Mussulman of India—the same who observed the mock siege—had, besides, to carry in his bride like the Roman. And in some districts of Abyssinia—in parts of which the sham fight (though in a disintegrated form) is still kept up both after the wedding and before it—it was proper that the bridegroom should carry the bride on his shoulders the whole way from her house to his own (Bruce's *Travels.* Vol. VII., p. 67. 1804). In this last example, too, if the distance was great, it sufficed to carry the bride entirely round her own house, which shows us the form, as it were, in process of dwindling, under the influence of convenience. Such cases as this would assure us as to the meaning of similar acts in other cases, were that doubtful; would show us, for example, why the Bedouin must force his bride to enter his tent (Burckhardt's *Notes.* Vol. I., p. 108. 1830); why, in Egypt, when the bride arrives at the bridegroom's door, he issues forth, " suddenly clasps her in his arms, as if by violence, and runs off with her as a prize" into the house. (Burckhardt, *Arabic Proverbs.* P. 116. 1830.) In all such cases what is done is analogous to what is prescribed to the Hindoos in the Sutras. At a vital stage of the marriage ceremony a strong man and the bridegroom forcibly drew the bride and made her sit down on a red ox-skin; and this was one of the essential ceremonies in the constitution of the Hindoo marriage.

In many cases the bride is required to show reluctance to enter her new home. An instance has occurred to us among the Slavs, in which a pretence was made of dragging her in, and she was ultimately bribed into entering. Cases have also been noticed in which she had to make some pretence of hiding herself. In many parts of Italy, Gubernatis tells us, the bride, on the wedding-day, has still to go through a ceremony of weeping—and the same has been noted in many other places. Other forms—some of them much more marked than that—in which the symbol of capture still appears in modern Italy, have been noted by Signor de Gubernatis (*Storia comparata degli usi nuziale in Italia e presso gli altri popoli Indo-Europei.* Milan. 1869.) The pretence of tearing the bride from the arms of her mother, which occurred among the plebeians at Rome, is mentioned by him as being marriage custom in Sardinia, and also at Casalvieri.

NOTE B.

PROBABLE ORIGIN OF THE NAME RACSHASA.

WE have seen (pp. 42, 43) that, in the code of Menu, one of the eight legal forms of the marriage ceremony was that by capture *de facto*, and called Racshasa, and that this marriage was permitted to the military class. It is curious that the name of this species of marriage should be that of a race of beings—the Rakshasas—whom we find playing an important part, and that connected with a legend of a capture, in the mythic history of the Hindoos. The story of the *Ramayana* may be said to be that of the carrying off of Rama's wife, Sita, by the Rakshasa, Ravana, and of the consequent war carried on by Rama against the Rakshasas, ending in their defeat and the recovery of Sita. (See Williams's *Indian Epic Poetry.* Pp. 74-76.) Wilson (*India Three Thousand Years Ago.* P. 20. Bombay, 1858) speaks of the Rakshasas as "a people, often alluded to, from whom the Aryans suffered much, and who, by their descendants, were transferred in idea to the most distant south, and treated by them as a race of mythical giants." He ranks them with the Dasyus, Ugras, Pishachas, and Asuras, as indigenous barbarian races or tribes, which had to be overcome before the Aryans could effect a settlement in part of Hindustan. Lassen takes the same view. "The *Ramayana*," he says (Lassen, Vol. I., p. 535; we quote from Muir's *Sanscrit Texts,* Vol. II., p. 425), "contains the narrative of the first attempt of the Aryans to extend themselves to the south by conquest; but it presupposes the peaceable extension of Brahmanical missions in the same direction as having taken place still earlier. . . . The Rakshasas, who are represented as disturbing the sacrifices and devouring the priests, signify here, as often elsewhere, merely the savage tribes which placed themselves in hostile opposition to the Brahmanical institutions. The only other actors who appear in the legend, in addition to these inhabitants, are the monkeys, which ally themselves to Rama and render him assistance. This can only mean that, when the Aryan Kshatriyas first made hostile incursions into the south, they were aided by another portion of the indigenous tribes." Dr. Muir can find no authority for saying that the word Rakshasa was originally the name of a tribe. At the same time (*Texts*, Vol. II., p. 434), he inclines to hold the descriptions we have of them as having more probably originated in hostile contact with the savages of the south, than as the simple offspring of the poet's imagination. He notices (*Texts*, Vol. II., p. 426) that, even in the Vedic period, the Rakshasas "had been magnified into demons and giants by the poetical and superstitious imaginations of the early (Aryan) bards." He quotes from the *Ramayana* a passage which represents them as cannibals—feeding on blood, men-devouring, changing their shapes, &c.; and another, in which they are described as "of fearful swiftness and unyielding in battle;" while Ravana, the most terrible of all the Rakshasas, is stigmatised as a "destroyer of religious duties, and ravisher of the wives of others." Dr. Muir adds, that the description of the Rakshasas in the *Ramayana* "corresponds in many respects with the epithets applied to the same class of beings (whether we take them for men or for demons) who are so often alluded to in the *Rig Veda*," and that it is quite possible that the author of the *Ramayana* may have borrowed therefrom many of the traits which he ascribes to the Rakshasas.

But how came the name of a legal mode of marriage to be that of such a race of beings? The only answer that we can make is a surmise—viz., that while the system of capture had not as yet died out among the Kshatriyas, or warrior caste of the Aryans, it was perfect among the races to which the name Rakshasas was applied; and that what was *their* system gave its designation to the exceptional, although permitted, marriage by capture among the Kshatriyas. This is the more probable, since, so far as we can ascertain, there is nothing in the name—Rakshasa—itself descriptive of the mode of marriage.

From another point of view, it may be observed that the Rakshasas hold nearly the same place in Hindu tradition that giants, ogres, and trolls occupy in Scandinavian and Celtic legends. They are supernatural beings—robbers and plunderers of human habitations—men-devourers and women-stealers. The giants and ogres of the north share the characteristics of Ravana. The cruel monsters are always carrying off kings' daughters. As Rama's exploits culminate in the recovery of Sita, so the northern giant-slayer is crowned with the greatest glory when he has rescued the captive princesses and restored them in safety to the king's—their father's—palace. Are we to hold all such beings—giants, ogres, trolls, &c.—wherever they occur, as representing savage races, between whom and the peoples in whose legends they appear as supernatural beings there was chronic hostility?

KINSHIP IN ANCIENT GREECE.

KINSHIP IN ANCIENT GREECE.

THE scheme of the development of systems of kinship which I propound in *Primitive Marriage*, and the truth of which I propose to test in the case of the ancient Greeks, is briefly as follows:—(1) That the most ancient system of kinship in which the idea of blood-relationship was embodied was the system of kinship through females only; (2) that in the advance from savagery this system was succeeded by a system which acknowledged kinship through males also, and which (3) in most cases passed into a system (agnation) which acknowledged kinship through males only [1]; finally (4), that agnation broke down, and there was again kinship through females as well as through males.

I conceive that the causes of this progress—excepting the last step of it, which is undoubtedly the result of the growing influence of humane and equitable considerations—are to be found in the successive stages of the development of systems of marriage. And I conceive that marriage was at first unknown; and that its

---

[1] [See note on p. 126.]

earliest form was that species of polyandry which now prevails among the Nairs, in Malabar—to one wife several husbands, not necessarily related to one another. When this was the form of marriage, there was no certainty of male parentage, and the idea of blood-relationship could only be developed into the system of kinship through females. There being no regular cohabitation of husbands and wives, families consisted of mothers and their offspring; the headship of families was in mothers, and the right of succession thereto in daughters. What family property there was went ultimately to the daughters and their children, in whom the family was prolonged; a man's heirs were his brothers, in order of age, and, after them, his sisters' children. The consolidation of this primitive family system led to the shifting of the form of marriage from the Nair (in many cases through the British) to the Tibetan species of polyandry—the sons of a house taking a wife between them into the family of their mother. This change, while it left fatherhood uncertain, destroyed uncertainty as to the paternal blood in children, all the possible fathers being of the same blood. It thus introduced kinship through males. It involved the breaking up of the primitive form of the family, and led in time to the transference of the government from the mother to the eldest male of the family. The supremacy of women depended on non-cohabitation with their husbands; its overthrow was the necessary consequence of cohabitation. The family, as I have said, was originally prolonged in the children of the daughters; the sons' wives were in other houses, the continuers of other families. But now the daughters passed as wives into foreign houses, and the sons found representatives of their family in their own children. The headship of the family could thus no longer descend from mother to daughter; and it was lost to women, though, in virtue of their having once possessed it, they would long retain a high position, and exercise much of that authority amongst men which had been assigned to them by the earlier system. The males, therefore, took the upper hand, and among them the first place was naturally assigned to the eldest. The first in age and authority, the first to marry, and frequently a father before his brothers reached maturity, it came to be feigned that all the children were his, and in time he assumed many of the powers of a paterfamilias. The headship of the family now devolved from brother to brother, and failing brothers, on the eldest son of the brotherhood. Then, a practice of monandry arising, the younger brothers made separate marriages, and Tibetan polyandry died out, leaving behind it the Levirate—the obligation on brothers to marry in turn the widow of a brother deceased, which will be familiar to the reader as having existed among the Jews.[1] The Levirate next died out, as being opposed to ideas of propriety derived from the practice of monandry. And thus the family slowly assumed either the form to which we are accustomed, or that which it had in Rome. It is unnecessary for my

[1] [See note at p. 109.]

purpose to say anything here of the causes of the growth of agnation. The changes in the form of the family would, of course, in every case be gradual, and not be effected throughout the whole of any community at once.

This theory is supported by a very considerable amount of evidence, of which it is impossible in this place to give even a summary. As regards the initial stage of the progress which it declares, I may, however, state, that polyandry has been traced at points all over the world, both ancient and modern; and that, in most cases, there has been found the system of kinship through females only, or traces of that system. That system is found to prevail amongst the great majority of existing rude races, with not a few of which the primitive form of the family is still preserved. And, lastly, traces or traditions of polyandry, and of the system of kinship through females only, have been found in the records of all the historical races. What I now propose is, to see whether a somewhat minute examination of the history of ancient Greece will yield evidence for or against the theory.

If the reader will look back at the scheme of the development of systems of kinship given at the outset, he will see that the phenomena of kinship in the second and in the fourth stages of the progress must be the same; that there must be correspondences between the phases of transition from the second to the third, and from the third to the fourth stages of the progress; and that where the phenomena of kinship exhibited in any period may belong to the second or to the fourth, or to a phase of transition from the former, or to the latter, we must examine the periods antecedent and subsequent to it, in order to ascertain to which stage the phenomena really belong.

I propose then, firstly, to inquire into the state of Greek kinship as it appears in the Homeric poems; secondly, to glance at the history of kinship in post-Homeric Greece; and, thirdly, to see what light can be thrown on its pre-Homeric history by a study of Greek traditions, and of the congeners of the Greeks.

I. In no respect has life in the Homeric times so modern an aspect as in regard to the position of "wedded wives." The number of the wives acquired by capture, and the frequent mention made of women either as the end or the cause of war, remind us that there is something peculiar in the position of women, and even in the relation of the "wedded wife" to her lord. But for this, the general description of the married state might suggest to us the wedded life of our own fathers and mothers.

The position and fortune of the wedded wife are usually equal, sometimes superior, to those of her husband. Not unfrequently he owes to her his rank and wealth; always she possesses a dignified place and much influence. It is needless to cite examples of this. The poet often assumes a perfectly chivalrous tone in alluding to the wives of his heroes.

In Homer we find acknowledgment of the blood-ties through both the father and the mother. There is not a hint in the poems of the relationship between mother and child being less sacred or complete than that between father and child. On the contrary, in several passages, as I shall show, that relationship is represented as the more sacred of the two. And it is certainly always so depicted, where it is depicted at all, as to exclude the idea that it was not perceived to be a blood-relationship. Anticleia's grief for the absent Ulysses, and the meeting with her shade in Hades, are perfect pictures of filial and motherly tenderness. It would be hard for any one to read them, and imagine that in an age when blood-ties were at all thought of, the tie of blood was wanting to complete the bond between that mother and son.

Homer prefers the father in tracing genealogies, without denying the mother her place. On the other hand, it is clear that the Greeks had not been long accustomed to pedigrees traced through fathers. Few of the Homeric genealogies ascend many steps till they terminate in an unknown or divine father. Had pedigrees through fathers been old inheritances of the noble families which figure in the Troica, the divine parentages, whatever else besides uncertainty of fatherhood they may imply, could not possibly have been either so numerous or so commonly credited.

1. I instance the pleading of Lycaon in the *Iliad*, as containing proof of kinship through the mother, and proof that the tie through the father did not, in the same degree, infer the rights and obligations of kinship. This Lycaon was a son of Priam, by Laothoë, daughter

of Altes, King of the Leleges. She was one of Priam's numerous "wedded wives," and had by him two sons, Lycaon and Polydorus, the latter already slain by Achilles, who had come forth to avenge the death of Patroclus, his friend and kinsman.[1]

Lycaon, being assailed by Achilles, begs for his life, his main plea being that he is not related to Hector on the mother's side;

> Ἄλλο δέ τοι ἐρέω, σὺ δ' ἐνὶ φρεσὶ βάλλεο σῇσι,
> Μή με κτεῖν', ἐπεὶ οὐχ ὁμογάστριος Ἕκτορός εἰμι
> Ὅς τοι ἑταῖρον ἔπεφνεν ἐνηέα τε κρατερόν τε.

> "Yet I'll say
> This to thee, and cast it thou in heart;
> Do not slay *me*, since not from the same womb
> Am I as Hector is, who killed thy friend,
> At once both kind and brave."[2]

The appeal is to the well-known law of blood-feud, for though the assault takes place in battle, it is made in the thirst for vengeance. What, then, is the meaning and effect of the appeal? Is it this:—"Hector and Hector's kindred are alone amenable to your vengeance, for it was Hector who slew your friend. I am neither kith nor kin of Hector. True, we have, as you know, the same father. But I put it to you, what does that matter? He is not my brother uterine (ὁμογάστριος),

---

[1] The friendship of Achilles and Patroclus overshadows their affinity. But according to tradition the affinity was undoubted. Æacus and Menœtius were brothers uterine—sons of Ægina; and the former was the father of Peleus, the latter of Patroclus.

[2] The translations of the Homeric passages are all from Norgate.

my relative through the mother"? At least, it implies that being a brother by the same father did not mark him out one of those specially liable to be slain as a relative of the wrong-doer. The pleading was ineffectual, but it remained unanswered save by the sword. "Patroclus has died. I too, the magnificent Achilles, must soon die. You had as well go, my friend. So there." And the keen sword smote at the collar-bone beside the neck. Achilles was avenging the death of a dear friend as well as a kinsman; and the limitations imposed by the law of blood-feud, appealed to by Lycaon, were powerless to restrain him. Should it be thought that the inference made from this case is too large, it must at any rate be allowed that the passage proves—(1) that the blood connection between the mother and son was fully acknowledged; (2) that the connection through the father and mother made a closer kinship than that through the father only, which would not have been the case had agnation been established. And as it is obvious that Lycaon could not have urged his plea had he and Hector been uterine brothers, even had they been sons of different fathers, it becomes probable (3) that the blood-tie through the mother alone was practically, at this time, a stronger one than that through the father alone.

Further on, Priam speculates as to the fate of Lycaon and Polydorus. "If they yet live captive with the Greeks," he says, "then surely we shall ransom them with brass and gold; for the money is in the house, as the aged Altes gave abundance with his daughter."

There is here a further note of relationship between mother and child. The mother's wealth was specially applicable for ransoming *her* sons. We may infer that in the household of the polygynous Priam, the children of a wife, whatever other rights of inheritance they had, were heirs to her wealth.

It may be said that Lycaon's plea refers solely to a state of feeling prevailing on the Asiatic side, and peculiar to a people who practised polygyny. But if it was of no force from Homer's point of view, he either would not have stated it, or he would have made Achilles meet it with an answer. The reply of Achilles is irrelevant, being substantially what I have stated, with the addition that he had made up his mind to spare no child of Priam. It must be assumed that the plea appeared of force to Homer's auditors, and that could only be through their knowing what a difference the want of a perfect kinship should have made. On the Greek side, as well as on the Asiatic, there was, owing to the system of " captive wives," abundance of room for the distinction between the paternal and maternal tie, and for its practical recognition in cases of blood-feud.[1] That Lycaon is presumably of strictly

[1] I know no better illustration of the incompleteness of kinship through the father, at the stage of development in which I conceive the Homeric Greeks to have been, than is afforded by the story of Amnon and Tamar, in the Book of Samuel. Tamar was Amnon's half-sister by the same father; yet they were marriageable. 2 Sam. xii. 13 : "Speak to the king, for he will not withhold me from thee." And see v. 16. Her uterine brother Absalom revenged the rape of Tamar by slaying Amnon. He then fled to the kindred

Greek ancestry on both sides of his parentage, is a fact on which I shall not rest an argument.

2. In the *Iliad* we have evidence of the existence of kinship through the mother in the story of Tlepolemus, the Rhodian leader, son of Hercules and Astyoche. This man, having inadvertently slain his grand-uncle Licymnius, the brother of Alcmene, mother of Hercules, had to flee, "for the other sons, and grandsons too, of mighty Herakles had threatened him." Not threatened to deliver him up to the kindred of Licymnius, but to avenge the death. Now, what had they to do with the matter as avengers? Nothing except on the footing that they were of the kindred of Licymnius; for, by old law, the right of vengeance belonged to the kindred of the slain. They were therefore (being of the kin of Hercules) of the kindred of Alcmene and of her brother Licymnius. That is, *some* Hellenes—for this is a strictly Hellenic story—recognized the blood-tie through the mother as creating the right and obligation of the blood-feud.— *Iliad*, ii. 656, *et seq.*

3. Helen, when she surveys the warriors from the wall, looks for, but cannot see, Castor and Pollux—

αὐτοκασιγνήτω, τώ μοι μία γείνατο μήτηρ.

"Mine own brethren,
Whom both, as also me, one mother bare."

---

of his mother, viz. to the court of Talmai, King of Geshur. (2 Sam. iii. 3, and xiii. 37.) In *Primitive Marriage*, p. 61, I point out how the occurrence of cases of this sort among the aborigines of Australia is one of the chief impediments in the way of the homogeneity of the groups being destroyed.

She cannot believe that they have not accompanied the Greeks; but if they have not, it must be because of the shame and blame resting on her, their sister. There is a legend which connects the three through a common father, Zeus; but that is not alluded to: Homer represents her thoughts as wholly fixed on their common mother.

A similar passage occurs in the nineteenth book of the *Iliad*. Briseïs is represented as bewailing, over the dead Patroclus, the accumulated woes which she has had to suffer—the loss of her husbands and of "three beloved brethren too (one mother bare us)."

τρεῖς τε κασιγνήτους, τούς μοι μία γείνατο μήτηρ.

This would scarcely have been repeated if the poet did not feel its power to stir tender chords in the hearts of his auditors. He always marks the distinction of κασίγνητος καὶ ὅπατρος and ὁμογάστριος as an important one. And he is not content with simply denoting the uterine tie. The verse swells, as with feeling, in referring to it. On the other hand, the word ὅπατρος, which he uses twice, is both times used abruptly, as if to state a fact unconnected, or at least not specially connected, with the feelings.

A passage in the twenty-fourth book puts it beyond dispute that Homer attaches superior importance to the tie through the mother. Apollo, addressing the gods in favour of granting burial to Hector, strongly disapproves the savage manner in which Achilles has treated the body. There is usually an end, he urges, of tears and wailing for human losses, even when they are the greatest, as when one loses—

<blockquote>
φίλτερον ἄλλον . . .
Ἠὲ κασίγνητον ὁμογάστριον, ἠὲ καὶ υἱόν.

"One right dear,
Either a brother born of self-same womb,
Or even a son."
</blockquote>

Here a brother "of the self-same womb," and a son, have the foremost place among dear relations. Why not a brother—ὅπατρος—of the same sire? Clearly because such brothers were not so closely and tenderly connected. That is, we must conclude that Homer regarded the blood-tie through the mother as closer and dearer than that through the father.[1]

4. The beggar Arnæus got his name through his mother. Was it customary among the lower classes to name the children after the mother? Have we a hint of such a custom among the higher classes in the following passage?—

<blockquote>
"Then in their palace
Anon the father and the lady mother
Did call their child 'Alcyone' for surname;
</blockquote>

---

[1] *Iliad*, iii. 235; xix. 290 *et seq.*; xi. 257; xii. 371; xxiv. 45. In *Odyssey*, iv. 224, Homer places in the same category sorrow for a mother, father, brother, or son—naming the mother first. One is reminded by the passages cited in the text of the special love and tenderness felt by Joseph for his brother Benjamin, "his mother's son": "His bowels did yearn upon his brother, and he sought where to weep, and entered into his chamber and wept there." How cold by comparison was his feeling for his brothers-german!—Gen. xliii. 29.

> Because, forsooth, her mother had the fate
> Of mournful Alcyon, and like her did weep
> When the far-darting king, Apollo Phœbus,
> Carried her daughter off."

This is from the tale of Meleager, and therefore very old. We shall find that the custom of naming children after the mother prevailed among the Lycians; and shall be able to show that it anciently prevailed among many of the Greek tribes.—*Odyssey*, xviii. 5; *Iliad*, ix. 556, et seq.

5. In the sixth book of the *Iliad* we have the genealogies of Glaucus and Sarpedon. Sisyphus begets Glaucus, who begets Bellerophon, who marries the daughter of Prœtus, King of Lycia, and by her begets Isander (who is slain), Hippolochus, and Laodameia. Then Hippolochus begets Glaucus; and Laodameia, embraced by Zeus, brings forth Sarpedon. Sarpedon is the leader of the Lycian allies, and Glaucus is but one of his lieutenants! The daughter's son is the chief, and the agnate the inferior. I shall recur to this when I come to treat of the Lycians. It points to a system of succession, through females, which prevails among nearly all rude races, and which, we shall find, continued to be in full force among the Lycians long after the Homeric period.—*Iliad*, vi. 150—210.

Here, meantime, I suspend the examination of the poems. I think I have succeeded in showing that Homer had no idea of there being no affinity between mother and child; that, on the contrary, he regarded uterine connections generally as especially close and tender. I have shown that there are traditions in the poems which prove that among some Hellenes affinity through the mother founded the blood-feud, and gave rights of succession; that among the "Pelasgi," and possibly Hellenes in Troy and Lycia, the tie through the mother was superior to that through the father, and that the latter was not regarded as a perfect kinship.

I may say here that did we know that my scheme of the normal development of systems of kinship was correct, and were the question this,—Finding in Homer's time kinship through mothers as well as fathers, was the stage of advancement one of departure from the system of kinship through females only, or of advance from agnation?—the question might be answered without further inquiry. I do not find a single trace of agnation—a single legend which gives a hint that it ever existed. I find some hints of kinship through the mother having been the only kinship. I find the whole circumstances of the people barbarous. The heroes are magnificently accoutred and armed; but their battles, and even those of the gods, tend to degenerate into stone-bickers. Their funeral orgies are those of the Viti and some Scythic peoples mentioned by Herodotus. Achilles, the hero of their imagination, is a sulky and implacable savage; Ulysses, their model wise man, is cunning, treacherous, and profligate. It would not be believed that this people had reached a point which the Romans only reached late in their history through the persistent efforts of a line of illustrious prætors. The question is not, however, what I have now stated. It is the much more important and difficult one whether I can show, to any high degree of probability, that the Greeks came through the earlier stages specified in my scheme.

II. What, then, is the post-Homeric history of kinship in Greece? And does it supply an argument in favour of the view that the Homeric Greeks were advancing from the system of kinship through females only to the more modern system of agnation?

It can be shown that in post-Homeric Greece there grew up an opinion unfavourable to the idea of kinship through the mother. The *law*, perhaps, never recognized agnation; but it made a close approach to doing so.

1. By Solon's time the next of kin on the father's side, to the fourth degree, succeeded before any right of succession (*ab intestato*) opened to the kindred of the mother; and, on both sides of the house, males and the children of males, cut out females and their children even of a nearer degree. The law provided that the estate of one dying childless and intestate should only pass to the next of kin on the mother's side, "si nulli supersint paterni proximi ad sobrinorum usque filios." This cannot be said to have been very unfriendly to the maternal relatives. I find, however, that by the time of Isæus, in this field the greatest of Athenian jurists, the law had so far changed, that Isæus denies a mother any place among the heirs of her son. In the celebrated suit about the succession of Hagnia it appears that the

mother of Hagnia claimed the succession (1) " tanquam cognata," she being the sister of his cousin Stratius. Being defeated in this claim, her advisers next demanded the estate for her (2) "tanquam matri filii." In this claim also she was defeated, on the ground, as Isæus states, that a mother had to her son no affinity carrying any legal right. Μητέρα εἶναι συγγενέστατον μὲν ἦν τῇ φύσει πάντων, ἐν δὲ ταῖς ἀγχιστείαις ὁμολογουμένως οὐκ ἔστιν. It follows, of course, *à fortiori*, that none of her kindred—no one on the maternal side of the house— could have any right of inheritance. This, practically, is agnation. Bunsen combats the position taken up by Isæus, and explains the lady's failure on other grounds. Isæus is, however, the greater authority; and Bunsen's argument, as I read it, turns chiefly on Solon's law, without making allowance for the change in the law in the interval between Solon and the suit.—Leges Atticæ (S. Petiti, 1741), vol. iii. p. 51 ; tit. vi. θ'; Bunsen de Jure hæred. Athen., p. 23; Isæus, ed. Schömann, p. 145.

2. But whether the opinion that there was no affinity between mother and child was ever realized in Greek law or not, there is no doubt that such an opinion came to be current in later Greece, as a new view, and was the subject of controversy. I have said there is no hint of such an opinion in Homer. Neither is there in Hesiod.[1] The view (which is stated in the *Orestes* of

[1] Is Hesiod to be regarded as serious when he speaks of the general uncertainty of male parentage in his own, " the fifth age " ? *Works and Days*, 182.

Euripides) receives, so far as I know, its earliest and best expression in the *Eumenides* of Æschylus, who distinctly represents it as a new doctrine.

The *Eumenides* exhibits kinship through the mother surviving as a subject of controversy. The plea which succeeds in the trial of Orestes is that he was not of kin to his mother Clytemnestra. On the other hand, success is only attained after much argument. The jury are equally divided on the plea, and Orestes gains his cause by the casting vote of Athene.

The basis of the suit is the claim of the Erinnyes to the right of punishing matricides. This was their function, by special ordination, as representing a time when kinship through the mother was unquestioned. The claim is disputed. Would they, asks Orestes, drive from his home the slayer of a wife that had killed her husband? The Erinnyes answer—

"That would not be kindred blood shed by the hand of a relation."

"What," asks Orestes—

"Do you call *me* related by blood to my mother?"

On this they open upon him with reproaches. Would you disown so dear a relationship? Did she not bear thee, murderer, in her womb? They are shocked at his impiety; and their horror increases on discovering that he is not alone in holding the new view—that it is adopted by the gods.

Apollo is clear as to the law of Zeus respecting kinship. "The bearer of the so-called offspring," he contends, "is not *the mother* of it, but only the nurse of the newly-conceived fœtus. It is the male who is the author of its being; while she, as a stranger, for a stranger preserves the young plant for those for whom the god has not blighted it in the bud. And I will show you a proof of this assertion; one *may* become a father without a mother. There stands by a witness of this in the daughter of Olympian Zeus, who was not even nursed [much less engendered or begotten] in the darkness of the womb." Pallas accepts this view of the matter, and records her vote in favour of Orestes.

On judgment being pronounced against them, the Erinnyes are plunged in despair

>   Ἰὼ θεοὶ νεώτεροι, παλαιοὺς νόμους
>   Καθιππάσασθε, κἀκ χερῶν εἵλεσθέ μου.

"Ye younger gods, ye have over-ridden the old laws, and have taken him out of my hands."

The lamentation and wail of dishonour are afterwards repeated with outcries which farther fix the attention on the fact that the new doctrine was subversive of old beliefs.

"That I should be treated thus! alas; *I of the ancient views*, and should have an abode in the land, forsooth, unhonoured and detested! Thereat I breathe out my fury and full resentment."

Now, were the views of kinship found in this play those which prevailed in the time of Æschylus, or those which, as he imagined, prevailed in the time of Orestes?[1]

It is most unlikely that the poet would have composed a drama in which were to be exhibited in conflict two sets of opinions, both archaic, and with neither of which his auditors might have any sympathy. Thus I think the idea is excluded that the play is an attempt to reflect the spirit of the age of Orestes. Moreover, Orestes is pre-Homeric, and neither in Homer's time, nor presumably before it, since we have no trace of it in the Homeric or Hesiodic poems, had the Greek mind thought of agnation. If, then, the new views did not prevail in the time of Æschylus himself, they were yet certainly post-Homeric; and, assuming this, it is immaterial to my argument whether Æschylus applied to

---

[1] The solemn adjudication in the *Eumenides* that there is no kinship between mother and child, and the acquittal on that ground of Orestes, seem to me in remarkable contrast to the Homeric account of Epicaste (*Odyss.* xi. 270),—

"Next beauteous Epicaste,
Mother of Œdipus, I saw; a deed
Heinous did she, through witlessness of mind.
To her own son got married; his own father
Slew he in fight and spoiled, and her he married."

The gods made known the matter far and wide among mankind. Epicaste hanged herself and left behind for Œdipus "full many a woe, as heavy indeed as through a mother's curse the avenging furies e'er bring to pass." In the *Eumenides* the furies have nothing to do with matricides, there being no blood-relationship between mother and child. Who can doubt but that in the mind of Homer the whole horror came out of the closeness, as he conceived it, of that as a blood-relationship.

the story of Orestes an opinion current in his own day, or one that had prevailed so recently as to be sufficiently familiar to allow it to be made the pivot of a dramatic plot. I would incline, however, to think, were there no other means of settling the matter, that the only satisfactory explanation which can be given of the almost balanced state of contrary opinions in the *Eumenides* is, that it reflects the state of popular feeling and belief respecting kinship in the time of Æschylus himself.

We know that the new view was adopted by several philosophers who (speaking roughly) were the contemporaries or immediate successors of Æschylus. That the act of generation, the begetting, was wholly the father's, and that the mere nutrition was the mother's, is said to have been the opinion of Pythagoras and Plato. Plutarch, in one place, represents these philosophers as holding ἀσώματον μὲν εἶναι τὴν δύναμιν τοῦ σπέρματος (like mind on its commencement), which transforms σωματικὴν δὲ τὴν ὕλην supplied by the mother; and, in another place, in speaking of that view of the Cosmos which conceives it to be compounded of two factors, mind and matter, he says, Plato calls mind the conception, idea, model, and *father;* and matter the mother, *nurse,* or seat and region capable of births. It would probably be found that Greek speculation went no farther than to give the father the first and the mother a subordinate place in the act of generation, and correspondingly to elevate the father's relation to the children and depress that of the mother. Chrysippus, however, is said to have held the extreme view propounded by Apollo in the *Eumenides.* "The fœtus is nourished in the womb like a plant; but being born, is refrigerated and hardened by the air, and its spirit being changed it becomes an animal." This constitutes the mother the mere nurse of her child, just as a field is of the seed sown in it.—Plutarch *de Plac. Phil.* 5, 4; *De Is. et Os.* 56 (Plut. *Oper.* Lips. 1778, vol. vii. 471); *De Stoic. Repug.* Id. vol. x. 350.

That such views prevailed among the thinkers in or about the time of Æschylus—to whose time also Isæus who denies the right of inheritance to the mother's side, may be referred—favours my opinion that the *Eumenides* reflects the feeling of the author's own day. And whoever adopts that opinion must agree with me in holding that we have proof in that drama, read in connection with the Homeric poems, that kinship through the mother had been in Homer's time undisputed among the Greeks, and had come, by the time of Æschylus, to be a subject of controversy, and to a great extent, if not wholly, to be ignored.

3. We have a confirmation of this in the change which took place in the status of women in post-Homeric Greece.

Where the ruder forms of the family system prevail, the position of women is necessarily very high. The truth of this might be illustrated by numerous instances. And their position is gradually lowered as those changes take place which oust them from the headship of families, and deprive connections through them of importance. They first lose the headship of families; next they are denied equality; and, lastly, on agnation being firmly established, they sink almost to the level of slaves.

I have already had occasion to notice the high position of women in the Homeric age. "We find," says Mr. Gladstone, "in Homer the fulness of the moral and intelligent being alike consummate, alike acknowledged on the one side and the other [*i.e.* on the female and on the male]. The conversation of Hector and Andromache in the sixth *Iliad*, of Ulysses and Penelope in the twenty-third *Odyssey*, the position of Arete at the court of Alcinous, and that of Helen in the palace of Menelaus, all tell one and the same tale." "Women in the Homeric age," says Mitford, "enjoyed more freedom, and communicated more in business and amusement among men, than in after ages has been usual in those Eastern countries; far more than at Athens in the flourishing times of the commonwealth. Equally, indeed, Homer's eloquent eulogies and Hesiod's severe sarcasms prove women to have been, in their days, important members of society."

It is notorious that in later Greece all this was changed. In Sparta alone, where the old customs were best preserved, did the women retain anything of their old dignity and influence.[1] Everywhere else they were

---

[1] "Spartan mothers," says Müller, "preserved a power over their sons when arrived at manhood, of which we find no trace in the rest of Greece."—*The Dorians*, Book iv. chap. v. § 1. Again he says (*Ibid.* § 5) that the Dorians generally, and more at Sparta than elsewhere, preserved most rigidly and represented most truly

degraded. At Athens they were confined to home, and their liberties restricted in a fashion quite Oriental. Even the idea of marriage, as Mr. Gladstone observes, was, in post-Homeric Greece, greatly lowered. "The very name of γάμος, with its kindred words, underwent a change of sense, and was made applicable to such a relation as that established between the Greek chieftains in the war of Troy and their captives, in cases where they had wives already." Elsewhere he observes: "In truth, it would seem not only as if before Christianity appeared, *notwithstanding the advance of civilization*, the idea and place of women were below what they should have been, but actually as if, with respect to all that was most essential, *they sank with the lapse of time.*"—*Studies on Homer*, vol. ii. 517, 518.

I claim this lowering of the position of women in post-Homeric Greece as evidence that the change in the popular feeling about kinship, *which is proved to have taken place*, took place in post-Homeric times. Looking at the degradation of women as *an effect*, we see that no causes could well have produced it, so long as relationships through women preserved their old importance. On the other hand, we can discern a sufficient cause for that degradation in the gradually-increasing preponderance of male kinship, and in the changes in the marriage system—of which anon—which made

the customs of the ancient Greeks. We shall hereafter see that they preserved, among other things, much of the family and marriage systems to which the early influence of women was owing.

possible that preponderance. So that we have here a circumstance confirmatory of the conclusion at which we had previously arrived.

On the whole, looking to the double kinship in Homer, and the hints he furnishes of the former superiority of female kinship; to the high position of women in Homer, and their subsequent degradation consentaneously with the appearance and growth of the principle of agnation, does it not appear probable that in the Homeric times the Greeks had but just left behind them the system of kinship through females only, along with all the other features of social and family life which the presence of that system implies?

III. Let us now see now far the conclusion at which I am pointing is confirmed by the traditions of the Greeks and a study of their congeners.

Bachofen, in his *Das Mutterrecht*, goes over this field. He conceives that he has found proofs of "mother-right"—the primitive female government—not only in all the early Greek settlements, but in every branch of the Indo-Germanic family. For my purpose it must suffice to glance at some facts respecting the ancient populations of Persia and Media, from which, according to some writers, the Greeks were derived, and to make a rapid examination of the customs and traditions of the Greeks themselves in a few of their principal settlements.

We shall find that in Persia there was anciently general incestuous promiscuity. We shall find in ancient Media various forms of marriage, including polyandry, but no law of incest, and no conjugal fidelity. In Sparta we shall find monandry without conjugal fidelity, alongside of polyandry in the form in which it now prevails in Tibet; in Troy, the Levirate; and in Athens, sister-marriages and traces of the Levirate. Farther, we shall find among the Lycians, whose affinity to the Greeks was so pronounced, the system of female kinship prevailing down to the time of Herodotus, and shall adduce evidence that that system—the result of promiscuity, or the lower polyandry—anciently prevailed in Attica, and in Crete, and in several other Greek settlements. It is quite consistent with my views that in all these quarters monandry, and even the patria potestas, may have prevailed at points. What I maintain is, that anciently in the Greek settlements these phenomena were exceptional.

1. The incest of the ancient Persians is a familiar fact; the evidence of it is reviewed at considerable length by Selden, and was a few years ago carefully sifted by a writer in the *Fortnightly Review*. They not only allowed the union of brother and sister of the full blood, but even of mother and son, and father and daughter; and in some cases they required such unions for the production of persons qualified for religious offices. I know no account that can be given of such a total absence of restrictions on marriage, except that the Persian customs were those of savage hordes, that somehow (probably owing to their practice of polyandry) never became exogamous, and so never attained to the idea of incest. That Persian marriages were anciently

polyandric, I conceive to be proved by their having the Levirate. The Medes had no better manners than the Persians. Strabo says they had marriage in various forms, including polyandry; but marriage meant little with them, if Xanthus is to be believed, that they had no law of incest, and freely interchanged their wives. If the Greeks were really offshoots of the poorer and hard-pressed portions of the hill-population of Media and Persia, we may believe that when they set out for Greece they were in bad training. And I am not aware that there was any race between them and their new home from whom they could learn much.[1]

2. What Xanthus says of the Medes, Xenophon says of the Lacedæmonians. They had no conjugal fidelity. A Spartan husband had no scruple in calling on a friend, or even a stranger, to be the father of his

[1] Selden's *Jus. Natur.* chap. xi. art. "Consanguineous Marriages"; *Fortnightly Review*, No. xii. p. 715; Kleker, *Zendavesta*, iii. p. 226; Strabo (Amsterdam, 1707), ii. 798; Xanthus, *apud* Rawlinson, *Herod. Life*, cxlviii. I have discussed in *Primitive Marriage* the connection between polyandry and exogamy, and shown how the former may prevent the rise of the latter. I have also discussed the connection between polyandry and the Levirate, and have, as I believe, shown good reason for holding that the latter is a relic of the former. The three well-marked stages of polyandry may respectively be termed the Nair, the British, and the Tibetan. In the British, or second of the three stages of polyandry, fathers and sons usually had a wife in common, and no such idea had been formed as is conveyed by the word incest. The solidifying of such customs as prevailed in ancient Britain, and their perpetuation after marriage had become monandric, would be sufficient to explain the strange peculiarities of Persian and Median manners described above.

children; it was proper for a Spartan matron to be mistress in two houses. Nay, they had polyandry in the Tibetan form; for we are told by Polybius that the brothers of a house often had one wife between them. This is interesting, as we thus see exhibited in Sparta, at one and the same time, promiscuity in its highest polyandric form, and lingering round a growing practice of monandry.—Xenophon, *Rep. Laced.* 1, 9; Polyb. *Frag. ap. Maii Collect. Vet. Scriptt.* vol. ii. p. 384; Grote's *Greece*, vol. ii. 520, 536, 556; Müller's *Dorians*, book iii. ch. 10, § 3.

It has been usual to throw discredit on the statement of Polybius about the Spartans, as on that of Cæsar about the Britons, of Tacitus about the Finns, and of Strabo about the ancient Irish. But it will not do to put aside these statements as if those able ancients were men of no sense; as if the military officers and political agents of the Roman Empire, for instance, were not as trustworthy authorities as our own officers and agents in India, from whom we know of such customs existing in our own day. As the statement of Polybius is in itself probable, considering all we know of the Lacedæmonians, we must accept it, and believe that the Spartans practised this form of polyandry. And as it is admitted that the Spartans longer than any other Greeks preserved the ancient customs of the Greeks, we are entitled to infer that this species of polyandry had prevailed as a form of marriage among the race at large. Even if we had not the statement of Polybius, I should have considered that we had evidence that the Spartans anciently practised polyandry, in that legend which represents Lycurgus as declining, on purpose to set an example to his countrymen, to marry his brother's widow, and so cut out from the succession his brother's son. This is a tradition of the decay of polyandry in the royal house of Sparta. It is a declinature of the rights and obligations of the Levir;[1] for by the marriage, according to the story, Lycurgus would have legally succeeded to the throne, notwithstanding the appearance of a male child of his brother—a law of succession derived from polyandry. And I would have inferred that though polyandry began so early to die out in the upper ranks, yet, in all probability, it lingered into the historical period among the poorer folk, so that it might have been the subject of observation and record. And I believe Polybius the more readily that I had made these inferences before I knew of his statement.

3. In the legends of the house of Priam we have some instances of brothers succeeding to their brothers' widows. Helen, on the death of Paris, fell to his next brother, Deiphobus; and Andromache, widow of Hector, became ultimately the wife of Hector's only surviving brother, Helenus. As to Helen, it is said the right of succession to her was the subject of dispute between Helenus and Deiphobus. She properly fell to the elder of the rivals. As the pleading of Lycaon assures us of the superiority of the tie through the mother on the Trojan side—a note of polyandry—we

[1] [See note at p. 109.]

may the more readily believe that we have here a tradition of the Levirate.[1]

4. At Athens we have strong evidence of the system of female kinship, and therefore of some degree of promiscuity, in the sister-marriages permitted by law. A man might marry a sister by the same father, but not a sister by the same mother. Ἐξεῖναι γαμεῖν τὰς ἐκ πατέρων ἀδελφάς (*Leges Atticæ*, lib. vi. t. i. ή). Assuming that the Greeks were anciently exogamous—*i.e.* forbidden to marry those who were counted to be of the same blood with themselves, we must accept this law as proof that in Attica there was kinship originally through the mother only. It represents the system of female kinship as regulating intermarriages after it had lost importance in regard to successions. But other Attic laws equally point out the ancient state of the Athenians. For example, there is Solon's provision for the case of an ἐπίκληρος that had married an old man. "Dotalis fœmina, si maritus, qui eam sibi jure vindicavit, coire non posset, cum mariti adgnatis concumbito" (*Leg. Att.* lib. vi. t. i. ιγ'). This is not the Levirate, but it somewhat resembles it; and it is identical with the provision in the code of Menu for the interference of an authorized "sapinda" to discharge the duties of the Levir where the Levir was incapable. The provision for securing progeny in either case remands us to a state of society for its origin in which polyandrous ideas of propriety must have prevailed. Such a thing could never be dreamed of in an age of monandry and conjugal fidelity.

[1] [As to this also, see note at p. 109.]

5. Having now found promiscuity and polyandry in those districts from which the Greek races are believed to have been derived; polyandry and traces of promiscuity in Sparta, where the ancient Greek customs are believed to have been best preserved; and traces of polyandry in Troy and Attica, we might expect to find in the Greek legends numerous indications of the ancient supremacy of women, as well as of the system of kinship through females only. And we do so to an extent that is quite remarkable. Volumes might be filled with the minuter items of evidence.[1] Let me here give a single example of the sort of facts which I have in view before proceeding to the evidence on which I mainly rely. I refer to the Homeric legend of Meleager, which, read in the light of tradition, shows that at one time, among some Hellenes, heirship was vested in the mother's kindred, and not in the father's. No evidence need be adduced to show that this legend is Hellenic.

The legend of the Boar-hunt, and of the quarrel and war that rose out of it, is rapidly, and in some respects imperfectly, related in Homer. The purpose which Phœnix has in telling it is to induce Achilles to lay aside his wrath, by illustrating the dangers of over-

[1] Facts of the sort I have in view are to be found in abundance in Cyprus, the home of Aphrodite; in Lemnos, celebrated for the cruelties of its women; in the legends of Danaus and Atreus, and, indeed, in almost every Greek genealogy. They are to be found everywhere in connection with the Greek oracles and with religious rites. I need scarcely add that the legends of the Amazons contribute their quota.

indulgence in anger; and this end is fully served, consistently with some points of the story being left not a little obscure. The origin of the war, for instance, is thus described, immediately after the account of the ravages of the boar, and its slaughter by Meleager and his friends :—

> "And 'twas for sake of him,
> E'en for the boar's head and the bristly skin,
> The goddess brought about a mighty clamour,
> And war-cry 'twixt the lofty-souled Ætolians
> And the Curetes."

How the clamour arose is not stated, but the cause of Meleager's wrath is explained. He was angry at heart against his mother Althæa, because of her imprecations :

> "Who invoked the Gods, indeed, in her deep grief
> At blood-shed of her brother; and full oft
> The bounteous Earth, yea, smote she with her hands,
> Down sinking, knees to ground, and drenched with tears
> Was all her bosom, as she called on Hades
> And dread Persephoneia, to bring Death
> Upon her son."

Thus Homer's account is that the war rose out of a dispute between the Ætolians and Curetes, as to the boar's head and bristles, and that Althæa had cursed Meleager because he had killed her brother; but it is not part of the account that the brother of Althæa was killed at the hunt, or because he preferred a claim to the trophies of the chase. Phœnix, I may add, tells the story as one of several "tales of the olden times," which might be made to illustrate his theme, and as being one which he remembers.

Μέμνημαι τόδε ἔργον ἐγὼ πάλαι, οὔτι νέον γε.

"I do remember this, a matter of yore
(Nothing of late, at least)."

We may assume that Homer here made an old legend—old even in his time—serve his poetic purposes, and related it only so far as his purposes required.

But all the post-Homeric accounts are agreed that Althæa's brothers were slain by Meleager at the hunt; and from Hyginus we learn the cause of the quarrel. "When Meleager, having killed the boar, was for making over to Atalanta the chief spoils, his uncles on the mother's side took them away from her, asserting their right as next of kin, if Meleager declined to keep the prize to himself." Here then is the origin of the dispute. Meleager's maternal uncles denied his right to grant away the spoils, and so extinguish their hope of succeeding to them. If he did not choose to keep the trophies which he had acquired by his prowess, they fell to those who would inherit them, supposing him to die. Seeing that Meleager had paternal relatives, this is a distinct tradition of a time when a man's heirs were on his mother's and not on his father's side of the house.

What Hyginus relates is not a new or different version of the Homeric story, but an addition to it. It is in keeping with the Homeric account; moreover it consists (as I hope to show) with the statement that the legend belonged to "the olden times" even when Homer sang. And it is certainly (as we have seen) an addition which could not have been made in the time of Hyginus, nor indeed in the post-Homeric period. We have seen that the farther we advance, leaving behind the Homeric stage, the more monstrous and incredible would such a claim on the part of a mother's brothers have appeared. We must accept the tradition, therefore, as evidencing a time when inheritances descended from a man to his sister's children, and when *e converso* a man's maternal uncles were among his nearest heirs.[1]

[1] *Il.* ix. 525 *et seq.*; Hyginus, *Fab.* 229 and 174; and see Grote's *Greece*, vol. i. 200. In parting with the story of Meleager and the boar-hunt, let me ask what is *the meaning* of the boar, and of the collection of the flower of Greece—the whole of its chivalry—to put him down? It seems ridiculous that any mortal boar should cause such trouble and require an army of warriors to kill it; that the victory over it should ever after rank among the proudest exploits of the nation. And what is meant by the oracle enjoining Adrastus to give his daughters in marriage, one to a boar, the other to a lion; which was complied with by their marrying Tydeus and Polynices respectively? What is meant by the relations of Pasiphaë with a bull—the result the Minotaur; by Jupiter in the form of a bull carrying off Europa; by Phorbas attaining the supremacy in Rhodes by freeing it of snakes; by the conversion in Ægina of the ants—μύρμηκες—into men, the Myrmidons; by Cecrops being half a snake: by the stories of the dragon's teeth at Colchis and Thebes; by the numerous *horse* names in Homer, and a score of such-like facts? Is it at all possible that, most anciently, there were among the Greeks tribes with *totems*,—Bull, Boar, and Lion tribes; Snake, Ant, and Dragon tribes?—Here are a few names of Red Indian (American) tribes drawn from the fauna of their country—Wolf, Bear, Snake, Deer, Snipe, Eagle, Hare, Rabbit,

I now propose, first, to glance at some facts indicative of the ancient supremacy of women in families; secondly, to see how far the system of kinship, through females only, can be traced through the custom of naming children after the mother; and, thirdly, briefly to consider the most ancient Greek traditions of the primitive state, in their relation to my argument.

First. 1. Evidence of the ancient predominance of women among the Greeks is to be found in the number of their female divinities, and especially in the number of their Eponymæ. Looking to the Greek theogony, and accepting that view of systems of polytheism which represents them as resulting from the fusion of tribes or races, and the combination, in one Olympus, of the divinities which, before fusion, the tribes or races respectively worshipped, we must believe that many of the Greek tribes anciently worshipped only female divinities. And it is in accordance with this that five of the eight divinities of *immemorial* Greek worship were female—Here, Persephone, Athene, Demeter, and Aphrodite. (*Studies on Homer*, vol. ii. p. 395.) As to the Greek Eponymæ, their number is remarkably Crane, Duck, Sable, and Pike. It might be worth the while of some one with leisure to see how the facts bearing on this question would look when collected and marshalled. There are dozens of existing races, some of them comparatively advanced, whose tribes are thus named. Why may it not have been so among the ancient Greeks?

[The suggestion made in the preceding paragraph was afterwards developed by the author in a series of papers "On the Worship of Animals and Plants" (*Fortnightly Review*, 1869—70)—which will be republished in a new series of *Studies in Ancient History*.]

great, considering the disposition of the later Greeks to substitute male for female pedigrees. Among the Eponymæ are Salamis, Corcyra, Ægina, Thebe, the daughters of the river Asopus (Diod. iv. 13; Paus. ii. 5, § 1), Messene, Sparta, Athene, and Mycene—all of them belonging to the pre-historic period, whereas we know that many of the Eponymi of the genealogists were invented within historic times. Sparta is older than Spartus; Mycene than Myceneus. Mycene as an Eponyma is mentioned by Homer; Myceneus, who supplanted her, is, as Mr. Grote points out, the creation of post-Homeric Greece. How came it that there were so many goddesses in the early times, that so many cities and tribes were named after women? Must we not hold that women were anciently of high social importance? Is there not the suggestion that they were the chiefs of the groups of kindred?

2. Not only were the tribes named after women; they explained their affinities to one another by pointing to the relationship of their primitive mothers. The daughters of Asopus were carried off in various directions by gods, and became the mothers of tribes, which were thus kindred to one another. The kinship was no mythological dream, but a practical fact; the myth was its explanation. Let us, for example, take the case of the Thebans and Æginetans. When the Thebans, says Herodotus (v. 80, 81), in the sixty-eighth Olympiad, were hard pressed in war by Athens, they were directed by the Delphian oracle to ask assistance of their next of kin. Recollecting that Thebe and Ægina had been

sisters, they were induced to apply to the Æginetans as their next of kin; and the Æginetans gave them aid, first by sending their common heroes, the Æacidæ, next by actual armed force. How much of truth there is in the myth explaining this connection between the Thebans and the Æginetans is immaterial; it is enough for us that this tradition of the pre-historical period represents the two peoples as tracing their affinities through women — looking back to women as the heads of the families from which they sprang, and seeking their next of kin on the mother's side. A similar case is that of the Lycteans in Crete, who claimed affinity with Athens and with Sparta. In both cases the affinity was traced through mothers only, the fathers being wholly disregarded.[1]

[1] We find, by the way, a case something like that of the Thebans and Æginetans in connection with the story of Boreas and Oreithyia. On the invasion of Xerxes the Athenians were told by the oracle to invoke the aid of *their* son-in-law. They remembered Oreithyia and invoked Boreas, who sent a north-east wind, which wrecked the Persian fleet. I may farther observe that the Æacid genealogy establishes a connection between Ægina, Salamis, and Phthia. That between Ægina and Salamis we know: they were daughters of the river Asopus. Was the connection of these and Phthia also established through women?

Though I rest an argument upon *the reception* of these tribal affinities through first mothers among the Greeks, it must not be supposed that I believe that tribal affinities were really created through the sisterhood of first mothers, or that any one of the Greek tribes was really composed of all the descendants of one woman or one married pair. I believe that the social unit, if one may so speak, was not the family, but the tribe; that the operation of exogamy—the law forbidding the marriage of persons of the same

The female divinities, the Eponymæ, the traditions of tribal affinities through women, seem all to be indications of the ancient system of female kinship.

Second. Let us now see how far we can directly trace that system in Greece through the custom of naming children after the mother. This custom is an unmistakable " note " of the system of kinship through females only. Many illustrations of the connection between the two will be found in *Primitive Marriage.* To name one or two must suffice at present. The native Australians have female kinship only; among them children always belong to the family of their

stock—and of the system of kinship through females only, produced the division of the tribe into gentes (the word is convenient), consisting of persons born of mothers of the same stock; and that within the gens, when circumstances had developed the feeling of a closer relationship between persons born of the same mother, there arose the family, consisting at first of a mother and her children. This view is in harmony with all that is known of the history of property. The subject is discussed, though not so fully as it should have been, in *Primitive Marriage*, chap. viii. Affinity between two tribes would, on this view, be created through the marriage system having produced within both of them a number of gentes of the same stock. A family system in which the mother was the family head, her children the heirs, and her daughters the continuers of the family and gens to which she belonged—her husband or husbands being strangers to the gens—would account for women attaining a considerable position, and also for their being reputed to be, as they really were, the means of allying tribes to one another. I hope that before long I shall succeed in showing by satisfactory evidence that this view of the growth of society is supported by the facts of ancient Greek history. It seems highly probable that the names of the first mothers, through whom tribes were reputed to be connected, were really gentile names.

mother, and take her family name. The American Indians again, having the same limited kinship, their children also take the *totem* or family name of the mother. The Kocch in Northern India, the Celts in ancient Britain; in fact, a great array of cases, ancient and modern, might be cited to establish this connection. But those cited will suffice if the reader takes along with them the fact that, among ourselves, in all European countries, wherever practically, or in the eye of the law, there is kinship only through the mother, as in cases of illegitimacy, it is customary to call children by the name of the mother. This, while it is the natural consequence of the non-acknowledgment of the tie through the father, cannot, so far as I can see, be the consequence of anything else. And so far as I know, the custom of naming children after the mother has never been found in a case where relationship to the father was fully acknowledged. If it be a clear sign of exclusively female kinship that children should take the mother's family name, it is *à fortiori*, a note of it that they should be called by a matronymic.

We saw an instance of naming μητρόθεν, in Ithaca, in the case of the beggar Arnæus, and reasons to suspect another in the aristocratic house of Idas and Marpessa Evenine. I now proceed to show that what in these two cases may have been exceptional was *the custom* of the Lycians, the Athenians, the Cretans, and Messenians.

(*a*) As regards the Lycians, whose close affinity to

the Greeks appears undoubted, we have the testimony of several witnesses. Herodotus says of them, καλέουσι ἀπὸ τῶν μητέρων ἑαυτοὺς καὶ οὐκὶ ἀπὸ τῶν πατέρων. "If any one," he proceeds to say, "asks his neighbour who he is, he will declare himself born of such a mother, and will reckon up the female ancestors of his mother;[1] and if a female citizen should marry a slave, all her offspring are deemed wellborn; whereas, if a male citizen, and even the chief one amongst them, should take a foreign wife or a concubine, the children are without rights." Not the name only, but the status also, was taken from the mother. To like effect writes Nicolaus Damascenus, Λύκιοι τὰς γυναῖκας μᾶλλον ἢ τοὺς ἄνδρας τιμῶσι, καὶ καλοῦνται μητρόθεν, τάς τε κληρονομίας ταῖς θυγατράσι λείπουσιν οὐ τοῖς υἱοῖς. "The Lycians honour their women rather than their men, and are called after the mother. They leave their inheritance to their daughters, and not to their sons." Heraclides Ponticus represents them as having been accustomed from of old to be ruled by their women, ἐκ παλαιοῦ γυναικοκρατοῦνται; while Plutarch attests that they had the custom of naming children μητρόθεν. Plutarch relates a fable of the origin of the custom among the people of Xanthus, which he concludes by saying, διὸ καὶ νόμος ἦν τοῖς Ξανθίοις, μὴ πατρόθεν, ἀλλ' ἀπὸ μητρῶν, χρηματίζειν. This fable seems to be referred to by Pausanias,

---

[1] Have we a hint that this method of forming pedigrees had not gone wholly into disuse among the Homeric Greeks, in *Odyss.* i. 223?

but curiously enough as a Tröezenian and not a Lycian tradition.¹

(β) The ancient Attic traditions are full of recollections of female supremacy. It is not my purpose to attempt to show this, which could only be done by examining, at great length, a variety of old legends. My present business is with the tradition that at one time in Athens marriage was unknown in its modern forms, and that children were named after their mothers. This tradition is given by Justinus, Suidas, and Varro.²

The Athenians, says Justinus (ii. 6), "Ante Deucalionis tempora regem habuere Cecropa, quem, ut omnis antiquitas fabulata est, biformem prodidere, quia primus marem fœminæ matrimonio junxit." To the same effect Suidas (*sub voce* Προμηθεύς).

---

[1] See Herod. i. 173; Müller's *Fr. Hist. Gr.* 5, 461; Heracl. *Pont. de reb. pub. fr.* 15; Müller's *Fr. Hist. Gr.*; Plutarch *de Mul. Virt. cap. Lyciæ;* Pausan. ii. 32, § 7. As there is ground for suspecting an affinity between the Greeks and Egyptians, I notice what Herodotus (ii. 35, 36) says of the latter : "No necessity binds sons to keep their parents when they do not choose; whereas daughters are obliged to do so, even if against their choice. This custom Rawlinson declares to be incredible. No doubt it was a relic of the Lycian stage, in which the daughters were the heirs. The custom is now in full force among the Kocch, with whom the women are the heads of families (see *Primitive Marriage*, p. 151). I need hardly say that in the Lycian customs we have the fullest explanation of the superiority of Sarpedon to Glaucus.

[2] As a specimen of the class of legends to which I refer, I may cite that of the origin of the Ioxidæ. They traced through Ioxus and Melanippus to Perigune, the daughter of Sinis, as their primitive mother, and from her derived their custom of reverencing as holy and worshipping certain marsh plants. (Plut. *Theseus*, chap. iv.)

"Under the government of Cecrops," says Varro (*apud August. de Civ. Dei*, xviii. 9), " a double wonder sprang out of the earth at the same time ; in one place the olive-tree, and in another water. The king, in terror, sent to Delphi to ask what he should do. The god answered that the olive-tree signified Minerva (Athene), and the water Neptune (Poseidon) ; and that it remained with the burgesses to choose after which of the two they would name their town. Cecrops called an assembly of the burgesses, both men and women, for it was then the custom to let the women take part in the public councils. The men voted for Poseidon, the women for Athene ; and as there were more women than men by one, Athene conquered. Thereon Poseidon was enraged, and immediately the sea flowed over all the lands of Athens. To appease the god the burgesses found it necessary to impose a threefold punishment on their wives. They were to lose their votes ; the children were to receive no more the mother's name ; and they themselves were no longer to be called Athenians after the goddess." "Ut nulla ulterius ferrent suffragia, *ut nullus nascentium maternum nomen acciperet*, ut ne quis eas Athenæas vocaret." . . . "In mulieribus quæ sic punitæ sunt, et Minerva quæ vicerat victa est ; nec adfuit suffragatricibus suis, ut suffragiorum deinceps perdita potestate, et alienatis filiis a nominibus matrum, Athenæas saltem vocari liceret, et ejus deæ mereri vocabulum quam viri dei victricem fecerant ferendo suffragium." Thus the tradition is, that before the struggle for the mastery in the city, between Athene and Poseidon,—of which we have so many accounts—children in Attica, as in Lycia, bore the names of their mothers, and the women, as a body, were named after the goddess so long as they were called Athenians. They were then true burgesses; afterwards they were only burgher's wives. The tradition at once affirms that children at Athens were anciently named after the mother, and illustrates the high position anciently held by women among the Greeks.[1] It is a tradition of a genuinely archaic state, and I believe it to be a myth founded upon fact. When did it take shape? It certainly was not the invention of later Greece. Athene is here the representative and champion of what Bachofen calls "mother-right." In the *Eumenides* it is Athene who by her vote decides that a child is not of kin to its mother!

(γ) The Cretans, according to Plutarch, spoke of Crete not as their fatherland but as their "motherland"; they said not πατρίς, but μητρίς. In his treatise as to whether an old man should have the government of a state (ed. Lips. 1777, vol. ix. p. 166) Plutarch says: "Suppose that thou hadst a Tithonus for father, who was immortal, but on account of his great age always required care, thou wouldst doubtless not hesitate or find it burdensome to treat him

---

[1] Strabo (ix. 402), on the authority of Ephorus, relates a story in some respects similar to that of Varro, which suggests that the Bœotian women had anciently the same standing and privileges as the women of Athens.

kindly, and do everything for his support, inasmuch as he had for long done so much good to thee. But thy fatherland, *or as the Cretans are wont to say, thy motherland*, is immeasurably older and has far greater rights than even parents."

It would follow from the custom of tracing pedigrees through mothers, in conjunction with the notion of Autochthonism, that a man giving his pedigree must at last arrive at his first mother, his native land, and that he must call his country motherland, and not fatherland. That the Cretans thus spoke of their country points to the prevalence in Crete, in ancient times, of the custom of naming children from the mother. That colonists should call their original home Metropolis (μητρόπολις) is a different matter; yet even this word, as it implies a preference for the mother, must have come into use prior to those times in which, as we have seen, the kinship between mother and child was disputed.

There are numerous hints of the system of female kinship in the Cretan legends. I shall just notice one at which I have already glanced. The Lycteans considered themselves a Lacedæmonian colony, and kindred of the Athenians. The Athenian connection went back to those women whom the Pelasgic Tyrrhenians carried off from Cape Brauron, and only the mothers of the colonists were Spartans. In neither case did the Lycteans take any notice of the fathers. (*Plut. de Mulier, Virt. cap. Tyrrhenæ.*)

(δ) The evidence of the Messenians having had the

custom of naming after the mother is similar to that just seen in the case of the Cretans, but is a degree more indirect. It is to be inferred from the dream of Comon, the Messenian leader, and its interpretation as recorded by Pausanias, that the Messenians called their native place μητρίs and not πατρίs. Comon dreamed that he lay with his dead mother and she came to life. "The dream signified that Messene should be recovered again." The Messenians, it will be remembered, had an Eponyma, Messene.[1]

It is almost needless to repeat that we must believe that the system of kinship through females only prevailed wherever it was the custom to name children after the mother.

Third. It only remains to consider whether any, and what conclusions as to the early history of kinship in Greece can be drawn from the body of tradition preserved among the Greeks, declaring what were, in the earliest times, the condition and habits of their ancestors.

All Greek tradition represents the early inhabitants

---

[1] Pausan. iv. 26, § 3. Bachofen suggests that out of the idea of a common motherland rose the conception of the general brotherhood of members of the State. He notices the old Roman definition of parricide as derived from that conception. "Nam paricida non utique is, qui parentem occidisset, dicebatur, sed qualemcumque hominem indemnatum. Ita fuisse indicat Lex Numæ Pompilii regis, his composita verbis; si quis hominem liberum dolo sciens morti duit, paricida esto." The suggestion is ingenious, and in some cases the conception of the general brotherhood of citizens may have had such an origin.

of the country as emerging from the depths of the savage state. The legends of Arcadia are equally distinct as to the starting-point of the race with those of the Æolid house of Athamas. Less horrible than these, but equally unambiguous, and to the same effect, are the traditions of Crete and Attica. Everywhere the Greeks believed in a past of savage rudeness, and cherished the memories of those who helped them to take the first steps of progress. Their ancestors, according to their legends, were cannibals, and offered human sacrifices to the gods; were ignorant of agriculture, and lived on roots and shell-fish; had no marriage and no laws. Then came one who taught them to prune the vine and to plough the soil; and another who gave them marriage, laws, and social order. The legends which have handed down the names of these reputed founders of society were received as true by the mass of the people; but, of course, the conclusion that they are true cannot be founded upon the popular acceptance of them. There is no doubt whatever of their being of great antiquity. The fabled golden age of Hesiod, had it been a popular faith and not a mere poet's dream, would obviously not be inconsistent with these legends, would raise no shadow of obstacle to their reception, for they describe a state of things existing long after it is said to have vanished from the earth.

If a people were to emerge from a state of savageness, in which the association of the sexes had been subject to no regulation, nobody need be surprised if they did not, at a single step, arrive at a practice of monandry. Those who are acquainted with the usual circumstances of savage tribes would be very much surprised were they to do so. Owing to the practice of female infanticide, which the difficulties of subsistence force savages to adopt, and the liability to have their wives carried off by envious neighbours, the women in a group—even at a comparatively advanced stage—are usually much less numerous than the men; so that, for savages, to say nothing of other considerations, a general practice of monandry is, in the common case, if not invariably, physically impossible. Their first approaches to permanent cohabitation—the first regulated association of the sexes among them—must take the shape of a system of polyandry. I have already described three distinct types of polyandry, which I have severally called the Nair, the British, and the Tibetan; and I hold the British (notwithstanding incidents to us revolting) to be superior to the Nair, and the Tibetan to the British, because, in either case, the one admits of a better family system than the other. Since the two higher forms could only exist among a people who had, independently of them, acquired the idea of close kinship subsisting between parent and child, and between children of the same parent, it is obvious that a people with whom marriage and the family had been unknown could not at the first attempt arrive at either of these. For these they must have been prepared by the experience of a system like that of the Nairs, and possibly one still ruder, under which it would be possible for children of the same mother to acquire the feelings of relationship, and become bound to one another by a sense of common interests. The Tibetan polyandry once reached, an improving race would slowly advance, as we know many races have done, from it to monandry; and with monandry, when established, there would most probably remain, in the Levirate, a trace of their previous customs.

With such a people, at the Nair stage, women would (as among the Nairs) be the heads of families, daughters the heirs and continuers; and the position of women, if the system lasted long, would become one of high consideration. There would be kinship only through the mother, because paternity would be uncertain: and men would, for distinction, be named after the mother as naturally as at a subsequent stage they were named after the father.

It would not be surprising to find a people with such a history, after the family and the system of kinship had taken a substantially modern shape, in some respects treating the uterine connection as closer than the tie through a common father; forbidding uterine brother and sister, for example, while allowing brother and sister german, to marry; to find their tribes tracing themselves back to common mothers, not to common fathers—their legends telling of a time when not the patronymic, but the matronymic, was in use; least of all, to find them, at the beginning of history, remarkable for good treatment of their women.[1]

We have seen that in the most polished of the states of Greece, long after the family system had assumed the modern form—after a movement which magnified the tie of common fatherhood, and depreciated that of common motherhood, had made considerable progress—marriage was still allowed between brother and sister german, while between brother and sister uterine it was prohibited. We have found that not a few of the Grecian tribes deduced their descent, not from a first father, but from a first mother; that through the kinship of their first mothers, some of them held that they were closely allied one to the other; and that in several cases the tradition was preserved of a time when men were named after their mothers. In addition

---

[1] It is no mere conjecture that a people advancing from the savage state should pass through the progress outlined above; for it can be shown that such has been the usual—and so far as we know it has been the invariable—history of improving peoples. It can be shown, on the one hand, that the successive stages pave the way for one another—the onward movement taking place under influences which can be assigned; on the other hand, that the customs and institutions of races comparatively advanced usually present many indications of an experience of the lower stages. And even the Nairs, whose marriage system is the rudest form of polyandry, are an improving people—there are improving influences at work amongst them. There is nothing to show that the position of their ancestors, at any former period, was better than theirs is now—nothing to contradict the hypothesis that *they* came out of the savage state.

to these unmistakable vestiges of a period when fathers were "nowhere," and mothers were the heads of families —when polyandry of the Nair type was prevalent, and there was kinship through mothers only—we have seen that the greater number of the most ancient Greek divinities were female, which—not to make too much of it—seems to be an illustration of the ancient importance of women. In the Homeric period, too, with a family system of modern structure—with double kinship, but yet a preference for the uterine tie—we have found that women had great influence, and were held in high consideration. Since they lost place after this, as the movement toward agnation went on,[1] and since this movement has always begun before the modern family

[1] This proposition requires a few words of elucidation. The movement towards agnation obviously rose out of—or rather followed upon—the growth and consolidation of the patria potestas (see Maine's *Ancient Law*, p. 149 *et seq.*). It was an indication of the growth of paternal authority; and as fathers continued to gain, it was natural that mothers should continue to lose. At the beginning of history, in most cases, we find the patria potestas already so firmly established that, with or without agnation, fathers had the power of life and death over their wives and children, and that these were as devoid of rights as if they had been slaves. It is not necessary to quote authorities to show that this has been found to be a result—usually a very early one—of the monandric marriage system. Agnation, where it exists, is always a sign that the paternal supremacy is complete. My argument at this point may be put thus: in a family system, in which the father is the head of the family, it is found that all authority falls, and probably in no long time, into the father's hands; the tendency of such a family system is found to be to exalt the husband and lower the wife. Such a system could not result in women being treated with great consideration, and if we find women among any people so treated under

system has lasted long, and has ever been found unfavourable to women, we must seek, in the circumstances of an earlier family system, the explanation of their position at the earlier time. And we have it in the position attained by women under the Nair form of polyandry, of which so many indications have already been pointed out. That suffices for the explanation, and I know of nothing else that is sufficient for it. It is so much the less difficult to believe that the Greek

it, the cause most probably is something earlier in the marriage customs of the people. Of course all this refers to a period long anterior to that at which humane and reasonable considerations are influential enough to procure for women some approach to an equality of rights.

[See, in connection with the earlier part of the preceding paragraph, note on p. 126. Reference may also be made to *The Patriarchal Theory*, ch. xiii. On the theory of agnation stated in this work, there was, with kinship through males, a tendency to agnation, but it had to overcome the resistance offered by the previous establishment of a system of kinship through females; and the circumstances which favoured it included the removal of the most effective (often, no doubt, the only effective) check upon the paternal power—the protection of the wife's kindred. On this theory, therefore, the paternal power was high wherever there was much likelihood of kinship becoming agnatic.

Among savage or barbarous peoples it is found with male kinship that the wife's position is often very low, and that a man can often do with his children pretty much what he pleases so long as they are young and helpless, though the interest in them of their father's relatives, that is the blood-feud, protects them more or less. Patria potestas, in the Roman sense—the highest power a savage could possess over wife and young children, in consequence of his freedom from control, recognised as a father's right by law over his wife and his children at all ages—has, nevertheless, been so rare that no clear example of it has ever been found except in Rome.]

tribes had an experience of this marriage system, that we have found the strongest possible evidence of its existence among the Lycians, their close kinsfolk; among whom, long after Homer's time, not only was the matronymic in use, but daughters were the heirs of families, and pedigrees were counted through female ancestors only. And, indeed, the shortness of the genealogies in Homer raises a suspicion that the Greeks themselves in Homer's time had not had long practice in counting pedigrees through males.

Again—not to dwell upon weak or doubtful matters, such as the apparent operation of the Levirate among the Trojans,[1] or the practice closely resembling it, found, long after Homer's time, at Athens—we have evidence, both direct and inferential, that the Tibetan polyandry prevailed in post-Homeric times in Sparta—the state reported to have best preserved the ancient customs of the Greeks. The evidence, direct and inferential taken together, seems sufficient to support this statement; its consistency with so much that we have seen of the customs of the ancient Greeks is an additional reason for receiving it. And again, the fact that Tibetan polyandry prevailed in Sparta is, in no small degree, corroborative of the conclusion, that the early Greeks generally were polyandrous. We have seen that this conclusion, supported on the one side by the Spartan customs, is, from another point of view, made probable by what has been handed down of the marriage customs of the Medians and Persians—the peoples to whom, in

[1] [See page 222, and note at page 109.]

all probability, the tribes of the Greeks are most nearly akin.

Let me now ask whether the facts of Greek history, summarized above, are not perfectly consistent with the tradition that the early Greeks emerged from a state of savageness in which marriage was unknown to them? The indications of the existence in Greece of the Nair family system seem to me irresistible; and the earliest family system of a savage people would almost certainly be of the Nair type. It is remarkable that so many traces of that system should remain, and no doubt there are many which have escaped my search; but if, as I think, those which I have pointed out support and verify the Greek tradition, on the other hand the tradition should make some persons more ready to believe that the family system, which has been so often tracked in ancient Greece, is really that of Nair polyandry, and the close relationship to the mother, which forms an incident of it, the system of kinship through females only.

If I have proved that the system of double kinship, which prevailed in the time of Homer, was preceded by a system of kinship through females only, then—since it cannot be disputed that the Greeks subsequently made a very near approach to agnation, if they did not actually reach it—the scheme of the development of systems of kinship propounded by me at the outset, and the truth of which I proposed to test in the case of the Greeks, has successfully stood that test.

THE CLASSIFICATORY SYSTEM OF RELATIONSHIPS.

THE CLASSIFICATORY SYSTEM OF RELATIONSHIPS.

CHAPTER I.

MR. MORGAN'S CONJECTURAL SOLUTION OF THE ORIGIN OF THE CLASSIFICATORY SYSTEM OF RELATIONSHIPS.

In the *League of the Iroquois*, published in 1854, Mr. Morgan gave an account of "the system of relationships" of that people, which he for a time considered as *an invention* of theirs, and peculiar to them. Afterwards finding this system, or one similar to it, among the other Indian nations, he thought it might be made a means of solving what he calls "the great problem of the Asiatic origin" of the Red Indians. He accordingly procured to be sent, with the sanction of the United States Government, to the agents of that Government in foreign countries, a letter explaining the Iroquois relationship system, accompanied by blank schedules of questions designed to elicit accounts of the systems of relationships in use among the peoples among whom those agents were severally stationed. His work on

The Systems of Consanguinity and Affinity of the Human Family[1] consists—(1, and chiefly) of the returns made in answer to this letter; (2) of expositions connected with or explanatory of the returns; (3) of a conjectural solution of the origin of "the classificatory system of relationships,"[2] as he has called the systems of the Iroquois type; and (4 and lastly) of an elaborate discussion of "the great problem" above mentioned. If Mr. Morgan had any other purpose in his inquiry than the solution of this problem, it was to ascertain "the parent tribe" of mankind, or, as he himself expresses it, "to re-ascend the several lines of the outflow of the generations, and reach and identify that parent stock from which we believe we are all alike descended." Since the results of an inquiry undertaken with such aims prove to be of great value for the purposes of scientific history, we may well admire the happy chance to which they have been owing.[3]

---

[1] Washington City, 1871.

[2] The system in use among ourselves he calls the Descriptive System of Relationships.

[3] See Mr. Morgan's circular letter, *Cambrian Journal*, vol. iii., second series, pp. 149—66. How antipathetical to Mr. Morgan's mind the historical method is, may be seen in his ascribing the origin of what he calls "the Hawaian custom" to a reformatory movement of society; and the origin of exogamy—which he calls the tribal organization—to legislation. In his view they were both of them "institutions designed to work out the amelioration of society." This in his latest work: the same spirit breathed in his earliest. "By the formation of societies and governments," he says (*League of the Iroquois*, p. 56), "mankind are brought largely

The "conjectural solution" above mentioned, which alone concerns us here, is comprised in twenty pages of the work (pp. 474—94); and was suggested to Mr. Morgan by his friend Professor McIlwaine. It is a supposition that in the progress of society certain stages occurred in a certain order, as the *normal* stages in the evolution of marriage and the family; or, to use Mr. Morgan's own words, it is "an assumption of the existence and general prevalence of a series of customs and institutions which sprang up, at intervals, along the pathway of man's experience, and which must, of necessity, have preceded a knowledge of marriage between single pairs, and of the family itself, in the modern sense of the term."

The stages comprised in the series are fifteen in number, and are stated thus (p. 480):—

I. (The starting-point.) Promiscuous intercourse.

II. The intermarriage or cohabitation of brothers and sisters.

III. The communal family (first stage of the family).

IV. The Hawaian custom—giving

V. The Malayan form of the classificatory system of relationship.

VI. The tribal organization—giving

VII. The Turanian and Ganowánian systems of relationship.

under the influence of the social relations, and their progress has been found to be in exact proportion to the wisdom of the institutions under which their minds were developed."

VIII. Marriage between single pairs—giving

IX. The Barbarian family (second stage of the family).

X. Polygamy—giving

XI. The Patriarchal family (third stage of the family).

XII. Polyandria.

XIII. The rise of property, with the settlement of lineal succession to estates—giving

XIV. The civilized family (fourth and ultimate stage of the family)—producing

XV. The overthrow of the classificatory system of relationship, and the substitution of the descriptive.

It will have been noticed that by means of the first four of these stages Mr. Morgan undertakes to explain the "Malayan form" of the classificatory system of relationships, which is the form of that system found in the Sandwich Islands, and one or two other places. "The first four customs or institutions being given," he says (p. 480[1]), "the origin of the Malayan system can be demonstrated from the nature of descents, and the several relationships shown to be those actually existing." Then by means of the same stages in connection with the sixth stage, "the tribal organization," he undertakes to explain the "Turanian" and "Ganowánian" forms of the classificatory system—the "Turanian" being the form found

---

[1] The reference is to Mr. Morgan's work on *The Systems of Consanguinity and Affinity of the Human Family*, whenever the page only is given.

among the Hindus, the Chinese, and others, and the "Ganowánian" being that found among American Indians.[1] It may be taken as indisputable that, these three forms explained, the origin of the classificatory system is explained; and that done, the other varieties of the system present comparatively few points of difficulty. I propose then to examine, in this chapter, the explanations which Mr. Morgan offers of the origin of those forms. In the next chapter I shall suggest a new explanation of their origin.

The main features of the Malayan system of relationships, the form of the classificatory system which stands first for explanation, are the following :—

1. The children of my several brothers and of my several sisters are my children, and *their* children again are my grandchildren.

2. All the children of several own brothers and all the children of several own sisters are brothers and sisters to each other, and all the children of these

---

[1] The terms "Turanian" and "Ganowánian" are, as employed by Mr. Morgan, new and not very apt. His "Turanian family" comprises "the people of South India, who speak the Dravidian language, and number upwards of thirty millions; the people of North India, who speak the Gaura language, and number upwards of one hundred millions; the Chinese, who are supposed to number upwards of three hundred millions; and the Japanese, who are included provisionally, numbering about thirty millions" (p. 385). The "Ganowánians" are the American Indians, the name being compounded of two Indian words, and meaning "the bow-and-arrow people."

collateral brothers and sisters are brothers and sisters: and so on.

3. All the brothers of my father and of my mother are my fathers, and all the sisters of my father and of my mother are my mothers.

4. All the children of my several collateral brothers and sisters are my children, and *their* children again are my grandchildren.

5. All the brothers and sisters of my grandparents are my grandparents.[1]

Another feature of the system is that the brothers-in-law of my father and of my mother are my fathers, and their sisters-in-law are my mothers, and to this Mr. Morgan thus refers (p. 483) when closing his solution:—"The several marriage-relationships may be explained with more or less certainty on the same principles." But he does not attempt to explain the marriage relationships.

The means by which Mr. Morgan undertakes to account for those relationships are, as we have seen, the first four of his series of stages, or rather (the first being the assumed starting-point), the second, third, and fourth of these stages, of which he says that they all came slowly into existence, and were "of still slower diffusion among the nations as they progressed in experience."

He offers no evidence of the former prevalence of intermarriages of brothers and sisters as a general custom, or of the existence of the "communal family."

---

[1] See pages 482 and 483, from which the statement is abridged.

His case is, that if we can explain the Malayan system on the assumption that such a general custom, and such a family-system once existed prior to or along with the "Hawaian custom," then we must believe that they did formerly exist.

As to the brother and sister marriages he puts the case thus high: "Without this custom," he says (p. 488), "it is *impossible* to explain the origin of the system from the nature of descents. There is therefore a *necessity* for the prevalence of this custom amongst the remote ancestors of all the nations which now possess the classificatory system, if the system itself is to be regarded as having a natural origin." The "communal family" is a sort of corollary from this necessary fact. It was a group of brothers and sisters living in what Sir John Lubbock calls "communal marriage," the husbands and wives knowing they were brothers and sisters, and dwelling sufficiently on their close blood-bond to elaborate a system of relationships from it while yet the incestuous communism lasted.

The "Hawaian custom," as described by Mr. Morgan, was a custom according to which several own brothers, and their wives, or several own sisters and their husbands, lived in a "communal family,"—the husbands and wives in either case being unrelated by blood. He mentions it (p. 457) "as now for the first time announced," on the authority of Mr. Andrews, a judge at Honolulu, and cites the Rev. Artemus Bishop as a corroborating witness. The statements made by both these gentlemen, however,—they relate to the Sandwich

Islands,—are not of the nature of testimony, but are guesses to explain the Malayan system, about which they were giving information to Mr. Morgan. Mr. Andrews says only that "the relationship of *Pinalua* is rather amphibious. It arose from the fact that two or more brothers with their wives, or two or more sisters with their husbands, *were inclined* to possess each other in common; but the modern use of the word is that of dear friend or intimate companion." What Mr. Bishop says does not necessarily refer to a custom of that sort at all. He says that "the confusion of relationships (among the Hawaiians) is the result of the *ancient* custom among relatives of the living together of husbands and wives in common." This statement, putting the strongest construction upon it, may as well refer to what Mr. Morgan calls the "communal family" as to the "Hawaiian custom." The latter custom, therefore, —of which "no trace has been found in any part of Asia or America," as Mr. Morgan admits, and no evidence anywhere in the world,—must be regarded as a pure assumption made to explain the Malayan system. It is in the same case as the "communal family," and marriages of brothers and sisters, *i.e.* it is a "stage" for which there is no evidence.

What Mr. Morgan claims to have shown (p. 483) by means of the marriages of brothers and sisters, the "communal family" and the "Hawaiian custom," is, (1) That the Malayan system of relationships is a system of blood relationships; and (2) That every relationship in the system can be explained from the nature of descents, and be shown to be the one actually existing (when the system was formed), as near as the parentage of individuals could be known. Let us see how far he has succeeded.

1. *The Malayan system of relationships is a system of blood relationships.*

Mr. Morgan *assumes* this, and says nothing of the obstacles to making the assumption. No doubt he conceives this fundamental fact to be proved, as the stages required for his explanation are proved, by the success of the conjectural solution in the second branch of his undertaking.

2. *Every relationship in the Malayan system can be explained from the nature of descents, and be shown to be the one actually existing, as near as the parentage of individuals could be known.*

It will suffice if we attend to a few only of the relationships in the system; for it is plain that they can all be explained, if it can be explained—1, Why all the brothers of my father and all the brothers of my mother are my fathers; 2, Why all the sisters of my father and all the sisters of my mother are my mothers. Let us note Mr. Morgan's explanations of these facts, and also to what customs the explanations are referred (see pp. 481–83).

1. My father's brothers are my fathers, because they all cohabit with my mother. One of them is certainly my father, and it is uncertain which. Therefore they are all called my fathers. [The reference

S

may be either to brother and sister marriages or to the " Hawaian custom."]

2. My mother's brothers are my fathers, because " my mother is the wife of all her brothers." [The reference is to brother and sister marriages.]

3. My father's sisters are my mothers, because they and my mother are wives to my father and his brothers. [The reference is to brother and sister marriages.]

4. My mother's sisters are my mothers, because they are, along with my mother, the wives of their brothers. [The reference is to brother and sister marriages.]

All the references are to brother and sister marriages, unless under No. 1 the reference is to the "Hawaian custom." But it is not necessary to resort to the "custom" in explanation of this case, and it is obvious that the "custom" could be of no avail to explain the other cases. Indeed, Mr. Morgan says (p. 439), "The existence of this custom ('the Hawaian') is not necessary to an explanation of the origin of the Malayan system." The Malayan system is found, then, to be explainable by brother and sister marriages solely ; and the "Hawaian custom" is, consequently, without even such support as having a share in the solution could give it.

As to the sufficiency of the explanation, need it be pointed out that Mr. Morgan has failed, and must have failed with Nos. 3 and 4 ? The explanation of my having several mothers is not *of the same sort* as that of my having several fathers. The several persons in Nos. 1 and 2 are called my fathers because they are all the husbands of my mother. One of them is certainly my father, and it is uncertain which; and I am called the son of each of them, agreeably to this condition of my uncertain descent. This reasoning is familiar, and (so far as it goes) is all that could be required. But why are the several women in Nos. 3 and 4 called my "mothers"? Mr. Morgan says it is because they are the wives of my fathers, and, in the absence of a term in the language to denominate their exact relation to me, they must be called either my "mothers" or nothing, and, *e converso*, I must be called their "son." But this is giving up his case. This is an explanation on the ground of poverty of language (of which no proof is adduced—nay more, which there are facts to disprove), not an explanation from the nature of descents.[1] And, indeed, if a man is called the "son" of a woman who did not bear him, his being so called clearly defies explanation on the principles of natural descent. The imputed relationship is not, in that case, "the one actually existing as near as the parentage of individuals could be known"; and accordingly Mr. Morgan's proposition is not made out.

Even had Mr. Morgan been able to surmount the difficulties presented by the fact of a man having several mothers, he would still have been far from explaining the peculiarities of the Malayan system. Among the peoples with whom that system is in actual use, a child's father's brothers are different persons from

[1] See *post*, pp. 273 and 279.

his mother's brothers; and the father's sisters are different persons from the mother's sisters; and the relations in law also of a father and of a mother are usually distinct persons from the brothers of the father and of the mother. How then came a boy to be called the "son" of each of several *distinct* sets of persons —his father's brothers, his mother's brothers, and his father's and mother's brothers-in-law? Of such facts as these—which were the facts he had to do with— Mr. Morgan offers positively no explanation. He has not even attempted to connect them with the relationships which would have been developed in his "communal family." In the "communal family," the men and women being brothers and sisters, the father's brothers and the mother's brothers would have been the same persons, the father's sisters and the mother's sisters the same persons; all the descriptions of persons who under the Malayan system are called fathers would have been coincident, and all the descriptions of persons who under it are called mothers also coincident. How, agreeably to the nature of descents, came the relationships that could have been developed in this family group, of persons all of one blood, to be applicable to relationships in family groups of the existing type, in which husbands and wives are no longer brothers and sisters, and the bloods are diverse? It is reasonable to believe that Mr. Morgan never saw this difficulty. In what manner, had he seen it, could he have overcome it? Could he have maintained that, while the "communal family" lasted, the different descriptions of persons referred to, several of which would have been then coincident in a single person, were distinguished in idea the one from the other; so that, when the "communal family" passed away, the nomenclature which had applied to those sets of persons while they were yet coincident and ideally distinguished merely, readily extended to them when they became distinct? Surely not. It is incredible that in the sort of family contemplated, brothers should come to regard each other not only as brothers but as brothers-in-law; or to be regarded by their children, while addressed by the name of father, as also father's brothers, mother's brothers, and father and mother's brothers-in-law. Mr. Morgan's other course was to pass on from the "communal family," in which the several descriptions of persons would have been coincident, to the family founded on the "Hawaian custom," in which they would have been to some extent distinguished, and show how what lay in germ in the earlier stage was unfolded in the later. But this also he has not attempted; and, as we have seen, the "Hawaian custom" is only an hypothesis like the "communal family" itself.

The explanation offered of the origin of the Malayan system, then, is, to say the least, unsatisfactory so far as it goes, and stops a long way short of being an explanation of the origin of the system. It is simply inconceivable how the system could have been developed from that to which Mr. Morgan refers us as the germ of it.

Let us next see how, with the Malayan form given, Mr. Morgan accounts for the "Turanian" and "Ganowánian" forms of the classificatory system. In these forms, which agree with the Malayan in all other respects (see pp. 485–86),

(1) All the children of my several sisters, myself a male, are my nephews and nieces.

(2) All the children of my several brothers, myself a female, are my nephews and nieces.

(3) All my father's sisters are my aunts.

(4) All my mother's brothers are my uncles.

(5) The children of my several uncles and aunts are my cousins.

(6) The children of my male cousins, myself a male, are, in the "Turanian" form, my nephews and nieces; and the children of my female cousins are my sons and daughters.

(7) The children of my male cousins, myself a male, are, in the "Ganowánian" form, my sons and daughters; and the children of my female cousins are my nephews and nieces.

It will be enough to see the explanations offered at two leading points. Here they are :—

Myself a male, my sisters' children are my nephews and nieces.

"Reason.—Under the 'tribal organization,' brothers and sisters not being allowed to intermarry or cohabit, the children of my sisters can no longer be my children, but must stand to me in a different and more remote

MR. MORGAN'S CONJECTURAL SOLUTION. 263

relationship. Whence the relationships of nephew and niece" (p. 485).

In considering the sufficiency of this Reason, we must remember that, in Mr. Morgan's scheme, the "Hawaian custom," which is introduced as "*giving* the Malayan form of the classificatory system," appears before the "tribal organization."[1] This custom is represented as having given own brothers, in the run of cases, wives unrelated to them; and own sisters, in the run of cases, husbands unrelated to them. It must be assumed not to have made brother and sister marriages unlawful, since, by the hypothesis, it is reserved for the "tribal organization" to make them unlawful.[2] But brothers and sisters having, *de facto*,

[1] For the argument, it is of no consequence that, in point of fact, the "Hawaian custom" has, in Mr. Morgan's explanation, nothing to do with *giving* the Malayan form. It cannot be overlooked that Mr. Morgan's scheme represents the custom as an institution of "slow growth, and still slower diffusion among the nations," precedent to the appearance of the tribal organization.

[2] Mr. Morgan says, "*It is to be inferred* that the tribal organization was designed to work out a reformation with respect to the intermarriages of brothers and sisters, from the conspicuous manner in which it accomplishes this result." This is said on the view that he had proved by his solution that these "communal marriages" of brothers and sisters were anciently universal. As no trace of them can now be found, he asks us to notice how conspicuously exogamy did its work—whether we can doubt, looking to the total disappearance of "communal marriages" of brothers and sisters, that exogamy had its origin in a reformatory movement to put an end to them. The reader, by referring to page 139, will find that Mr. Morgan there pretty fully explains the tribal organization as being exogamy, and also its connection with female kinship. He says (p. 140), "In a number of Indian nations descent is *now* limited to

under the custom, in the run of cases, ceased to intermarry or cohabit, the children of a man's sisters, as a rule, would not have been his children. This being so, were. Mr. Morgan's Reason sufficient, the "Hawaian custom," in *giving* the Malayan relationships, should have given them identical with the Turanian. The representation, however, is that this effect was not produced, and that the custom allowed the children of a man's sister to be still accounted his children, the children of a man and those of his sister to be still accounted brothers and sisters.

But the "tribal organization," as the reader may see (p. 490), is simply exogamy, the prohibition of marriage between persons of the same tribe of descent, or having the same family name or totem. And exogamy prohibits marriage between brothers and sisters only when they are children of the same mother, or of mothers of the same blood. It follows from this that a man's son and his sister's daughter, while reputed brother and sister, would have been free, when the "tribal organization" had been established, to intermarry, for they belonged to different tribes of descent. The man and his sister being of one blood, the son of the former and the daughter of the latter must, so far as the Hawaian

the male line, with the same prohibition of intermarriage in the tribe, and the son succeeds to the father's office. There are reasons for believing that this is an innovation upon the ancient custom, *and that descent in the female line was once universal in the Ganowánian family."* That kinship should change to the male line is what should be expected, according to the hypothesis set forth in *Primitive Marriage.*

custom prevailed, have been of different bloods, whether kinship were traced through males or females only; for the hypothesis is that the man was married to women unrelated to him, and his sister to men unrelated to her. Similarly, it appears that the "tribal organization" would have left the greater number of reputed brothers and sisters free to intermarry. According to the Malayan system, and under the Hawaian custom, so far as it prevailed, a man would have for sisters the daughters of his fathers by mothers of various tribes of descent, and with every one of them he could intermarry, provided her mother was not of the same tribe as his own mother; the daughters of his fathers' own sisters, and with every one of them he could intermarry, for they were all, as we have seen, of a different tribe from his own; the daughters of his mother's own brothers, and with every one of them he could intermarry, for none of his mother's brothers had a relative for wife. Exogamy would cut him off from his own sisters, but from these he was already, *de facto*, cut off by the "Hawaian custom." The precise extent of the new restriction on marriage, then, would be that a man would be cut off from marrying those of his "sisters" who were the daughters of the own sisters of his mother. Thus we see that the "tribal organization," coming after the "Hawaian custom," would not, in the run of cases, prevent the marriage of reputed brothers and sisters; and so far, the features of the established system of relationships could not, or at least need not, have undergone a radical change. Mr. Morgan's Reason, then, is insufficient; and his own assumptions make it appear to be unfounded.

The preceding argument takes Mr. Morgan on his own ground, so far as it assumes "the Hawaian custom" to have been widely prevalent prior to the rise of exogamy. But even if we put that custom out of the field, Mr. Morgan's Reason will not acquire validity. The process by which exogamy would dissolve the communal families would be a process by which—the Malayan system not being instantly transformed—there would be produced several sets of "brothers" and "sisters" free to intermarry for one set that would not be so free; and therefore, so far as the Reason goes, the system of relationships should remain unchanged. The reader will readily see the truth of this if he keeps in view how many of the multitude of "brothers" and "sisters" born of the first exogamous marriages would be free to intermarry—kinship as a bar to marriage being counted through women only. Unless, then, we could assume—what seems wholly inadmissible—that exogamy could transform the system of relationships in the course of a single generation, it appears that, by the means specified in the Reason, it never could transform the system at all.[1]

[1] If exogamy anciently recognized a broader kinship than that through females only, it rested with Mr. Morgan to show that. But he has not tried to do it. On the contrary, we shall presently see that he explains one of the features of the "Turanian" form by supposing "brother" and "sister" marriage on a grand scale to continue after the rise of exogamy; viz. the marriage of "brothers" to those of their "sisters" who were, as we should say, "their cousins."

Now to take another case. In the "Turanian" form—

"All the children of my male cousins, myself a male, are my nephews and nieces, and all the children of my female cousins are my sons and daughters."

Reason.—"Unless I cohabit with all my female cousins, and am excluded from cohabitation with all the wives of my male cousins, these relationships cannot be explained from the nature of descents."

Mr. Morgan has no custom or other reason to account for my ceasing to cohabit "with all the wives of my male cousins," who, according to "the privilege of barbarism," were my wives; and he offers no explanation of my being, as a matter of course, husband to all my female cousins, who used to be my sisters, notwithstanding the prohibition of marriage between brothers and sisters.

Again: in the "Ganowánian" form, "all the children of my male cousins, myself a male, are my sons and daughters; of my female cousins, are my nephews and nieces."

Reason.—This deviation, says Mr. Morgan, "in all probability has a logical explanation of some kind. If it is attributable to the slight variation upon the privilege of barbarism above indicated, a singular solution of the difference in the two systems is thereby afforded."

The "slight variation" indicated is that the Red Men of America cohabited with all the wives of their male cousins, and were excluded from cohabiting with all their female cousins. Here there was room for imagining some reformatory movement in America counter to that which Asia had witnessed. But Mr. Morgan suggests no cause for such a variance in the marriage laws of the two continents, and hints at no evidence—apart from his solution—that there ever was such a variance.

Looking more closely at the Reasons given in the two cases last noticed, we reach results, some of which, had he perceived them, would have gratified Mr. Morgan. The Reason in the "Ganowánian" case makes me and my male cousins—who used to be "brothers"—have our wives in common, and these wives are no longer our female cousins who used to be our "sisters." We, who used to be "brothers," have in common our wives, who are strangers to us in blood. Here we have "the Hawaian custom." Our female cousins—formerly our "sisters,"—from whom we are excluded, are no doubt living in communism with stranger husbands. Surprising as these results are, those derivable from the Reason in the Turanian case are still more remarkable. This reason makes me and my male cousins cohabit with our female cousins: it is thus that our female cousins' children are sons and daughters to us their male cousins. But cohabitation has ceased to imply marriage; for our female cousins, who used to be our wives, are our wives no longer, albeit we cohabit with them. We have *wives* however, and the peculiarity is that we, who are still communists with our female cousins, are either interdicted altogether from cohabiting with our wives, or each of us has wives with whom he alone has a right to cohabit. If the latter view must prevail, monandry appears too soon for Mr. Morgan's scheme of development; if the former, we have a new "singular solution" of the difficulty. It should not surprise us if in this wild dream—not to say nightmare—of early institutions, cohabitation having ceased to imply marriage, marriage should have ceased to imply cohabitation.

No more need be said of explanations which not even their author can think satisfactory.[1]

In attempting to explain the origin of the classificatory system, Mr. Morgan made two radical mistakes. His first mistake was, that he did not steadily contemplate the main peculiarity of the system—its classification of the connected persons; that he did not seek the origin of the system in the probable origin of the classification. To attempt to solve the problem by explaining the relationships comprised in the system in detail, was to take securities for failure. The second mistake, or rather I should say error, was to have so lightly assumed the system to be a system of blood-ties. From the second error he almost certainly would have been safe had he not fallen into the first.

In the explanation of the system which I shall presently offer, the importance of attending to the classification of the related persons will be made sufficiently apparent. No more need here be said on that head. But the examination I have made of Mr. Morgan's solution may be fitly closed by some remarks on the

[1] [See Note B appended to this Essay.]

assumption that the classificatory system is a system of blood-ties. For the following reasons I think that assumption was an error :—

(1) It is apparent, on the slightest inspection of Mr. Morgan's tables, that "son" and "daughter," in the classificatory system, do not mean son or daughter "begotten by" or "born to"; that "brother" and "sister" are terms which do not imply connection by descent from the same mother or father; and that "mother" does not mean the bearing mother. From the analogies of the case, we must believe that "father" does not mean the begetting father. It would be most extraordinary if "father" had had that meaning on the first emergence of men from the state of promiscuity, which is the Malayan case. These facts surely ought to have strongly suggested that the classificatory system cannot be a system of blood-ties at all, for it appears inconceivable that the most stupid savages could form a system of blood-connections, disregarding the limitation of connections set by the obvious fact of motherhood.[1]

(2) The suggestion received from the non-natural senses in which the terms of relationships are employed is confirmed by the consideration that all, or almost all, the peoples using a form of the classificatory system, have, besides, some well-defined system of blood-ties—

---

[1] It seems almost incredible," says Mr. Darwin of Mr. Morgan's explanations at this point, "that the relationship of the child to its mother should ever be completely ignored, especially as the women in most savage tribes nurse their infants for a long time."—*Descent of Man*, second edition, p. 588.

the system which traces blood-ties through women only, or some other. It is inconceivable that any people should have at the same time two and entirely different systems of *blood* relationship. And it may be confidently affirmed that in every case it is the system which is unquestionably a system of blood-ties, and not the classificatory system, that alone is of practical force —which regulates the succession, for instance, to honours or estates.

Of the fact that the system of kinship through females only existed among many peoples having the so-called "classificatory form of relationships," there can neither be doubt nor dispute. I make Mr. Morgan himself a witness as to the Iroquois. An Iroquois child is a relation of its mother, but not of its father. Mr. Morgan even goes so far as to say that among this people "no right in the father to the custody of his children's persons or to their nurture was recognized." Husband and wife having separate rights of property, the wife's property passes on her death to her children; but when the husband dies, his property does not pass to his children. It passes to his sister's children—"his near relatives in his own tribe."[1] A man's brother by the same mother is his near relation, and all who are related to him through his mother—tracing blood through women only—are his relations. Those relations share with him the obligations of the blood-feud, and stand by him in all his quarrels. His brother by the same father only is not his blood-relation at all, if

[1] The *League of the Iroquois*, p. 327.

their mothers are not kindred, and may be arrayed against him in his quarrels. The two are not only not of the same kindred; they are of different tribal, and, it may be, of different national connections. "If a Cayuga woman," says Mr. Morgan, "married a Seneca, her children were Cayugas, and her descendants in the female line, to the latest posterity, continued to be Cayugas, although they resided with the Senecas, and by intermarriage with them had lost every particle of Cayuga blood. In the same manner, if a Mohawk married a Delaware woman, her children were not only Delawares but aliens."[1] And what is true of one tribe or nation of the American Indians is, speaking broadly, true of all. "It is noticeable," says Schoolcraft, speaking of the Indians generally, "that they trace blood-kindred and consanguinities to the remotest ties—and that where there is a lapse of memory or tradition, the totem is confidently appealed to *as the test of blood affinities*, however remote. It is a consequence of the importance attached to this ancient family tie that no person is permitted to change or alter his totem, and that such a change is absolutely unknown."[2] The totem, here rightly called the test of kinship, is taken from the mother, who, belonging to a different tribe, has always a different totem from the father. But the "relationships" in the classificatory system have nothing to do with the totem, and embrace persons of numerous diverse totems.

[1] *League of the Iroquois*, p. 325.
[2] *Indian Tribes*, Part I. p. 420. Philadelphia, 1853.

Not only is the system of kinship through females only an undoubted system of blood-ties: it determines all successions; the transmission of honours and offices; the right of intermarriage; the tribal connection, and all the duties and privileges of blood-relationship. What duties or rights are affected by the "relationships" comprised in the classificatory system? Absolutely none. They are barren of consequences, except indeed as comprising a code of courtesies and ceremonial addresses in social intercourse.

(3) That the classificatory system is a system of mutual salutations merely, appears from many of its peculiar features. For one thing, the names for relationships are framed as for use in addresses. They want generality. The relation of brother to sister, for instance, is unnamed; in the Hawaian example of the Malayan form there is no name for brother or for sister. On the other hand, there are a variety of names for use in salutations between "brother" and "sister," according to the age and sex of the person speaking in relation to the age and sex of the person addressed. And this peculiarity is shown, I believe, in almost every example of the classificatory system. Then, for another thing, Mr. Morgan has not shown that these relationships are of any force or effect whatever *as* blood-ties, while he has shown that they are in daily use for the purposes of mutual salutation, and has explained why, among the "Ganowánians" at least, a system of terms for this purpose was indispensable—a necessity. "The American Indians," he says (p. 132), "always speak to each other,

when related, by the term of relationship, and never by the personal name of the individual addressed. In familiar intercourse, and in formal salutation, they invariably address each other by the exact relationship [of consanguinity or affinity] in which they stand related. .... It is not only the custom to salute by kin, but an omission to recognize in this manner a relative would, amongst most of these nations, be a discourtesy amounting to an affront. In Indian society the mode of address when speaking to a relative is the possessive form of the term of relationship; e.g. *my father, my elder brother, my grandson, my nephew, my niece, my uncle, my son-in-law, my brother-in-law*, and so on throughout the recognized relationships. If the parties are not related, then *my friend*. . . . There is another custom which renders this one a practical necessity. From some cause, of which it is not necessary here to seek an explanation, an American Indian is reluctant to mention his own personal name. It would be a violation of good manners for an Indian to speak to another Indian by his name." Surely all this points to the system being one of mutual salutations.[1]

In parting with Mr. Morgan I cannot refrain from making one or two observations on the scheme of progress which he has put forward in connection with his conjectural solution. Two stages only of that scheme are employed in the solution; the others are unsupported either by the solution or by evidence. Moreover,

[1] [See Note A appended to this Essay.]

the parts of his scheme are far from being consistent with one another. "The Barbarian family" (Stage ix.), for example, is exhibited "with the family name still unknown" (personal names *having* appeared), notwithstanding that exogamy, which strictly operates through totems and kobongs—in short, through "family names,"—had appeared (Stage vi.) a very long time, possibly thousands of years before. Polygamy again (Stage x.) is exhibited as springing out of the "Hawaian custom" (Stage iv.); "the strongest of several brothers taking to himself all the wives and refusing to share them longer with his brothers." A simple natural fact is thus explained by a "custom" not known to have ever existed. The marriage of single pairs, too (Stage viii.) had long before been exhibited as normal, and yet it had left the "Hawaian custom" vitality enough to beget polygamy as normal. We are even asked to observe how polygamy, "a reformatory movement," put an end to the Hawaian custom that had outlived a practice of monandry. Polyandry next is exhibited (Stage xii.) as one of the consequences of this "reformatory movement," and, as such, "requiring no farther notice." Lastly (Stage xiii.) appears, for the first time, the succession of sons to fathers, although a practice of monandry had (Stage viii.) been established ever so long, possibly many thousands of years, previously.

I need not say that the whole of this scheme collapses with the conjectural solution in connection with which it was put forward. That solution, assigning for the phenomena of the classificatory system causes not known to have ever operated, could not have ranked as a scientific hypothesis, however successfully the phenomena had been explained on the assumption that such causes were at one time in operation. Failing to explain the phenomena, the solution must sink below the level of reasonable guessing, to which level, indeed, it must have sunk, even had it explained the phenomena, if by any other set of mere conjectures the phenomena could be equally well explained. The space I have devoted to the consideration of the solution may seem disproportioned to its importance; but issuing from the Press of the Smithsonian Institution, and its preparation appearing to have been aided by the United States Government, Mr. Morgan's work has been very generally quoted as a work of authority, and it seemed worth while to take the trouble necessary to show its utterly unscientific character.

CHAPTER II.

THE ORIGIN OF THE CLASSIFICATORY SYSTEM OF RELATIONSHIPS.

IT cannot be doubted that the classificatory system in the Malayan form illustrates a very early social condition of man. We must also believe, from its connecting itself with the family, that it had its origin in some early marriage-law. Indeed, an examination of the leading points of difference presented by the various forms of the classificatory system leaves no doubt that the phenomena presented in all the forms are ultimately referable to the marriage-law; and that accordingly its origin must be so also.

Though a system of modes of addressing persons—which, for reasons already sufficiently explained, I take the classificatory system to be—must have grown up with greater freedom than a system of kinship that inferred rights and obligations, it seems reasonable to believe that the system of blood-ties and the system of addresses would begin to grow up together, and for some little time have a common history. If so, one should look to the same set of circumstances for the origin of both. Now the rise of the system of kinship through females only, and the subsequent development of kinship, have been made the subject of an hypothesis. It will be a test of that hypothesis to see whether, while explaining the history of kinships, it will also account for the rise of such a system as the classificatory system of addresses; and it will be confirmatory of any presumptions otherwise existing in its favour, should the hypothesis stand the test—especially considering that the phenomena of the classificatory system were not as yet collected when the hypothesis was framed.

I propose then to see whether the classificatory system can be explained on the hypothesis stated in *Primitive Marriage,* that the first form of the family was the Nair, founded on Nair polyandry, and the second the Tibetan, founded on Tibetan polyandry. These two types of marriage-law and of the family have been traced so extensively that in assigning them as causes of the phenomena of the classificatory system no one can question that I assign real, and not imaginary causes. And first of the classificatory system in its Malayan form :—

1. *Origin of the Malayan form of the classificatory system of relationships.*

As I propose to make more or less use in this exposition, by way of illustration, of the terms used in the Hawaian, which is the most complete, example of the Malayan form, it will be convenient to attend for a moment to a few of these respecting which we have (p. 452) some information from Judge Andrews :—

1. The Hawaians have no definite term for father

[or for mother] : mkûa, signifies parent, male or female. If we wish to say father or mother we add kane [kana], male, or wahina [waheena], female.

2. The Hawaian has no specific word for son [or for daughter]. Keiki signifies child, or originally *the little*: iki, little, small; the article *ke* has in modern times become prefixed.

To express the idea of son or daughter, the words kana = male, waheena = female, must be added. Son = little one male; daughter = little one female.[1]

3. The Hawaian has no word for brother [or for sister] in the sense of the languages of Western Europe. The word hóahanaŭ, from hóa, companion, and hanaŭ, born, is of common gender, and is seldom used in speaking of one born of the same parents.[2]

4. Wahine or waheena, which appears in Mr. Morgan's tables as meaning "wife," and is applied to a variety of different persons, as well as to a wife, *e.g.* wife's sister, brother's wife, &c., means literally "female," a woman; and kane or kana, which appears in the tables as "husband," "husband's brother," and "sister's husband," means literally "male," a man.[3]

---

[1] In the Indo-Germanic speeches the terms for "son" and "daughter" have the same meanings, viz. child male and child female. — See Dr. Deecke's *Die Deutschenwerwandschaftsnamen.* Weimar, 1870.

[2] Mr. Andrews simply adds, "I have used the terms hóahanaŭ and hóahanaŭ wahine [waheena] for brothers and sisters, because they may be so used, and without them *I could not go on with the degrees of relationships.*"

[3] While the language is thus poor in terms to denote persons of the highest importance in a system of blood-ties, it is rich in terms

5. There are of course no special terms for father's brother or mother's brother, or for father's sister or mother's sister. They are all equally *mkûa*, parents, distinguished as male or female by the addition of kana or waheëna; thus makua kana signifies a male parent, and makua waheena a female parent.

6. There are no terms for grandfather or grandmother. *Kupuna*, common gender, means an ancestor of any degree above that of mkûa. There are no terms for grandson or granddaughter. Moopuna, common gender, means a grandchild. With kana or waheena added, it means grandson or granddaughter.

Let us now contemplate the classificatory system, as it appears in the Hawaian example, apart from the details on which Mr. Morgan founded his solution. What we find is this, that "the Hawaians have held, pure and simple, to the five primary grades of relatives" (p. 454), according to the Chinese text: "all men who are born into the world have five ranks of relatives. My own generation is one grade; my father's is one; and my grandfather's is one. Thus above me there are two grades. My son's generation is one grade, and my grandson's is one; thus below me are two grades of relations: including myself in the estimate, there are

required in a nomenclature of courtesies. There are no terms for brother and sister, but there are terms by which a younger brother or a younger sister may address an elder of the same sex, and *vice versâ*; and terms by which a sister may address an older brother, and even a term by which a brother may address a sister older than himself. There are also terms for use in addressing various relations in law.

five grades." Let us arrange these grades to the eye, and name them as they are named in the Hawaian system.

1st Generation = Kupuna = my grandparents.
2nd Generation = Mkûa = my parents.
3rd Generation [no name], I and those of my generation.
4th Generation = Kaikee or Keiki = my children.
5th Generation = Moopuna = my grandchildren.

The names applied to the persons in each generation are, we have seen, of common gender. A man of the grade is named by adding kana = male, to the grade name; a woman, by adding waheena = female.

We do not know the meaning of the names of the grades, except that that of the fourth is "little ones," from "iki," little. The other terms have not been philologically examined, as it is desirable they should be, but their precise meaning is not essential to the present purpose, for we may be certain, meantime, that such a term in common gender as "mkûa" did not explicitly, at least at first, convey the idea of begetting father or bearing mother, much less both ideas in combination.

It is obvious that in these five grades there is a reduplication, and that all the real relationships can be illustrated from a family containing persons of three generations.

Let us then suppose a family of the Nair type to contain persons of three generations as follows:—

First generation, comprising one or more women,

and one or more men, with, say, one or more men or women remaining over from an earlier generation [1] (= Kupuna).

Second generation, comprising the children of the women of the first (= Mkûa).

Third generation, comprising the children of the women of the second (= Keiki).

This family is held together solely by uterine ties, and all its members, if they think of the matter at all, trace their descent back to a common mother. In the house there are no husbands of any of the women, and no wives of any of the men. The men have their wives in various other houses, and the women similarly have their husbands in various other houses. The group contains no "begetting" father of any of the children; but the men of the group are, of course, the natural protectors of all the children.[2]

In a household of this type, the women marrying while yet young, there probably would be found persons of as many as five generations, though, not to com-

---

[1] It is a feature of the system that these are "Kupuna" equally with the others.

[2] It is to a group of this sort that we must refer "avus" = protector = old man of the first generation in the family supposed above, *i.e.* "grandfather"; avunculus = younger protector = "mother's brother," "father" to all the children of his sisters = man of the second generation. Indeed, we may well believe, on the analogies of Indo-Germanic speech, that mkûa had the sense of "protector" or "guardian." "Father," and "brother" used as a general term, equally mean protector or guardian; and "mother's brother," as we have just seen, means the same thing. (See Dr. Deecke's work, *loc. cit.*)

plicate the matter, I take, as the case to deal with, a family with—practically—three generations only. It is obvious, that there being no common father or mother, the members of the family cannot be affiliated as in a family derived from a pair. Yet, in their intercourse they must have terms by which to address one another; and personal (individual) names not being in use—an invincible prejudice against the use of them being general among backward races [1]—the terms employed must be general terms, applicable " to the members of the family in classes." Indeed, apart from this consideration, it is obvious that they fall naturally into classes, and that the convenience of naming these would be the greater the more numerous the classes. What the name should be for those of the third generation in the household supposed is obvious enough. They are "the little ones" (keiki) of the family, but will be so called only by those of the second generation, which comprises their mothers, to whom they directly belong —the persons in that generation continuing to be called keiki by the generation above. Those of the first generation are as clearly "the oldest," whether they shall as a class be named from that fact or not. But they will be called "the oldest" (kupuna) only by those of the third generation—the second generation continuing to them the name applied to them when there was in the family a generation above them; some members of which, indeed, as we have supposed, may

[1] Schuyler, vol. i. p. 40, says even of the Kirghiz that they are not allowed to use the real names of their relations.

still survive. Those of the second generation will be to those of the third mkûa—say elders, which, in their turn, those of the first are to them. Lastly, to those of the first those of the third will be, say, "little ones' little ones" (moopuna). If any members of a generation earlier than the first survive, "the little ones' little ones" will probably class them with "the oldest," and not have a special term for them; while by "the elders" they will be properly named so far as they are of no more than one generation before the first. As the members of any class must address one another as well as members of the other classes, we shall see a necessity for a new series of terms. The class name comprising them all, they will address one another by terms varying with the seniority, or juniority, or sex of the person addressed. And these terms will be of use in all the classes.

Suppose such a system of class names in use in the Nair families of a district, and I think we may see the origin of the Malayan system, by considering what would be the effects upon the nomenclature of the transition from Nair to Tibetan polyandry. We shall see that whatever the class names signified at first, keiki inevitably must come to signify child; mkûa, parent; moopuna, grandchild; and kupuna, grandparent.

Though I have supposed this typical Nair family to be of one household, *i.e.* under one roof, the supposition has been made for the sake of clearness merely. It is a supposition, however, which the facts of primitive life would fairly justify. At the same time it is obvious that the filiation of the members of such a family to one another, and their arrangement in classes for that purpose, are independent of their all having a common home, and would, if once established, survive the resolution of the family into sub-groups in separate homes.

That resolution was an inevitable consequence in time of the special blood-bonds between mothers and their own children, and between uterine brothers and sisters. Accordingly, the Nair household would in time come to be constituted, as it is described by Buchanan, a mother and her sons and daughters living together under the same roof, together, of course, with the daughters' children. The various ways in which this separation of homes would be brought about are sufficiently explained by the authorities cited in *Primitive Marriage*, p. 100 ; and at p. 104 it will be seen that I have explained how the separation of homes would not at once have the effect of disrupting the family bond between those who, if the separation had not occurred, would have been all of one family. They would long remain and be classed as members of one family, as if they were all still of one household.

Let us now see how the type of the family must have been altered in the course of the transition from Nair to Tibetan polyandry.

The cases which would favour a beginning of Tibetan polyandry would be those in which a mother and her sons and daughters had a home to themselves. The sons and daughters when grown up would, notwithstanding the separate home, remain affiliated to their mother's family (call it A), and would class in it, say, as mkûa.

If, now, we suppose the brothers to take a wife into their home from another family (B), and their wife and their sisters to have children—the sisters by their Nair husbands—we shall have the following results:—

1. The wife having entered family A as a member by marriage, must class in that family with her husbands and their sisters. She will therefore be of class mkûa in A; but by birth she is already of class mkûa in B.

2. The children born to her and her husbands' sisters are keiki in A. Some of them are her own children, and will call her makua waheena—and all the children can have but one name for her. She will be makua waheena to all the children of A; but by birth she is makua waheena to all the children of B.

3. The men of B (class mkûa) are makua kana to their sisters' children by immemorial usage, and will long continue to be so after these are born to her in another family. Her keiki will call them makua kana; but that is what they call the men of A (class mkûa).

4. Similarly, the women of B (class mkûa) will continue to be makua waheena to their sisters' keiki, though born in A. The keiki of A will call them makua

waheena, which is what they call the women (class mkûa) of A.

5. The new relationship thus introduced will, through the force of old custom, have full effect throughout all the classes in the connected houses. The elder people who are mkûa to those persons in both houses who are mkûa to a woman's keiki, will to these keiki be kupuna, and the keiki to them moopuna. The wife's children will thus class as keiki in the fullest sense in both families.

When Tibetan polyandry has come to supersede, or greatly preponderate over, Nair polyandry, the men (class mkûa) of a household will, as a rule, be all brothers uterine, and the women (class mkûa), except any wife, will, as a rule, be sisters uterine. The sisters, when of age, leave the household to become wives in other homes, and the brothers take into their home a wife between them. Whatever the various class names meant originally, they will now acquire definite significations, as if they were relative to descents. The brothers' wife will be own mother to all the keiki in their house; the brothers will be their fathers; and the keiki will be own brothers and sisters. The keiki will still call their mother makua waheena, however, and their fathers makua kana. And these terms will come accordingly to mean father and mother respectively. But these class names being, by force of custom, as comprehensive as formerly, it will follow that the father's sisters, in whatever family they are as wives, being "makua waheena" to their brothers' children, will be their "mothers," and so, too, on precisely the same grounds, the sisters of the own mother of the children will be. Their father's brothers will, of course, be their "fathers,"[1] and so will their mother's brothers. Farther, the keiki, classing as such at once in the family of their birth, and in that of their mother's birth, will come to be "brothers and sisters" of all the children counting as keiki in the two families, *i.e.* of their father's sisters' children, and their mother's sisters' children, and mother's brothers' children, and, of course, of their father's brothers' children, should any of the brothers make separate marriages. In short, they will as keiki be "brothers" and "sisters" of all the children of every person entitled to be classed as mkûa, in any family, with their mother or mother's sisters or brothers, or their father or father's sisters or brothers. And these new and widely-extended relationships will, through the force of custom, have their full effect throughout all the classes in the connected houses. Those who are mkûa, in any house, to those called makua kana or makua waheena by any children will, to the children, be kupuna, and the children to them moopuna. When in turn the keiki grow up and class as mkûa, the children of all of them, as far as the newly-extended class goes, will to their mkûa be moopuna, and the latter kupuna to these children. In short, the changes due to causes affecting only the classes of mkûa and keiki, broaden

[1] See *post*, p. 289. Their father's brothers, even if not co-husbands of their mother, would, as classing mkûa with their father, be to them **makua kana**, *i.e.* "fathers."

these classes without otherwise disturbing their relations to the other classes—ascending or descending.

Marriage relationships being now recognized, we may see how relatives in law come to be classed and take their place in the system. To explain this in one case will be to explain it in all. Take the husband of one's father's sister—father's brother-in-law. My father's sister is to me makûa waheena ; I to her am keiki. But her keiki are her husband's—if not as a direct consequence of usage, then by courtesy, which even among ourselves is strong enough to have such an effect. On another view, on a marriage, the wife classes mkûa in the husband's family, and the husband classes as mkûa in the wife's family. It is a direct consequence of this that my father's and mother's brothers-in-law should be to me makûa kana, *i.e.* " fathers," and their sisters-in-law makûa waheena, *i.e.* " mothers."

The reader will see that in this way every feature of the Malayan system is fully and simply accounted for. Also he will see, what I have pointed out in a footnote (*ante*, p. 288), that from the manner in which they are accounted for, they might as well be accounted for as consequences of the sons and daughters of houses of the Nair type making monandrous marriages, as by their making Tibetan polyandrous marriages. For my father's brothers, classing as mkûa with my father, will be to me makûa kana, *i.e.* " fathers," whether they are co-husbands with my father or not. But we shall immediately see strong reasons for believing that the system was mainly an effect of Tibetan polyandry, to the production of which

U

effect a growing practice of monandry could, from the nature of the case, oppose no obstacle. And I have presented the explanation of the Malayan form in its present shape accordingly. Speaking broadly, the explanation of the Malayan form comes to this : 1, A necessity or convenience for classifying kindred united in families while as yet husbands and wives did not live together within the same family; and 2, The broadening of the classes of kindred thus arising through the connection of families by marriage, on wives passing as a rule into the families of their husbands.

I now proceed to consider,—

2. *The origin of the " Turanian" and " Ganowánian" forms of the classificatory system.*

In these forms of the classificatory system every feature of the Malayan form remains undisturbed, except that the class of keiki has been disrupted, and certain of its members put in a new class as cousins ; and that along with cousinry has come the relationship of uncle and aunt to nephew and niece, and consequently a disturbance in the class of mkûa. Beyond this no change has occurred. If I formerly belonged to the class mkûa, for instance, the children of those who used to be my keiki, and have become my nephews and nieces, are still my grandchildren (moopuna). I to them am grandfather—kupuna,—and my mkûa are the kupuna of my nephews and nieces. When we seek the precise limits of the change, again, we see that the children of several brothers are classed together keiki as before; and so are the children of several sisters; and that the new class of cousins comprises only the children of several sisters, in relation to the children of their several brothers.

When we consider these facts a little, we shall see that those remaining classed together as keiki are all of one blood, tribe, or kinship, and that those classed as cousins are of different bloods, tribes, or kinships.

Recurring to my hypothesis: with female kinship still prevailing, the children of several brothers are necessarily of one blood, tribe, or kinship, namely, that of their mother, the wife of the brothers of a house under Tibetan polyandry. The children of several sisters are also necessarily of one blood, tribe, or kinship, namely, that of their mothers, who are of one blood. And the children of the brothers are, necessarily, of a different blood from the children of the sisters—if exogamy is the law. The brothers and their sisters being of the same blood, the brothers' children are of a different blood, for the brothers must marry a woman of a different blood from themselves, and their children are of the mother's blood.

In the Nair stage there had been but one blood in a family. Its members were all of one tribe or kinship; and could be of no other; for exogamy, if it were then law, would be of importance only in limiting the women of the house in their choice of husbands. This homogeneity of the family was destroyed at once on polyandry becoming Tibetan. The brothers' wife and her children were then of a different blood and kinship from that of the old Nair family to which the brothers belonged; and that fact could not fail to tell in time upon the system in use for the purposes of mutual salutation.

To the various ways and degrees in which the pressure of that fact upon that system was yielded to in different areas, we may refer all the differences in the forms of the classificatory system.

In proceeding to consider these differences as they appear in the "Turanian" and "Ganowánian" forms, it will be convenient, though merely for the purposes of exposition, to think of those forms as having been developed out of the Malayan form. We have no reason to believe, however, that they ever passed through what may be called the Malayan stage—no ground for doubting that they, in the course of a single movement, became what they now are. It may reasonably be supposed that exogamy was law as early as the Nair stage; and exogamy might have acted instantly on the system of addresses, as it formed itself under the influence of Tibetan polyandry. All the peoples having the classificatory system in the "Turanian" or "Ganowánian" forms are, or were, exogamous. Whether the Hawaians, and those few tribes connected with them by the Malayan form, are exogamous I cannot ascertain. If they are not, the Malayan form is precisely what it might, on that footing, be expected to be; if they are, the Hawaian case is a proof that the pressure of exogamy on the system might be resisted. We shall see in the other cases to be noticed that it was not a pressure incapable of being partially resisted; that in some cases its effects were less than, or different from what they were in others. At any rate, it will readily be seen that it is immaterial to the explanation now to be offered whether exogamy acted on the system of addresses instantly, or only began to act upon it after it had assumed the Malayan form. It is worthy of notice that exogamy *may* not, from the first establishment of the family, have been the law. As I showed in *Primitive Marriage* (pp. 116 and 124) many years since, an extensive practice of polyandry may long retard, and even prevent, the rise of exogamy.

We have seen that with exogamy prevailing, the children of brothers will be of a different blood from the children of their sisters—who represent the old Nair family. This is reason enough why the brothers' children should no longer be classed as keiki along with those of the sisters. Ceasing to be keiki along with them, they are put in a new class and called their cousins. Their fathers' sister becomes their aunt, and they her nephews and nieces; and, on the principle of reciprocity, the sisters' children become nephews and nieces to the brothers, and the brothers become their uncles.

The first five distinctive features (*ante*, p. 262) of the "Turanian" and "Ganowánian" forms are thus simply accounted for. It will be observed, however, that it was not *inevitable* that exogamy should produce all of these effects. For instance, the brothers are of the same blood as their sisters' children. It was not inevitable, therefore, that they should cease to be makûa kana to their sisters' children; and if they ceased to be so, it was only on the principle of reciprocity, because the sisters ceased to be makûa waheena to their children. But the principle of reciprocity was capable of a contrary application: the brothers continuing to be makûa kana to their sisters' children, that is, the sisters would continue to be makûa waheena to theirs. This explains what we find among the Crow and Minnitaree, and in one or more of the Athapascan nations of American Indians (see *Morgan*, p. 148). And in precisely the same way may be explained the absence of terms for nephew and niece among a few of the American tribes (*Morgan*, p. 148). The sisters' children being of one blood with their mother's brother may continue to be his keiki—after cousinry has been instituted. And they being called by him keiki, his children will, on the principle of reciprocity, be called keiki by his sister. This will be not inconsistent with a change in the relative terms—with the brother becoming uncle and the sister aunt to the children of each other respectively. It will be seen that, on the view I am taking, the institution of cousinry was inevitable—cousins being of different kinships—but that none of the other usual accompaniments of it were inevitable.

It remains for me to offer—

3. *Explanations of the differences between the " Ganowánian" and " Turanian" forms.*

These differences are noted *ante*, p. 262. They are as follows :—

(1.) In the Ganowánian form the children of my male cousins, myself a male, are my sons and daughters, and the children of my female cousins are my nephews and nieces.

(2.) In the Turanian form all the children of my male cousins, myself a male, are my nephews and nieces, while all the children of my female cousins are my sons and daughters.

What has happened in the first case is easily accounted for. I used to be makûa kana to the children of all my cousins when my cousins and I were of one class. I am now makûa kana to the children only of my male cousins—who used to be my brothers. Now, men are still makûa kana—" fathers "—to their brothers' children. I have ceased to be makûa kana to the children of my female cousins, who used to be my sisters; these children have become my nephews and nieces. And men are now uncles to their sisters' children. It appears, then, that though we have come to be called cousins, the disturbance due to the test of blood, while following the natural line so far as it goes, has been the least that, following that line, it could have been. My male cousin's son is called my son, as he formerly was, and as my brother's son now is. My female cousin's son has applied to him the term now given to my own sister's son. There has been no disturbance in the relationships arising to one brother through another, and (no doubt in some way as a consequence of that) there has been no disturbance, as there might have been, in the relationships arising to one male cousin through another. There has been a disturbance in the relationships arising to a brother and sister through each other; and the same amount of change has been made in the relationships arising between male and female cousins through each other. Here, then, is a simple case of imperfect development. Practically the relationships arising to cousins through each other are the same as if they had been brother and sister instead of cousins. In fact, attention among the "Ganowánians" seems to have been exclusively fixed upon the women as the persons through whom it was that blood ties were created; and no change was made in the case of relationships arising to men through other men.

The second case requires closer consideration, and it is necessary to set forth all the facts of it, which are given by Mr. Morgan in his analysis of the Tamilian system (*Morgan*, footnote, pp. 387, *ff*).

(*a*) Myself a male, my male cousin's children are my nephews and nieces.

(*b*) Myself a male, my female cousin's children are my children.

(*c*) Myself a female, my male cousin's children are my children.

(*d*) Myself a female, my female cousin's children are my nephews and nieces.

Under the Malayan form, the children in each case would be my children. Cases (*b*) and (*c*) are true to the Malayan form, *i.e.* I, a male, and my female cousin, are still addressed as parents of each other's children.

To begin with the simplest case, which is case (*d*). It is plain that my female cousin and I, a female, being of different bloods, her children also and I (kinship being traced through the mother) are of different bloods. The new terms evolved under the influence of the idea of blood are accordingly applied to my relationship with them. I become their aunt, and they become my nephews and nieces.

Take next case (*a*). My male cousin and I, a male, are strangers in blood. His children do not follow him in blood; but unless there is between them and me a connection not made through him, plainly they and I are strangers in blood, and the new terms applicable primarily to connections, not regarded as blood-relations, are those which are properly applicable to us. It was by no means, however, of necessity that those terms should be applied. A blood-connection between the children of male cousins, made in frequent cases through their mothers—a connection which would make them "brothers," and the one cousin, therefore the father, rather than the uncle, of the other's children —might have prevented the application of them, even in cases where no such blood-connection existed. And the mere force of ancient usage might have had the same effect. We have seen that among the American Indians the old terms were continued in this case. Except the difficulty of making any change, however, there can have been no powerful cause in action to retard the application in this case of the new terms among the "Turanians," and very probably there was some cause in action which, making it obvious in very frequent cases that a man's children and his male cousin's children were of different bloods, accelerated their application. A cause which might have so operated we shall immediately have to notice.

There remain the two cases (b) and (c) in which the Malayan form has been followed. They certainly are cases in which this could not have been looked for; for when a man's sister's son, though of his blood, has become his nephew, and his male cousin's son is also his nephew, it is extraordinary that his female cousin's son (who is not of his blood) should remain his son. It is safe to say that there must have been some powerful and widely-operating cause, the action of which in this case arrested change. That cause, too, must have been connected with the marriage system.

A prevalence of cousin-marriages in the early times of the Turanian peoples—for cousins not being of the same blood were free to intermarry—would be a full explanation. Where a male cousin married his female cousin, the children would truly be at once the children of the male cousin and of the female cousin.[1] And

---

[1] See Buchanan's *Journey from Madras through Mysore, &c.* vol. iii. p. 16, for a case in which a man was bound to marry one female cousin—his mother's brother's daughter. In this case a man's children were not his heirs. His heirs were his sisters and their children.

it is to the frequency of cousin-marriages, and of other marriages through which, though not between cousins, the one cousin's children were of the other cousin's tribe and blood (which brother's and sister's children never could be), that I think the preservation of the old terms must in those two cases be referred. In cousin-marriages, too, and other marriages having the same effect as cousin-marriages as regards blood—through which, that is, a man's children and his *male*-cousin's children would *not* be of the same tribe or blood—which would be the effect, for example, of two male cousins marrying each other's sisters) we may find the accelerating force that seemed to be required for the establishment between a man and his male-cousin's son of the relation of uncle and nephew.

There is nothing violent in the supposition of a frequency of cousin-marriages and other marriages having the same effect upon blood; indeed, in the small and scattered communities of early times, it is difficult to believe that cousin-marriages, being allowed, were infrequent. Something very far short of a practice of them might well suffice to preserve (in cases *b* and *c*) the nomenclature of address, which had immemorial custom in its favour; especially if supported by a frequency of marriages through which the same effects as regards blood would be produced—through which, that is, the children of a male cousin would be of the same blood as those of his female cousin. To believe in the frequency of marriages of the latter sort is simply to believe that the persons within a community between whom the *jus connubii* existed were given to marrying one another, which requires no effort; and this alone might have been almost enough to keep the old nomenclature in use.

It will be evident that the hypothesis that Tibetan polyandry succeeded Nair polyandry as a normal stage of progress is essential to my explanation of the Turanian and Ganowánian forms of the classificatory system. If brothers made separate marriages, I can see no reason why their children should not have been classed as cousins. If we could assume that there existed a pretty uniform practice of brothers of one family marrying sisters of another, or women of the same tribe or blood, we should have such a reason; but I am not aware of a practice of this sort on a scale to justify our making such an assumption. On the other hand, Tibetan polyandry we know to have been common, and to have left traces everywhere in the laws of succession; and we know it, moreover, in connection with the very fact to which the broadening of the class connections has been ascribed—the change from non-cohabitation of husbands and wives to cohabitation; from their being resident in different families, that is, to their residing together in the same family. Tibetan polyandry seems, then, essential to the explanation of the Turanian and Ganowánian forms. To the explanation of the Malayan it is not essential. But if, which is not impossible (though I have shown that it is not certain), all the forms had a common history, so far as their development to the Malayan form is concerned, it becomes very probable that Tibetan polyandry was a factor in determining the Malayan form. Moreover, if the Hawaians, and those connected with them by the Malayan form, are not exogamous, we may be sure they passed through a full experience of polyandry in all its phases; and this consideration increases the probability that the disruption of the family of the Nair type among them was not owing to a practice of monandry.

At any rate, I venture to think that all the features of the more primitive forms of the classificatory system have now been accounted for on a hypothesis which was framed independently of them, and while they were yet unknown, if it be not also proved that that hypothesis is absolutely necessary to the explanation of them. On the same hypothesis the Esquimo form of the classificatory system can easily be accounted for; but the consideration of this, and of the transition from the classificatory form to the descriptive, must be reserved for another occasion. My impression is that the study of that transition may yet be made to throw much new light on the primitive condition of man, and to *demonstrate* that all the races of men have had, to speak broadly, a development from savagery of the same general character.

APPENDIX.

APPENDIX.

NOTE A.

[THE CLASSIFICATORY SYSTEM.

[MR. MORGAN was not the first to describe the classificatory system of the Iroquois; and his account of it, though derived from his own observations and not from any authority, might, up to a certain point, have been taken bodily from Lafitau, who wrote in 1724. The use of its terms between relations was explained alike by both,[1] and Lafitau also showed that this was not peculiarly Indian but had prevailed among other peoples. In regarding the terms as for the use of blood relations only (see supra, page 274), and as always employed to denote blood-relationship, however, Mr. Morgan parted company with the earlier writer. For Lafitau distinctly mentions that, among the Indians, "my brother," "my father," "my child," "my nephew," and so forth, were conventional modes of salutation, severally addressed to people in proportion to the distinction in which they were held. He tells us that they were commonly applied—as relative age and station determined—not only to all fellow-tribesmen and friends but to strangers (and he might have said, even to enemies); and that this was because of the objection the Indians had to being addressed by name. The terms of the classificatory system were, therefore, according to Lafitau, not only used where there was no blood-relationship, but were terms of address universally employed; and were commonly used without thought of blood-relationship—to indicate not degrees of blood-relationship but simply degrees of

---

[1] *Mœurs des Sauvages Americains, Comparées avec Mœurs des Premiers Temps.* Par le P. Lafitau de la Compagne de Jesus. Paris, 1724. 2 vols. (See vol. i. p. 552.)

respect. "Communément," he says,[1] "les sauvages ne s'entendent pas volontier nommer par le nom qui leur est affecté, et la demande qu'on leur en feroit est une espèce d'affront qui les feroit rougir. En se parlant les uns aux autres, ils se donnent tous des noms de parenté, de frere, de sœur, d'oncle, de neveu, &c. observant exactement *les degrés de subordination et toutes les proportions de l'age* à moins qu'il n'y ait une parenté réelle par le sang ou par adoption; car alors un enfant se trouvera quelquefois le grandpere de ceux qui, selon l'ordre de la nature, pourroient être facilement le sien. Ils pratiquent la même civilité à l'egard des etrangers, à qui ils donnent, en leur parlant, des noms de consanguinité, comme s'il y avait une vrai liaison du sang, plus proche ou plus eloignée à proportion de l'honneur qu'ils veulent leur faire, coûtume qui Nicolas de Damas rapporte aussi des anciens peuples de Scythie."

Mr. Morgan's statement that every person who was not a relative was, among the Indians, addressed, not by any of the classificatory terms, but as "my friend," was consistent with his theory (which, indeed, could not have been formed without it) that the terms of the classificatory system were descriptive of acknowledged blood-relationships. But the theory and the statement fail together if we must accept the evidence of Lafitau. If Lafitau is right, the classificatory terms were, among the Iroquois, terms of address; everybody used them (that is, commonly used them) whether addressing a relative or not; and, in general, they certainly did not carry any implication of blood-relationship, but were used to indicate the respect due from the speaker to the age and station of the person spoken of. And that Lafitau was right (though, no doubt, the phrase "my friend" might have been used in speaking to a person who was not a relative) is simply unquestionable. One cannot read much of any early writer on the American Indians without finding the terms which it is natural for us to speak of as terms of relationship, and which it has become convenient to describe as classificatory, interchanged, as Lafitau said they were, between persons who clearly were not relations. And, indeed, it is doubtful whether any writer before Mr. Morgan ever thought of them except as forming a system of modes of address varying with the degree of deference demanded or desired to be shown. An apt example of the way in which they were used occurs in the *Documents Relative to the Colonial History of the State of New*

[1] *Mœurs des Sauvages Americains, Comparées avec Mœurs des Premiers Temps*, vol. i. pp. 75, 76.

York (Albany, 1853-58. Vol. iv. p. 758), where we find the Onondagas (Iroquois) solemnly offering to bind themselves to call the Mohawks (Iroquois) fathers if the latter joined them in a war against the Governor of Canada. It is perfectly clear that father was, in this case, to be used as a term of respect, and that the offer would have been meaningless had the term not had its recognised value simply as a term of respect. Mr. Morgan, curiously enough, has himself given excellent examples of this use of the classificatory terms between tribe and tribe. (See *Ancient Society*, p. 138, for the Iroquois; also p. 106.)

If farther illustration of their uses be wanted, it can easily be found in the *Relations des Jesuites*—writings of high authority about the manners of the Indians (though not all of equal authority), and which, though more concerned with the Hurons than the Iroquois, contain accounts of both (and, besides, they were really the same people). In the *Relations*—to take a few examples—we find Father Le Jeune saying : " As soon as they could see me from the village [Huron] everybody ran out, each calling me by my name. 'What, Echom, my nephew, my brother, my cousin, art thou come back?'" (*Relations des Jesuites.* Quebec Reprint. Vol. i. p. 29. Quebec, 1858.) They addressed him, that is, in the term of the classificatory system which was appropriate in each case. Again (the speaker this time is Simon le Moine, and the people were Iroquois)— " One regards me as his brother, another as his uncle, a third as his cousin—never had I so numerous a body of relatives." (Ibid. vol. ii. p. 13.) Once more, " The Huron chief," says Joseph Poncet, " addressing the Iroquois chief, his prisoner, says to him, 'My nephew,' for it is a term of compliment used among these peoples." The captive Iroquois replying, addressed the Huron as "my uncle." (Ibid. vol. ii. p. 21.) We find, too, an Iroquois, in trying to console Simon le Moine upon the death of two Frenchmen, speaking of them as Simon's nephews, and assuring him that when he wants nephews to build for him he will find that all his nephews are not dead— meaning that the Iroquois would help him. (Ibid. vol. iii. p. 37.) We find a great chief speaking of the French as his nephews (vol. i. p. 89); the chiefs of a village addressing Le Jeune as "my nephew," (vol. i. p. 84); a Huron chief addressing an Iroquois prisoner as "my nephew," and the Iroquois, when brought out for the torture, saying to the assembled Hurons, "My brothers, do your worst" (vol. i. pp. 110-113); another prisoner addressed as "my uncle," and answering "my nephew" (vol. i. p. 116); a Huron chief addressing a stranger as "my brother," and speaking of "my cousins of the two other nations" (vol. iii. p. 21); Father Jogues addressed by an old woman with whom he stayed as "my nephew" (vol. ii. p. 75); a present offered in the name of the young men of the Iroquois to "their uncle," the great chief of the French; Frenchmen also addressed by an Iroquois as "my brothers," and the governor spoken of as an eldest brother (vol. ii. pp. 22 and 28). These are instances enough to show that Mr. Morgan was wrong in supposing that the classificatory terms were only used between relations, and to denote blood-relationship; and enough to show that they were regularly used without thought of relationship, and between people who were not relations, one or another being used—age and station being both considered—according to the degree of respect to be conveyed.

Lafitau tells us that, even in his time, the Indians were said to have departed greatly from their ancient customs. It is intelligible—indeed it is certain—that they have changed very much since then; and this may explain the difference between Lafitau and Mr. Morgan. To study contemporary Indians towards the middle of the nineteenth century was not, by itself, the best way to learn the truth about Indian customs and institutions, when there were accessible copious records of these dating from more than two hundred years earlier.

It is not necessary, however, to go to early writers about the Red Men to find proof that Mr. Morgan entirely misconceived the classificatory system as used among them. In James's *Rocky Mountains* (1823) there occur (without any theorising) excellent casual illustrations of the way in which it was actually used. "The Big Elk," we find it said in one place (vol. i. p. 174), "made us a considerable harangue, with all the remarkable vivacity, fluency, and nerve of Indian eloquence, in which he said that he would address me by the title of 'father.' 'And you,' said he to Mr. Dougherty, 'whom I know so well, I will call brother.'" This is pretty well, but a few pages further on (vol. i. p. 185), we meet with something better. "They then serve out the food to the guests [this occurs in a description of a feast among Indians], placing the best portions of it before the chiefs. Each individual, on the reception of his portion, returns his thanks to the host in such respectful expressions as become his relative consequence, as "How-je-ne-ha, How-we-sun-guh, How-na-ga-ha, &c. (thank you, father, thank you, younger brother, thank you, uncle, &c.), after which they eat in silence." Here we find the classificatory terms used precisely as Lafitau said they were used, to express degrees of respect, and not degrees of relationship. After this, one finds, without surprise, that when the terms used between relations come to be expressly spoken of, the writer tells us of their use in addresses, and has nothing else to say of them; and shows, incidentally, that particular terms were used where there was a propriety in using them, whether there was blood-relationship or not. "The designations by which the Omawhaws distinguish their various degrees of consanguinity," he says (vol. i. p. 231), "are somewhat different in meaning from ours; children universally address their father's brother by the title of *father*, and their mother's brother by that of *uncle;* their mother's sister is called *mother*, and their father's sister *aunt*. The children of brothers and sisters address each other by the titles of brother and sister. . . . . A man distinguishes his wife's brother by the title of 'Tahong,' or brother-in-law, *and his son also by the same designation.* He calls the wife of his brother-in-law 'Cong-ha,' or *mother-in-law.* [These two must be mere terms of address.] A woman calls her husband's brother 'Wish-e-a,' or brother-in-law, and speaks of his children as her own. Her husband's sister she distinguishes by the title of relationship 'Wish-e-cong,' or sister-in-law. Men who marry sisters address each other by the title of brother. All women who marry the same individual, even though not previously related, apply to each other the title of sister."]

[In *Ancient Society* (published in 1877, after the appearance of the criticism here reprinted) Mr. Morgan seems to have allowed for the fact that the American Indians (and other peoples who have the classificatory system) use the classificatory terms freely in addresses; he remodelled his theories, apparently, to account for the terms being employed between larger classes than he had originally contemplated. He still, however, held to the untenable position that they were never used except between people who knew they were each other's relations, and never used by such people except to denote the relationship known to them as subsisting between them. And "where no relationship subsists," he said again, "the form of salutation is simply 'my friend.'" (*Ancient Society*, pp. 436, 441, 328.) It is for the classificatory system as thus misconceived of, that Mr.

Morgan tried to account in *Ancient Society*. If the misconception has to be admitted, his theories are worthless; since, even if well devised, they have been devised to account for that which is not the fact. It is clear that this was Mr. Morgan's own view.

If, moreover, the classificatory terms were freely used as terms of address, with nothing thought of but age and station, large suppositions about early marriage which transcend experience (and perhaps also probability)—even apart from the risk of their proving too much or something other than what is wanted—are not needed in accounting for those terms. If it be thought they must have originated in some form of the family, it is unnecessary to imagine a form of the family large and complex beyond anything which observation has informed us of. More modest suppositions will suffice; for there need not be any proportion—there may be any degree of disparity—between the nucleus in which the terms originated and the circle throughout which they were commonly used.]

[No Lafitau has written of the Blacks of Australia, and we have no casual records of their customs such as the *Relations des Jesuites* have given us for the Indians of the Canadas. There is evidence, however, that, among them also, the terms of relationship were commonly used as terms of address, and not to denote known relationships only.

The explorer, Eyre, had excellent opportunities of being informed on such matters, and his evidence, while given quite casually, is very clear as to this. "In their intercourse with each other," he says, "natives of different tribes are exceedingly punctilious and polite, the most endearing epithets are passed between those who never met before; almost everything that is said is prefaced by the appellation of father, son, brother, mother, sister, or some other similar term, corresponding to that degree of relationship which would have been most in accordance with their relative ages and circumstances."[1]

This shows that the terms of relationship were used among the Australians precisely as Lafitau says they were used among the Iroquois. They were interchanged between persons who never met before—not between some strangers only, but between all whom occasion brought together; and that, as Mr.

[1] Eyre's *Central Australia*, vol. ii. p. 214. 1845.

Eyre clearly conveys, not in recognition of relationship actual or probable, but for politeness' sake—the term used being that which "age and circumstances" showed to be proper.

Some confirmatory statements may be found in a work deeply imbued with Mr. Morgan's theories—Mr. Brough Smith's work, *The Aborigines of Victoria*. The most distinct of these is that of Mr. Bridgman (vol. i. p. 92), and it is virtually identical with Mr. Eyre's, though less detailed. "Blacks in their native state, before they pick up our manners and customs," Mr. Bridgman says, "never call each other by name. They always use a term of relationship"; which, unless no blacks ever spoke to each other except those who knew each other to be relations, is simply Eyre's statement over again. It appears, too, that Mr. Bridgman himself, in his intercourse with the natives, addressed them by the terms of relationship. To this may be added Mr. Wilhelmi's statement (vol. i. p. 87), that "forms and names strictly in use among relations only" are so used, through friendship, between persons who are not relations, that "it becomes totally impossible to make out who are really relations and who are not."

The theories of Mr. Morgan's ingenious disciple, the Rev. Lorimer Fison (*Kamilaroi and Kurnai*, Melbourne, 1880) are all, more or less, founded upon the fact that terms of relationship are in use among the Australians as terms of address. A correspondent, whose means of getting knowledge are usually very imperfect, reports, in answer to a question, that certain rather large classes of people, or whole populations, as the case may be, call each other brothers and sisters (or whatever other term suits their relative ages), and Mr. Fison forthwith assumes that throughout those classes or populations there is full acknowledgment of blood-relationship.

It may be added that the Australian terms of relationship, so far as they are known to us, are, even more clearly than the classificatory terms in general, framed for use in addresses; while some of them are now in certain cases within the family, obviously terms of address only, and others can never have been descriptive of relationships actual or probable, as, according to Mr. Morgan, they all were originally. Not a few are reciprocal. Among the Kurnai (Gippsland), for example, wehntwin is the term applied to a paternal grandfather, his brother, and so on; and it is also the term applied by such persons to their grandsons and grandnephews. It cannot, therefore, have been framed to describe either the relationship of father's father or that of son's son. It must have originated as a term of address between men and their connections on the father's side of the generation above the father. There is a term, nakun, similarly used between a mother's father and his brothers and sisters, on the one hand, and her children on the other; and there are also terms which are similarly interchanged between people and their paternal and maternal grandmothers and their respective brothers and sisters. Among the Kurnai also, the wives of two brothers call each other sister, which so used can only be a term of address; and, similarly, the husbands of two sisters call each other brother; while, to confirm the indications thus received, in the Bra-brolung section of the Kurnai, bra meaning husband and wrukut wife, a man and his sister's husband call each other bra, and a woman and her brother's wife call each other wrukut. (*The Aborigines of Victoria*, vol. ii. p. 328). The terms used between grandparents, &c., and grandchildren, given above, do not carry the suggestion of communal marriage with them; and this is even less the case with the terms used in the Port Fairy district. These, according to Mr. Dawson, are in a great many cases varied, according as the person addressed is married or single.[1]]

NOTE B.

[MR. MORGAN'S LATEST WORK.

[In a work published after the appearance of this criticism (*Ancient Society*, London, 1877) Mr. Morgan made some changes in, and additions to, his reasonings, enlarged his family systems, and remodelled his nomenclature. His first form of the family was now founded upon the "marriage in a group" of men and women of the same blood calling themselves brothers and sisters —of " brothers and sisters own and collateral "—of all brothers and sisters and cousins of the same grade or generation. This he named the consanguine family. And he made use of this alone (omitting at this stage the "Hawaiian custom") in trying to account for the Malayan nomenclature. The Hawaiian custom

---

[1] *Australian Aborigines.* By James Dawson. Melbourne. 1881.

was, in this work, re-named punaluan marriage (see page 256); the definition of the new term was expanded (as in the previous case) so as to admit collateral brothers and collateral sisters (that is, male and female cousins) into the punaluan married groups; and Mr. Morgan declared punaluan marriage good for explaining, not the Malayan terms, but the Turanian. Their sufficiency to account for the former of these consistently with the nature of descents, "as near as the parentage of children could be known," was now to form the reason for believing in the consanguine family and the group marriage of "brothers" and "sisters" out of which it was said to spring. Its sufficiency in accounting in like manner for the Turanian terms was to prove the prevalence at one time of punaluan marriage—the proof of which had, with the former name, been rested upon the help it gave in accounting for the Malayan terms.

And his view still being that the terms he was dealing with denoted actual relationships "as near as the parentage of children could be known," Mr. Morgan now perceived the difficulty it made for his view that there should be in the Malayan system no distinctive term for mother. He suggested that the affiliation of children to the group to which they belonged would be so strong "that the distinction between relationships by blood and by affinity would not be recognized in every case" (but he should rather have said in any case)—and that thus the distinction between a real mother and the many other women known by the same name escaped observation, or, at any rate, left no impression. This, however, is equivalent to saying that, from the nature of the case, note could not be taken in the consanguine family of the parentage of children in the cases in which it could be known. And it is an abandonment of the hypothesis.

As to punaluan marriage, the Hawaiian custom of the text expanded as above-mentioned, and the family springing from it, though there was nothing to show that they ever were prevalent among men unless their fitness to account for the Turanian nomenclature, it will be found that, in *Ancient Society*, Mr. Morgan did not use them in accounting for any one of the Turanian terms. Those Turanian terms which coincide, or partly coincide, with Malayan terms he had already tried to account for by the hypothesis of the consanguine family, and he did this over again; the others he tried to account for (*Ancient Society*, pp. 442—445) by means of exogamy alone. His reasoning was exactly what it would have been had punaluan marriage never occurred to him—so that this was, on his own showing, a purely gratuitous assumption. Not only that, it was an embarrassing assumption. Instead of finding it indispensable for his explanations—and so being enabled to justify it, more or less, as a hypothesis—he had carefully to keep it out of his reasonings. An obvious difficulty with it was that, on the assumption, there were two forms of the punaluan family (see page 255), and that neither could "as near as the parentage of children could be known," yield him, even with his own reasoning, both the Turanian sense of father and the Turanian sense of mother. In the case in which the husbands were not brothers, Mr. Morgan's reasoning would not account for a father's brothers being called fathers; in the case in which the wives were not sisters, it would not account for a mother's sisters being mothers. The punaluan hypothesis at this critical point was, even in Mr. Morgan's hands, worse than useless for explanation; and, accordingly, he could not use it for any purpose of explanation. He attempted, however, to make it consistent with his system, or not adverse to it, by giving it a farther expansion. He supposed that the punaluan marriage group included, as a sort of honorary members, all the brothers "own and collateral" of each of the husbands where they were not each other's brothers, and all the sisters "own and collateral" of each of the wives where they were not each other's sisters. That would make it, for the explanation of the terms for father and mother, equivalent to the consanguine family. More than this is needed, motherhood being admittedly recognized when punaluan groups first began to be formed—so fully recognized that children of the same mother could no longer marry one another. But, at any rate, this involved, and Mr. Morgan saw this clearly, that neither the Turanian nomenclature nor the Malayan had received the impression of the punaluan family, as described by him, or of the Hawaiian custom as he had originally conceived of it.

Mr. Morgan's consanguine family is, in fact, a tribe or body of kinsfolk, the members of which never made outside marriages, while within there was promiscuity or communal marriage, not between all marriageable men and women, but between all men and women of the same grade or generation. It is indispensable to the hypothesis (as Mr. Morgan points out) that people of different grades should have been kept apart from one another; so that the hypothesis supposes that, with an extreme of licence up to a certain point, there was combined an unprecedented severity of restriction. The men and women who cohabited so freely were those of about the same age only—the older people, the middle-aged, and perhaps even the youngish people, being strictly cut off from the young. With punaluan marriage, according to the hypothesis, cohabitation was similarly restricted to men and women of the same grade or age. This, in either case, because (a thing not surprising in itself, nor needing any wonderful explanation) the people who use the classificatory system consider age among other things in addressing one another.

Punaluan marriage, like consanguine marriage, was on the hypothesis, confined to the tribe, as well as to people of about the same age within the tribe. How it could grow up within a consanguine tribe, in which those who were free to marry were all, to begin, "brothers" and "sisters," is a matter left obscure by Mr. Morgan; nor could he have worked this out without coming upon fatal difficulties. It is needless to remark upon the discrepancy between punaluan customs as described in *Ancient Society*, and the laxities hinted at (p. 256) by Mr. Morgan's correspondent, Mr. Andrews.

Mr. Lorimer Fison (*Kamilaroi and Kurnai*, Melbourne, 1880), while not accepting the consanguine family, on which Mr. Morgan's whole system rests, professes himself a believer in punaluan marriage and the punaluan family. But Mr. Fison's hypothesis (as stated in the work above mentioned) is not quite the same as Mr. Morgan's. Mr. Fison's "intermarrying classes," by the way, have sometimes been taken for matter of fact; but they are a hypothesis only.]

BACHOFENS "DAS MUTTERRECHT."

BACHOFEN'S "DAS MUTTERRECHT."

Das Mutterrecht—an inquiry into the gynaikocracy of the ancient world in its connection with religion and law—the work of a Swiss jurist, published in 1861, announced to the world, for the first time, the discovery that a system of kinship through females only had everywhere preceded the rise of kinship through males.[1] The general exposition prefixed to this great work makes it possible to form a view of the scope of the evidence adduced of this as the true history of kinships, as well as a view of the causes of that history as they appeared to Bachofen. From the work itself, owing to peculiarities in its composition, one might well despair of being able

[1] It was in the spring of 1866 that I first heard of *Das Mutterrecht*, and then I found that I had been anticipated by Herr Bachofen in this discovery. No two routes, however, could be more widely apart than those by which Bachofen and I had arrived at this conclusion. I was led to it by reasoning on the exigencies of my explanation of the origin of the form of capture. To Bachofen the fact seems to have revealed itself as everywhere underlying the traditions, and especially the mythologies, of antiquity which his prodigious learning comprehended in all their vast details.

to form any such views;[1] and, indeed, even the general exposition referred to is of so mystic a nature that it is difficult to obtain from it distinct propositions. The account of Bachofen's scheme of human progress which follows is wholly founded on that general exposition :—

At first there were no laws regulating the intercourse of the sexes, and human beings lived in a state of hetaïrism. The women, by nature nobler and more sensitive than the men, were at last disgusted with this life, and under the impulse of a strong religious aspiration combined to put an end to hetaïrism and introduce marriage. They succeeded, and established monogamy,[2] but not without an appeal to force. Bachofen compares the Amazonian movements of later days with those by which marriage was first introduced. After referring to the myth of Bellerophon as suggesting an armed rebellion of the women of Lycia for the assertion of their rights, he adds: "The importance of Amazonianism, as

---

[1] Since this paper was printed I have obtained, and read with pleasure, Profesor Giraud-Teulon's *La Mère, chez certains Peuples de l'Antiquité*, which is founded on *Das Mutterrecht* itself, of the evidence contained in which it bears to be a brief and orderly exposition. The reader who might despair of mastering Bachofen's ponderous German quarto, will find the gist of it in *La Mère*, in some sixty pages of pleasant reading.

[2] The form of marriage which they introduced is not expressly mentioned by Bachofen, but the whole scope of his exposition shows that he believed it to be monogamy. This is, indeed, what he always means by marriage, a gradual evolution of modes of marriage not being within his contemplation.

opposed to Hetaïrism, for the elevation of the feminine sex, and through them of mankind, cannot be doubted."

It resulted, at once from the spiritual superiority of the women, which gave origin to the progress from hetairism, and the superiority in arms by which they conquered for themselves the benefits of a marriage-law, that in the families founded upon marriage, which grew up after the change, the women and not the men held the first place. They assigned this place to themselves, or had it conceded to them. They were the heads of families; the children were named after their mothers and not after their fathers; and all the relationships to which rights of succession attached were traced through women only. Farther, they assigned to themselves, or had conceded to them, the political as well as the domestic supremacy.

Even in the stage of hetairism, religion—albeit of a low "telluric, chthonic" type—exercised a beneficent influence, and was a cause, if not the prime one, of the state of hetairism being departed from. Thereafter, an improving religious faith was everywhere the accompaniment and, in a sense, the cause of the triumph of the women and of the improving social condition. On the rise and consolidation of the gynaikocratical power in the Greek area, Aphrodite made way for Demeter and Hera,—divinities in some sense, still, " chthonic, telluric," but which, in another sense, were *lunar* divinities, and in every way superior to their predecessor. " Wherever gynaikocracy meets us," says Bachofen,[1] " the mystery

[1] P. xv.

of the 'chthonic' religion is bound up with it, whether this connects itself with Demeter's name or lends to motherdom an incorporation in some divinity of a similar character." Lastly, religion is represented as fostering the cause of women, chiefly through its mysteries assigning a divine character, as it were, to motherdom as compared with fatherdom.

What was gained through religion was destined to be lost through it. The loss came in the Greek area through Dionysos promulgating that fatherdom alone was divine—the father the only true parent, the mother a *nurse* merely. The women at first opposed this new gospel, and fresh Amazonian risings were the common feature of their opposition. But the resistance was ineffectual, and the women, presently becoming converts to the new idea, were, after that, its warmest supporters. Their support cost them less in position than might have been expected, for Bacchanalian excesses, restoring in a measure the ancient hetaïrism, laid afresh the basis of gynaikocracy. It was before a very different and more modern religious thought that gynaikocracy was destined to disappear. This thought was "the immaterial, spiritual, Appollonic"—"*solar*"—conception of fatherdom. It secured what remained of the advantages of Dionysos' previous triumph, and combined it with the fruits of fresh victories never again to be lost. For it was a pure celestial thought that promoted pure practices only, and so was destructive of hetairism, and all that was founded thereon. Fathers now took the first places in the family and the state; children were named after them; and all relationships to which rights of succession attached were traced through fathers only: the "motherless" Athene became the symbol of the overthrow of motherdom and of gynaikocracy. Not that the cause of mothers ceased to be the subject of farther conflicts. There was, indeed, a succession of these, between the principles of various creeds, before the fruits of the victory of fatherdom were securely garnered. When the final triumph came, it was determined by an influence outside the domain of religion —namely, the all-powerful authority of the Roman jurisprudence.

Such, in outline, are Bachofen's views, as explained in the introduction to *Das Mutterrecht*. He often states that he regards religion as a mere expression of the circumstances of a people, but then he always refers to religion as a cause,[1] without telling us what were the circumstances it represented, and so has failed to put the stages of progress before us in the light of the causes determining them, except in so far as we may take some religion for such a cause. In other respects his methods and results are equally unscientific.

He saw *the fact* that kinship was anciently traced through women only, but not why it was the fact. Admitting him to be correct in thinking that women, revolting from hetairism, introduced monogamous marriage, surely it is a pure dream of the imagination

---

[1] At p. xiii. Bachofen calls religion "the only powerful lever of all civilization." His various views on this subject are, in fact, in no small degree inconsistent with one another.

that they effected this by force of arms. Were it true that marriage was, from its beginning, monogamous, kinship would certainly (human nature being as it now is) have been traced through fathers, if not indeed through fathers only, from the first. Will any one accept it as genuine history that this consequence of monogamy did not follow at first because the women *willed* it otherwise? That, apart from the force of some custom established by a more primitive and earlier marriage system, the children of a man and woman living together as husband and wife should be subject to the mother's authority and not the father's, be named after her and not after the father, be her heirs and not the father's, is simply incredible; and is surely not rendered credible by the statement that these singularities were the direct consequences of women having been victorious in a war with men. But this is Bachofen's view of the facts. He wholly failed to see that all those signs of superiority on the woman's part were the direct consequences (1) of marriage *not* being monogamous or such as to permit of certainty of fatherhood; and (2) of wives not as yet living in their husband's houses, but apart from them, in the houses of their own mothers. It can scarcely be doubted, moreover, that Bachofen has misinterpreted many of the facts bearing on ancient gynaikocracy.[1]

---

[1] Partly it is misinterpretation, partly exaggeration merely, of these facts, which may be charged against Bachofen. Sir John Lubbock appears (*Origin of Civilization*, p. 92) to dispute the facts altogether, asserting that, "among the lowest races of men,"

It remains, however, after all qualifications and deductions, that he, before any one else, discovered the fact that a system of kinship through mothers only had anciently everywhere prevailed before the tie of blood between father and child had found a place in systems of relationships. And the honour of that discovery, the importance of which, as affording a new starting-point for all history, cannot be over-estimated, must, without stint or qualification, be assigned to him.

woman's place is one of abject subjection, and he instances the case of the Australians. But obviously, such an instance tells in no degree against Bachofen, and indeed it shows a misconception of the evidence adduced by him. At present, it is not easy to say what the exact condition of the Australians is; but it is clear that they have monogamy and polygamy as their forms of marriage, and so that, with them, husbands are the heads of families. No case is producible of woman being ill-treated under a form of marriage which assigns to her the headship of the family. The reader will find an admirable review of the facts in connection with this matter, and with ancient gynaikocracy, in Professor Millar's *Origin of Ranks*, a work in which Bachofen has *almost* been anticipated, and that by a treatment of the facts in every sense strictly scientific. I became acquainted with this work, which has gone out of sight, in 1871, exactly a century after it was published. Mr. Millar was professor of law in Glasgow, a coadjutor of Adam Smith, and friend of David Hume. Adam Smith is said to have suggested to him to write the work I refer to, which every student of history should be acquainted with—*The Origin of the Distinction of Ranks*. Fourth Edition, Edinburgh, 1806; First Edition, 1771.

"COMMUNAL MARRIAGE."

"COMMUNAL MARRIAGE."

THE scheme of social progress propounded by Sir John Lubbock in his *Origin of Civilization* has, for its starting-point, a system of "communal marriage," which, though different from, reminds us of, Mr. Morgan's "Communal" family.

Sir John Lubbock (p. 91) uses for convenience, as he says, the term "communal marriage" to mean at least two distinct things, viz., the condition of man socially, (1) When "marriage did not exist"; and (2) When "all the men and women in a small community were regarded as equally married to one another." "Communal marriage" is thus, in one sense, an equivalent for promiscuity; while, in another, it denotes the initial stage of a progress which Sir John sketches, and means something very different from promiscuity. In the latter sense, it confers "communal rights" (see p. 97) on all the men of a community, and is thus—as a species of marriage conferring marital rights on many—contrasted with "individual marriage," which confers such rights on one person only. The two significations of the phrase are obviously inconsistent with one another, for the state of hetairism knows no "rights" in matters of sex.[1]

The speculation as to the size of the primitive groups, to which the second meaning of communal marriage points, is not developed by Sir John Lubbock. Once he enters on the exposition of his scheme of progress, he neglects the size of the communities and speaks of them as "tribes," which may mean groups of any magnitude. The other qualifying terms in the definition of communal marriage are similarly neglected. The phrase is used to denote "the primitive social condition of man,"—a condition under which, while it lasted, all the men of a group were "equally" the husbands of every woman in the group, and had, over her, *communal rights*.

The history which Sir John Lubbock has to give of marriage is that the communal marriage system at first prevailed universally; and that the communism was everywhere gradually abridged, and finally, in most quarters, destroyed, by individual marriages between men and their war-captives. "Even under communal marriage," he says, "a warrior who had captured a beautiful girl would claim a peculiar right to her, and, when possible, would set custom at defiance," *i.e.* appropriate her to himself as a wife. Were he to appropriate a girl of the group, "he would infringe the rights of

---

[1] See p. 91, *Origin of Civilization*. The references are all to this book, and to the third edition.

the whole tribe"; but he might appropriate a war-captive without infringing those rights, because—"the tribe had no right to her." The appropriation of war-captives as wives by individuals, accordingly, in Sir John Lubbock's opinion, instituted (1) monandry, *i.e.* the marriage of one man to one woman or to several women; (2) exogamy, since a man could only get a wife to himself from another group; and (3) the practice of capturing women for wives, since, the state of hostility prevailing, wives could only be obtained from other tribes by capture.

The evidence offered of the initial stage of this progress is in two branches : (1) what purports to be evidence of the communal marriage system deduced from recorded instances of communism in women ; and (2) what purports to be evidence of this system deduced from facts brought forward to show that, on a marriage, compensation was given to the men of the husband's group as for an infringement of their rights over the woman. The initial stage being assumed as proved by this evidence, the progress therefrom, through individual marriage founded on capture, bears to be demonstrated by general reasoning.

But the general reasoning turns on one principle, and the evidence, in its second branch, on another principle. The first principle is that a man might appropriate a war-captive to himself, because *over her the tribe had no right;* the other principle is, that the appropriation must be expiated, because it infringed *the right of the tribe to the woman.* The contradiction between these principles is obviously absolute, and that it exists is beyond dispute.[1]

The evidence adduced of ancient communism in women involves facts so few that we may recite them, noting their value as we go on.

I. *First branch of the evidence of communism in women.*[2]

1. *Of the population of the Andaman Islands*, Belcher states that it is the custom "for the man and woman to remain together till the child is weaned." But this (see Lubbock, *l. c.* pp. 74 and 133) means "pairing," *i.e.* monogamous marriage, for

---

[1] With Sir J. Lubbock, marriage means only monandry, beginning with and developed through marriages by capture. If monandrous marriages between persons of the same group have a history apart from such marriages between persons of different groups, Sir John has not written—he has not even made allusion to—that history. Had he done so, it might be believed that the cases in which expiation for marriage was required were considered by him, although he did not say so, as cases in which the man and woman were of the same group; and it is clear that the proof of the expiation and its purpose being forthcoming, the ancient communal right might be legitimately inferred from such cases. The marriage, in such a case, would infringe the communal right, while a marriage with a war-captive might not. But these are considerations which seem not to have in any degree occupied Sir John's attention. At p. 98 he says, "Mr. McLennan's view [of the origin of marriage by capture] throws no light on the remarkable ceremonies of expiation for marriage"; and again (at p. 116), "the explanation I have suggested [of the origin of marriage by capture] derives additional probability from the evidence of a general feeling that marriage was an act for which some compensation was due to those whose rights were invaded."

[2] See *Origin of Civilization*, pp. 82—90.

a term which may extend even to four years. It would permit of kinship through fathers.

2. *The Bushmen* are stated to be *without marriage.* Here is evidence of communal marriage in the first sense of the term.

3. *The Nairs.*—The facts are well known. They present one of the best known cases of undoubted polyandry.

4. The *Teehurs.*— They "live almost indiscriminately, and even when two people are regarded as married, the tie is but nominal." Here marriage of pairs is known; conjugal fidelity slight.

5. "*China before Fouhi: Greece before Cecrops.*"—The trite tradition that in these countries *marriage was unknown* till the reigns of Fouhi and Cecrops respectively is thus paraphrased : " In China, communal marriage is stated to have prevailed down to the time of Fouhi, &c."

6. *Marriage did not exist* among the Messagetæ, the Auses, or the Garamantes, or, at one time, in California or Peru.

7. *Queen Charlotte's Island.*—Mr. Poole says that " marriage is altogether unknown."

8. *The Sandwich Islanders.*—Inference made from the Hawaiian system of relationships that children " belonged to the group rather than to their parents." I do not clearly understand what this means in its bearing on communism. But my views of the Hawaiian system are before the reader.

9. *The Todas.*—Offered as evidence of communal marriage. But the Todas give us one of the best

vouched cases of polyandry, presenting both the Nair and the Tibetan types of polyandry.

10. *The Tottiyars of India.*—A case of " brothers, uncles and nephews, holding their wives in common."

11. *The Galactophagi.*—Nicolaus (cited from Bachofen) says, "They called all old men fathers, young men sons, and those of equal age brothers." But what does this do to prove communal **marriage**? And see my examination of Morgan's " conjectural solution."

12. *The Sioux, &c.*—Here we have a case of polygamy—the wives being sisters. The case of Jacob might as well have been cited.

13. (pp. 88—90).—*Cases of adoption,* supposed to have to do with the subject, but, so far as I can see, absolutely unrelated to it. The practice of adoption, indeed, is a proof of the existence of some settled form, not very primitive, of the family.

Looking back, we see that the cases referred to under Nos. 2, 5, 6 and 7, are cases in which the fact adduced is that marriage was altogether unknown ; under Nos. 3 and 9 are cases of unquestionable polyandry ; under Nos. 1, 4, and 12 are cases of the marriage of pairs, or of polygamy, where the consortship is, in No. 1, not for life, and in No. 4 unaccompanied by strict conjugal fidelity. There remain only Nos. 8 and 11, both of them connected with the Malayan form of the classificatory system—which, if I am right, implies Nair polyandry, followed by Tibetan, or by monandry ; No. 10, which goes for little ; and No. 13, the cases comprised in which seem to have no bearing on the matter in hand, and which, indeed, illustrate a settled family system—the family presided over by parents united in monogamous marriage. It is surprising to find adoption as practised in Rome cited as part of this evidence.[1]

II. *Second Branch of the Evidence of Communism in Women.*—It is Bachofen who is really responsible for the proof here tendered. His idea is that evidence of the primitive hetairism is afforded by the acts of expiation for marriage (individual marriage, that is), that continued to be performed, on marriage being instituted, for the appeasement of the outraged divinity who presided over and cherished hetairism. A marriage was, as it were, a violation of a religious command; and its exclusiveness could only be atoned for by a period of "choiceless abandonment of herself to all" on the part of the woman.[2] The notion in this form is purely fanciful. The facts connected with the history of religion give no countenance to the supposition that men in the stage of savagery had thought out for them-

---

[1] That this evidence was adduced if not as *proof*, at least as justifying the assumption of "communal marriage" in the sense in which it conferred "communal rights," the reader may see, on referring to the summing-up of evidence on p. 90. "Assuming, then, that the communal marriage system shown in the preceding pages to prevail, or have prevailed so widely among races in a low stage of civilization, represents the primitive and earliest social condition of man, *we come now to consider the various ways in which it may have been broken up, and replaced by individual marriage.*"

[2] See Bachofen's *Das Mutterrecht,*" p. xix.

selves any divinity of the type of Aphrodite, whom Bachofen chiefly contemplates in connection with hetairism. To this fancy of Bachofen, however, Sir John Lubbock has given a scientific turn by representing the expiation, compensation, or whatever it may be called, as being offered, not to the goddess, but to the tribesmen of the bridegroom. It is they, and they alone, whose rights he supposes the marriage to infringe, and to whom accordingly compensation should be given.

Now, if we were to find a large number of well-vouched cases in which, on a marriage, extraordinary freedoms with the bride were permitted to the men of the bridegroom's kindred, it might be plausibly maintained, in the absence of any more satisfactory explanation, that such cases furnished a proof of the sort that Sir John was in search of—that there was an assertion on the one side and a recognition on the other of an ancient right. But the cases ought to point clearly to this. The privileged persons should be men of the bridegroom's group only; and the cases should be capable of no simpler explanation than that which refers them to an ancient communal right.[1] Let us see, then,

---

[1] [There are cases which, in some measure, fulfil the other conditions here spoken of; but there is in every one of them a simpler explanation. With a single exception, they are cases in which the form of capture occurs; and there are none which show more clearly the origin of that marriage custom. In actual capture, among the Australians (to take a convenient example), "in any case where the abduction has taken place for the benefit of some one individual, each of the members of the party claims as a right a privilege which the intended husband has no power to

what are the facts adduced. The evidence is comprised in pp. 116—122 and pp. 510-11 of *The Origin of Civilization*, and is introduced by a general allusion to

refuse" (*The Aborigines of Victoria*. By R. Brough-Smith, vol. ii p. 316. Melbourne, 1878). And this is claimed by those persons only who have taken part in the capture; it is, indeed, a common war-right, exercised whenever, under any circumstances, capture of a woman is made by a war-party; so that it belongs to those who exercise it in the case mentioned as captors of the woman—and, accordingly, is not claimed by, nor allowed to, any others of the husband's friends or kinsfolk. In the cases referred to, after the bridegroom's party have been allowed to carry off the bride, there is precisely the same custom. Though the carrying off is but a form, they treat her as an Australian party treats a woman when they have carried her off by force for one of their number—or, as an Australian party would treat any woman who had fallen into their hands in warfare. With the form of capture occurring in these cases, it seems to be beyond question that this is a tradition from actual capture, that the members of the bridegroom's party (it may be, without any theory about it), have continued to them the right of captors. As in actual capture among the Australians, this is granted only to those who have been brought to carry off the bride; it is neither granted to, nor claimed by, any others of the bridegroom's kinsfolk or friends.

The case above alluded to in which the form of capture did not occur is a case in which it could not occur in any of the usual forms. It is that of an Australian people, the Kurnai. The Kurnai (who were exogamous) practised capture; they had marriage by exchange, with something very like a form of capture (*The Aborigines of Victoria*, vol. i., p. 84); but elopements were also common among them. And in their elopements, when a man and woman had arranged to run away together, the man summoned a party of his friends, as he might have done for a capture, and thereupon the woman was treated as she would have been if the party had helped him in carrying her off. There was no form of carrying her off— the circumstances did not admit of it; there is that difference the facts given by Dulaure, in his chapter on the Worship of Venus, to which Dulaure correctly thinks that these facts belong. Sir John Lubbock says he cannot but think that they "have a different and a deeper signification."

1. *Babylonian and Cyprian Custom*, reported by Herodotus (Clio, 199).—This custom was in Babylonia a feature and outcome of the worship of Mylitta. The freedoms allowed are not said to have been accorded to men of the bridegroom's group, or of the bride's group, but to "strangers." They, moreover, were not accorded on the eve of, or in contemplation of, marriage, or necessarily before marriage rather than after it, but by each woman "once in her life"; and it is expressly stated that they were accorded "for the satisfaction of the goddess." Herodotus says that a similar custom prevailed in parts of Cyprus.

between this case and the cases already noticed. But against this must be set the fact that the Kurnai actually practised capture. That considered, the connection of what happened with capture appears to be as unmistakable at least as it is in the other cases. It is, indeed, a form of capture in itself. And there could scarcely be better proof than it affords that a long and systematic practice of abduction preceded the practice of elopement among the Kurnai —influencing their wedding customs so deeply that even a willing bride was treated like a captive woman. Here again nothing was allowed to any persons except those whom the men brought to play the part of captors.

It is scarcely necessary to say that no custom of exogamous peoples, no custom, at any rate, which had its origin in war-capture, can help to sustain Sir J. Lubbock's theory of expiation for marriage, as he has himself stated it.]

2. *Armenian Custom*, reported by Strabo.— This custom was a feature of the worship of Anaitis—a phallic divinity like Mylitta—to whom males as well as females were dedicated. The daughters of good families were "consecrated" to this goddess, and often married well after a long period of service in her temple. In this case the women appear to have given themselves to the worshippers of the goddess indiscriminately.

3. *Nasamones*, "*and other Æthiopians.*"—The *jus primæ noctis* accorded among the Nasamones and Auziles to all the guests at a marriage indiscriminately. There is no indication that the guests were of the kinship of the bridegroom only, and it is not likely that they were.

4. *Carthage; parts of Greece; Hindustan.*—"Dulaure asserts *it* occurred" in these places—*it* meaning the custom which prevailed at Babylon.

5. *The Lydians.*—Sir John says: "The account which Herodotus gives of the Lydians, though not so clear, seems to indicate a similar law."

What Herodotus says is that the daughters *of the common people* in Lydia were prostitutes before marriage.

6. *The Thracians.*—Sir John says that their customs, "as described by Herodotus, point to a similar feeling," the feeling, I presume, that compensation was due for marriage.

Here are their customs (Herod., b.v. 5 and 6).—They are polygamous and have suttee; buy their wives and sell their children (male and female). "On their maidens they keep no watch . . . while on their wives they keep a most strict watch."

7. *Italy.*—Allusion by St. Augustine to the newly-married performing (harmless) acts recognizing the divinity of Priapus.

8. *Balearic Islands; the Mantas; Nukahiva.*—A custom said to prevail similar to that of the Nasamones.

9. *India, in various quarters.*—Virgins required to permit liberties in the temples.

10. *The Sonthals.*—Marriages take place once a year. A period of license for six days before among the candidates for matrimony.

11. *Case of profligacy* on the part of a woman of the Nandowessies, such as not " once in an age " any of their women was guilty of, though it was in accordance with an old custom. She entertained 40 warriors. It is not said that they belonged to any one tribe, or that the act had relation to her marriage.

12. *A series of instances of lending wives* (pp. 118–120).—The case of the Tapyrians, referred to by Sir John Lubbock, is not exactly stated. It is not said by Strabo that they were *obliged* to leave their wives, but that it was their custom "to surrender them, even when they had had two or three children by them, to other men, as Cato surrendered Marcia in our own times, &c." This may mean no more than that it was sometimes done. At any rate, there is no hint that the wives were surrendered only to men of the same tribe as the husbands.

13. A series of instances of courtesans being either

highly respected or " by no means despised." Sir John regards the class of courtesans as representatives of the "communal wives" of primitive times. The existence of this class admits of a simpler explanation (pp. 120–122).

Such is the evidence. Nos. 1, 2, 4, 7, and 9 include cases which specifically relate themselves to phallic-worship; Nos. 3, 8, and 10, cases referring to the "first night," or the days preceding marriage; Nos. 5 and 6, cases in regard to which the statements made seem not to be supported by the authorities; and Nos. 11, 12, and 13, cases which appear to be without bearing on the matter at issue. Not one case satisfies the indispensable conditions specified; not one is a case of privileges accorded to the men of the bridegroom's group only, in clear connection with marriage, and incapable of a simpler explanation than that which refers them to an ancient communal right. With reference to the cases of phallic origin—more particularly the Indian cases—I cannot help observing that they occur among peoples who had advanced far from the primitive state. Indian history carries us thousands of years closer to the communal stage, if it ever existed, than we now are; and, in India, the farther back we go, the less we find of this sort of thing. The germ only of phallic-worship shows itself in the *Vedas*, and the gross luxuriance of licentiousness, of which the cases referred to are examples, is of later growth. The lending of wives, again, is a mere proof that conjugal attachment depends on sentiments which develop but slowly, and which, as the case of

Cato proves, prevail only after monogamy has had a long and uninterrupted history. Of the cases comprised under Nos. 3, 8, and 10, which will make the strongest impression on the reader—though they prove nothing, in my opinion, for Bachofen or for Lubbock—this is not the place to attempt to offer an explanation. For the present purpose, it is enough to point out that they are not cases of privilege granted to the men of the husband's tribe. In the case of the Nasamones the freedoms allowed were granted to "the guests" present at the nuptial feast; in the case of the Balearic Islanders, to the "intimates and friends"—it is not said whether of the bridegroom, or of the bride, or of both; and in neither case is it stated whether the nuptial feast was given at the home of the bridegroom or of the bride. In neither case is a reference made to relatives or tribesmen. How entirely unconnected these cases may be, with either the propitiation of a divinity or compensation to the men of a tribe, the reader may see on reference to what Gubernatis has written on similar customs.[1] "È da notarsi," says Gubernatis, "come nell' antica credenza vedica si supponeva che un demonio nascondesse nella vergine, il quale ne venisse via col sangue"; in support of which he refers to Hymn 85, Book x. of the *Rig-Veda*. Where such a view prevailed, it is easily conceivable how for a time the post of husband should be ceded, and how the exercise of the *jus primæ noctis* should really be of the nature of a

---

[1] See *Storia comparata degli Usi Nuziali in Italia e presso gli altri popoli Indo-Europei*, pp. 197–8. Milan, 1869.

friendly or neighbourly act. Lastly, I have only to remark of the "communal wives," as Sir John courteously calls them, that if any inference is to be made from their standing in Athens, in the brilliant age of Pericles, as to the state of matters in the primitive groups, proof of primitive communism in women might as well be sought in London or Paris in our own day. Far back in the interval between savagery and the age of Pericles are the heroes of Homer, with their noble wedded wives.

I have now examined, in both of its branches, the evidence of ancient communism ("communal rights") over women on which Sir John Lubbock founds his speculation, and I submit that it has been proved to be of no value.

Let us now recur to, and try to choose between, the contradictory principles on which Sir John Lubbock relies in setting up his initial stage on the one hand, and demonstrating the progress therefrom on the other. The question raised is whether "*the tribe had no right to a war-captive,*" so that her captor might easily appropriate her, or whether "the tribe had a right to her," so that he could as easily appropriate a woman of the group as a war-captive.

This question must be answered by an appeal to the facts relating to the ancient practice of capturing women for wives, regarded in their bearing on the communal rights which, as Sir John asserts, at first everywhere prevailed. Of the practice of capture we know nothing, as regards the great majority of the ancient nations, except what we learn from the form of capture. The practice, then, must be assumed to have been what that form indicates. Now in almost all cases the form of capture is the symbol of a group act—of a siege, or a pitched battle, or an invasion of a house by an armed band; while in a few cases only, and these much disintegrated, it represents a capture by an individual. On the one side are the kindred of the husband; on the other the kindred of the wife. This is so manifest that it cannot be contradicted; it appears clearly from the examples of the form adduced in my paper referred to in the Preface to this work,[1] which are classed as they represent sieges or battles or armed invasions. It also sufficiently appears from the collection of examples of the form furnished by Sir John Lubbock himself. Moreover, all the cases we have illustrating the practice of capture in its transition to a symbolism, are cases of the same sort—actual conflicts, in which the woman is the prize of victory and the combatants are on one side the kindred of the man, on the other the kindred of the woman. Such are the cases recorded by Olaus Magnus, and such is the case of the Mirdites, of which Mr. Tozer has recently given an excellent account. Lastly, the facts of actual capture, as they appear both in ancient literature and among existing races, prove the same thing; the captures usually occur in the course of raids upon enemies made by tribes or their war-parties. Even as capture is

---

[1] See Appendix to *Primitive Marriage*.

practised in Australia, the captures are usually made by two or more persons acting in concert. Our conclusion must be that in the most primitive times, of which, through this symbol, we have a far-off reflection, the capture of women for wives was usually the act of a group or of a detachment from a group.

But if women were commonly captured by the men of a group, or parties of them, and there was communism in women, I do not see how an individual who had captured "a beautiful girl" could appropriate her more easily than he could appropriate any beautiful girl of his own group for whom he had a fancy. War-captives being usually obtained by group-acts, or quasi group-acts, capture would be recognized as a regular mode of adding women to the group, subject to the customary rights of its male members; and there would be no man in the group who had not exercised the communal right over women taken by others. If, in this state of affairs, one were to capture "a beautiful girl," and plead the capture as a reason why he should be permitted to keep her to himself exclusively, he would be met by the answer that he had been used to benefit by captures made by others, and so was bound to allow others to benefit by that which he had made. And I do not see that to this he could reply. The case would go against him in a court of strict justice; tried by savages in a stage so low as we are asked to believe in—possession of "a beautiful girl" turning on the decision—it would be heard with impatience and settled by force. "Men surely would reserve to themselves exclusively their own prizes," says Sir John. They might wish to do so, no doubt, but power is not always proportioned to inclination. It was not Achilles who got Chryseis.

The correct view, then, seems to be that, granting communism and a practice of capture, the individual captor would have no exclusive right to a war-captive. Our conclusion must be that, even had there been proof of the general prevalence of what Sir John Lubbock has called the communal marriage system, the history he offers of the disruption of that system would have to be rejected.

Were the practice of capture to give an individual captor a right to exclude the custom of the tribe as regards his captive, it would surely give a similar right to several joint captors as regards women taken by them. If, then, it led to individual marriages, it must much more frequently have led to polyandrous arrangements. In thinking of these, again, we may be sure that those entitled to have one or two women exclusively to themselves would not forego the benefits of the custom, over *all* the women in the group, for this right —of the same communal type—over one or two. And we must ask, would the individual captor be likely to forego those benefits for the exclusive possession of one? Unless he did so, there could be no commencement made of the training of the men in those habits which develop the sentiments that foster monandry. But if he did so, he would in effect be no longer of the group, even did he remain in it with his wife, which it is scarcely conceivable he should do, and his example would accordingly be ineffectual for the group's improvement.

We have seen that Sir John Lubbock has not only failed to show that the initial stage of his scheme ever existed, but has failed also to make it in any the least degree probable that it ever existed. And we have farther seen that even had he shown that stage to have existed, he has failed to show, by reasoning that will bear examination, how it came to be departed from. With his explanation of the origin of monandry fall his explanations of the origin of exogamy, the practice of capture, female infanticide, and all the customs with these connected.

DIVISIONS OF
THE ANCIENT IRISH FAMILY.

DIVISIONS OF
THE ANCIENT IRISH FAMILY.

In his recent work on *Early Institutions*, Sir Henry Maine draws attention to the singular distribution of certain members of the old Irish family in four divisions. The reciprocal rights of succession of these divisions to each other's property is the subject of a number of regulations contained in the *Book of Aicill*, and various scattered scraps of information regarding the divisions are to be found elsewhere in the first three volumes of the *Senchus Mor*. In the preface to the third volume of that work we find the following account of the divisions:—" The most remarkable custom described in the *Book of Aicill* is the fourfold distribution of the family into the 'geilfine,' 'deirbfine,' 'iarfine,' and 'indfine' divisions. . . . Within the family seventeen members were organized in four divisions, of which the junior class, known as the 'geilfine' division, consisted of five persons; the 'deirbfine' the second in order, the 'iarfine' the third in order, and the 'indfine' the senior of all, consisted respectively of four persons. The whole organization consisted, and could only consist, of seventeen members. If any person was born into the 'geilfine' division, *its eldest member was promoted into the 'deirbfine'*; the eldest member of the 'deirbfine' passed into the 'iarfine'; the eldest member of the 'iarfine' moved into the 'indfine,' and the eldest member of the 'indfine' passed out of the organization altogether. It would appear that this transition from a lower to a higher grade took place upon the introduction of a new member into the 'geilfine' division, and therefore depended upon the introduction of new members, and not upon the death of the seniors."

This account seems correct, according to all the facts yet disclosed, except that, for "persons," "men," or "male persons," should have been substituted, and that, perhaps, it should have been stated that the organization might consist of fewer, though it could not include more, than seventeen persons. (*Senchus Mor*, vol. iii. p. 333.)

Sir Henry Maine considers this strange arrangement to be "a monument of that power of the father which is the first and greatest landmark in the course of legal history." (*Early Institutions*, p. 216.) Any man of a sept, he thinks, might become a root from which might spring as many of these groups of seventeen men as he had sons. "As soon as any one of the sons had four children, a full geilfine sub-group of five persons was formed, but any fresh birth of a male child to this son, or to any of his male descendants, had the effect of sending up the eldest member of the geilfine sub-group, *provided always he were not the person from whom it had sprung*, into the deirbfine. A succession of such births completed in time the deirbfine division, and went on to form the iarfine and the indfine." (*Idem*, p. 210.) The fifth person in the geilfine sub-group was the father of whom the other sixteen men in the organization were descendants, and Sir Henry thinks that this person always remained in that sub-group, and was its chief—"the geilfine chief"—or paterfamilias. The geilfine sub-group, consisting of the natural or adoptive sons (or descendants) immediately under the power of the father, was his "hand-family"; the other groups consisted of the emancipated descendants, "diminishing in dignity in proportion to their distance from the group [*i.e.* the geilfine], which, according to archaic notions, constitutes the true or representative family." (*Idem*, p. 217.) Why the "hand-family" should consist of five persons only Sir Henry explains by a reference to Mr. Tylor's views on finger-counting, and to *five* being "a primitive natural maximum number"; but he offers no explanation of the fact that the other divisions consisted of four persons each only, although he seems to have been impressed by the fact as remarkable, and says (p. 210), "The essential principle of the system seems to me a distribution into fours."

The accounts we have from ancient writers of the habits and customs of the early Irish would justify a strong belief that they knew nothing of—could have known nothing of—the patria potestas or a family system at all resembling the Roman. And the learned editors of the *Senchus Mor* (vol. ii. p. lv.) state, as the result of their study of early Irish family law, that no trace of the patria potestas is to be found in that law. "The Irish law," they say, "demands for the mother a position equal to that of the father, and there is no trace of the exercise of that arbitrary power which was wielded by a Roman father over the members of his family." If, then, Sir Henry Maine had really discovered in the fourfold division of the ancient Irish family a proof that the patria potestas was formerly known to the Irish, the fact would be of the highest interest. It would show how little trust we should put in mere impressions drawn from recorded facts, and what a powerful instrument of research comparative jurisprudence is, compared with direct historical inquiry by means of records and documents.

There are, however, overwhelming difficulties in the way of Sir Henry's explanations. Some objections to them, though by no means, in my opinion, the most important, he himself has seen and stated with his usual clearness and candour.

1. The supposition that the geilfine division consisted of a father and four sons, or descendants real or adoptive, and that the father always remained in the division, is contrary to what is expressly stated; namely, that on any person "being born into the geilfine division [the division being full] its *eldest*

member was promoted into the deirbfine." (*Senchus Mor*, vol. iii. p. cxl.)¹

2. Emancipation could but account for two divisions at the most—the emancipated and the unemancipated.

The emancipated having once passed out of the power of the father, that power could not again be exercised on them. It must then have been by some other power than that of the father, that the men, supposing them sons of the head of the geilfine division, were grouped outside of the "hand-family," and made to pass on from group to group. Sir Henry has failed to indicate what that power was, or on what rule or principle it was exercised, and of course he has failed to account for there being four divisions.

3. All the information we have respecting the divisions represents them as existing together as an organization. There is no authority for conceiving that *all* the members of the deirbfine, iarfine, and indfine divisions were originally members of the geilfine group; or that a geilfine group could exist except in relation to the three other groups co-existing with it. The only case mentioned in which a man passed from one division

---

¹ How can the following passage be reconciled with the supposition that the father of four sons or descendants forming, together with him, the geilfine division, was the geilfine chief? "That every one who is head or chief of the *geilfine* tribe be of the people of the tribe; *i.e.* he is the head of the tribe before men, *i.e.* the person who is most experienced." (*Senchus Mor*, vol. ii. pp. 279-81.) If the chief were the progenitor of all the others, how could he fail to be of the people of the tribe? But by the time this was written, the office of chief had become elective.

to another occurred when a new man entered the organization of seventeen men, and when, in consequence, a man had to go out of that organization; so that the organization is assumed as complete already before the commencement of the transference of the seniors from division to division; and of the senior member of the indfine division "into the community." These are the only cases of transference for which there is authority.

4. Emancipation would disinherit the emancipated; but our knowledge of these divisions is mainly derived from the laws of succession to property which connected each of them with all the others.

5. It is essential to Sir Henry's explanation that the geilfine division should be at once "the highest and the youngest." (See *Early Institutions*, p. 216.) It was unquestionably the youngest, as the indfine was the oldest. This is expressly stated, but I can nowhere find it called "the highest." It was certainly, as we shall see, the least-favoured division but one as regards successions, if, indeed, the law can be said to have shown a preference for one division over another.[1] The editors of the *Senchus*

---

[1] Sir Henry says (*ut supra*, p. 216), "the geilfine group is several times stated by the Brehon writers to be at once the highest and the youngest." He gives no reference to passages in which this is stated, and I can only say, as I have said above, that after a careful search I have not found any such passage. As regards successions, he has plainly fallen into a misconception of his authorities. At p. 223, in endeavouring to assign the origin of "Borough English," he says—"It appears to me that the institution [Borough English] is founded on the same ideas as those which gave a preference [in successions] to the geilfine division of the

Mor, as we have seen, speak of the eldest member of the geilfine class as being "promoted" to the deirbfine, and clearly consider the "indfine" as the highest division; for of the transitions from division to division they speak as, in every case, a "*transition from a lower to a higher grade.*" (*Senchus Mor*, vol. iii. p. cxl.)

6. The case is provided for, of the geilfine division becoming extinct and its property being distributed between the other divisions. The extinguishment of the "hand-family," with the "paterfamilias," by death nowise affected the fourfold organization. Other men from the family stepped into the vacant places and formed a new geilfine division, related to the other divisions precisely as its predecessor had been. This clearly appears from the provisions of the code for the simultaneous extinguishment by death of the indfine and geilfine divisions. (*Senchus Mor*, vol. iii. p. 333.) Their property was to be divided in certain proportions between the iarfine and the deirbfine divisions, but *on this condition*, that "the whole number of seventeen men should then be forthcoming"; which is explained to mean that the indfine division and the geilfine division should be instantly filled up anew by fresh men "out of the family if it were numerous enough

---

Celtic family." But as clearly appears by the table, p. cxli. vol. iii., *Senchus Mor*, the deirbfine was the most favoured in successions, the iarfine next, and the geilfine third in order. The law had, indeed, no preference, and that the deirbfine fared so well was due to the fact that property (with trivial exceptions) *descended* from the higher divisions to the lower, and ascended only when it could go no lower. (See pp. 493–5.)

for the purpose." If the seventeen men were not forthcoming, there was no partition of the property between the remaining divisions. In that case it went to the nearest of kin. We thus see that the divisions did not contain the family, but were an organization within it composed of certain members of the family, whose places, when a division became extinct, could be filled up by other members of it. The organization need not have been more than temporarily deranged by the extinction of the geilfine group. But if Sir Henry's view were correct, the whole organization should have collapsed on the death of the paterfamilias and all the members of his "hand-family."

These objections are fatal to Sir Henry Maine's account of the system. He has failed to throw light either on its purposes or its principles. He has made no single feature of it clear in the light of Roman law, and, after all his ingenious reasonings, has left its main features as mysterious as he found them.

What then was the real nature of this divisional arrangement? The fragment in the Book of Aicill which treats of it occurs under the heading "What is the reciprocal right among families?" Towards the close of the answer to this question there is a passage, apparently of later date than the rest, without bearing on the question discussed, but bearing directly on the constitution of the organization, and the rights, between themselves, of the members of the several "families." This passage, which is very obscure, is undoubtedly our chief authority on the matters it deals with. Sir Henry Maine's view of the divisions turns on an interpretation of it which must be put aside as incorrect; and, so far, the way is clear for a fresh and wholly different interpretation.

The passage referred to is an instance of the incorporation in the text of "the opinion of lawyers" on a hypothetical case, which, to judge from other such cases scattered about in the code, may have been fanciful as well as hypothetical. All the same, it may be possible to gather from it what the lawyers understood about this family system. The case is strictly in two parts, which are run into one another, but may be put separately and presented thus:

1.—"If the father is alive and has two sons, and each of these sons has a family of the full number, *i.e.* four, it is the opinion of the lawyers that the father would claim a man's share in every family of them, and that in this case they form [1] [*Irish* and literally, *there are*] two geilfine divisions."

2.—"*And* if the property has come from another place, from a family outside, though there should be in the family a son or brother of the person whose property came into it, he [in the opinion of the lawyers] shall not obtain it more than any other man of the family."

From the first part, which bears upon the genesis

---

[1] The words "they form" have clearly been adopted in the text on that reading of it which the editors, though not without hesitation, have followed equally with Sir Henry Maine.

of divisional organizations, Sir Henry Maine has inferred that any man of a sept might become the root of as many divisional organizations as he had sons; that as soon as one of his sons had four children, a geilfine sub-group of five persons was formed, and hence that a geilfine division consisted of a father and four sons. This is the interpretation which must be rejected. How then is the case to be construed?

The leading point of the opinion is that "the father would claim a man's share *in every family of them*," and it is added, as if it were consequential on that view, that "*in this case*¹ there are two geilfine divisions." What families are referred to? They cannot be the two geilfine divisions, for the reference is in terms applicable to several families and inapplicable to two; and is, moreover, followed by a reference to these divisions as if they were distinct from, or only among the number of, the families. For the same reasons the reference cannot be to the two families of the sons, apart from certain members of them forming two geilfine divisions.

Remembering that a division is never mentioned except as co-existing with three others in an organization, may we not infer that if in this case there were two geilfine divisions, there must have been eight divisions in all? As the divisions are constantly called "families," and are specially so called in the heading to the fragment in which this case occurs, we should then have to conclude that the point of the opinion is

---

¹ If a father and four sons formed a geilfine division, what room was there for these qualifying words?

that in the family of the father there would be formed two divisional organizations, and in all "eight families," in each of which the father would have right to "a man's share"—whatever that may mean.

How does this view consist with the facts of the case? A turning-point of Sir Henry Maine's interpretation is in the words "a family of the full number, *i.e.* four," which he correctly takes to mean four sons. Now this number is directly related to the number of divisions in a divisional organization, while it can be connected with the number of persons in the geilfine division only by the assumption, which we have seen to be unjustifiable, that the common progenitor of the other members of the organization always remained in that division. The words, "a family of the full number, *i.e.* four," *may* have been used then in reference to the number of brothers needed as a basis for the fourfold organization. Let us follow this idea and see to what conclusions it will lead.

What is contemplated is plainly the formation of divisional organizations within the family as derived from the father. There being two sets of four brothers each among his grandsons, it is clear that bases have been formed, in the opinion of the lawyers, for two such organizations. On the view I am putting, each brother in a set of four, whether he was already himself a father or merely regarded as a possible father, was assumed by them to represent a division or "family"; the eldest, the indfine; the next, the iarfine; the third, the deirbfine; and the youngest the geilfine.

Altogether there were thus represented eight divisions or "families" (comprised in two divisional organizations) in each of which the father had right to a man's share.

We need not now inquire what kind of property was vested in a division, or how or why it was vested; but when we ask how the father could have such a right in the several "families," it is plain that the lawyers must have held him to be actually, as common senior to them all, or otherwise constructively, a member of each of the families. Again, the reasoning which would support this view would clearly constitute each of the two sons of the father a member of each of the four families which *his* sons represented. We are thus led to think that in the opinion of the lawyers there were already, actually or constructively, three men, related as father, son, and grandson, in each of the eight divisions. Assume that this gives us, so far, the true idea of the composition of the divisions, and it may be inferred from the analogies of the case that the fourth man in each division would be a son of the brother who represented it, and the fifth man in the geilfine divisions a grandson of the youngest brother in each set of brothers. We thus arrive at the conclusion that the divisions formed in the way contemplated by the lawyers would each come to consist of a father, son, grandson, and great-grandson; and in case of the geilfine division, of a father, son, grandson, great-grandson, and great-great-grandson! Singular as this result is, it is directly deducible from the first branch of the case pronounced upon by the lawyers, when construed on the assumption that the words "a family of the full number, *i.e.* four," have reference to four brothers as presenting a basis for the formation of a divisional organization.[1]

But all the authority there is on the subject goes to show that this singular inference gives a correct description of the composition of the divisions. Besides being called "families" they were called "tribes," and the relationship connecting the members of a division was called geilfine tribe relationship. Now what this was is expressly stated. The editors of the second volume of the *Senchus Mor* expressly say (vol. ii. p. xlvi.) that the geilfine tribe relationship "was that of a father, son, grandson and great-grandson, and grandsons to the fifth generation, and in what was called the reverse line [? any other division]—*i.e.* the brother of the father and his sons to the fifth generation"; and there is what seems to be a confirmation of this statement at vol. ii. p. 209, where the relations of a chief to the chief "next" to him are discussed.[2]

Sir Henry Maine, indeed, says (*Early Institutions*, p. 211): "The Brehon writers speak of its [the geilfine division] consisting of a father, son, grandson, great-

---

[1] According to my interpretation the father is the most important man in both of the organizations formed within his family. On Sir Henry Maine's view he was outside both, and the only one of the kindred omitted. Of this violence done by himself to the principle of the patria potestas Sir Henry justly remarks (p. 219), that it has no analogy in Roman law.

[2] Mr. W. F. Skene is of opinion that these divisions existed only in the families of the chieftain class. See his edition of Fordun, article on "Tribe Communities."

grandson, and great-great-grandson, which is a conceivable case of geilfine relationship, though it can scarcely be a common one." If our reading of the passage under consideration is correct, it was, actually or constructively, the *only* one—when the division was full, *i.e.* when all its possible members were in being; and this, moreover, enables us to see why a division should be called a "tribe." It consisted of the heads of four or five families, lineally (or quasi-lineally) connected, *i.e.* of a man and three or four others representing the whole group of his descendants to the fourth or fifth generation.

If we conceive one of the organizations, initiated as in the case pronounced upon by the lawyers, to be completed (1) through the death of the father and his two sons, leaving a set of four grandsons in their places, each as the oldest member of his division; and (2) through the filling up of the divisions by the birth of descendants to the several grandsons, the following table will then represent the organization :—

Indfine.	Iarfine.	Deirbfine.	Geilfine.	
A_1	A_2	A_3	A_4	Fathers and Brothers.
B_1	B_2	B_3	B_4	Sons and First Cousins.
C_1	C_2	C_3	C_4	Grandsons and Second Cousins.
D_1	D_2	D_3	D_4	Great-Grandsons and Third Cousins.
			E_4	Great-Great-Grandson.

The seniors of the divisions are A_1, A_2, &c., the brothers who constituted the "family of the full number, *i.e.* four"; and the other men in the divisions along with them respectively, are their first-born sons, grandsons, &c. : A_1 is the eldest of the four brothers, A_2 the next eldest, and A_4 is the youngest. The following features of the system now become intelligible :—

1. It is at once obvious why it is said "the geilfine division is the youngest and the indfine division is the oldest."

2. We can see a reason why, as a rule, there should be four men only in a division, and why there should be a fifth man in the geilfine division.

The age of marriage among the ancient Irish was seventeen years—the age for finishing fosterage. Thus A_1 would be at least fifty-four years old before his great-grandson D_1 would be born; and he would be between eighty and ninety years old before E_4 could have a son, which would be the signal to A_1 to "go out into the community." As a rule, then, there could be only four generations of *men* in existence at a time, and represented in the divisions.

The fifth man—or rather boy—in the geilfine division must have been added to postpone the going out "into the community" of the senior of the indfine. When he went out, he became, as we shall see, a pensioner on his division, and were he to go out when E_4 was born, he might be a charge on that division for a term of years. Before E_4 could have a son, however,

A_1 would be a very old man. Indeed, the "going out" must have been rare. The law, however, provided for it, as it did for the divisions not being full, and even for their becoming extinct. Whatever the purposes of the organization were, the existence of the whole number of the seventeen men was not essential to them, and in the eye of the law a division existed so long as there was one man in it. (*Senchus Mor*, vol. iii. p. 333.)

3. So far as the organization was an artificial institution, it may have been a sufficient reason for limiting the number of divisions to four, that there were four men only in a division. More probably the reason was that four was, on the average, the full number of sons in a family.

4. We have a clue to "the self-acting principle," as Sir Henry Maine aptly calls it, according to which the eldest member of each division passed into the next on a new man "coming up" into the geilfine division. Among the Irish the next brother, or other nearest male agnate next in seniority to a deceased chief, succeeded to the chieftaincy in preference to a son. We can therefore understand how they should provide for the succession of brother to brother, in order of seniority, in the headship of divisions, and, failing brothers, for the succession of cousin to cousin (of the same class) in order of seniority. It accords with this succession law that when A_1 "went out," A_2 should succeed to him as head of the indfine division; that A_3 should succeed A_2 as head of the iarfine, and A_4 succeed A_3 as head of the deirbfine. But we saw that

before A_1 went out he would be very old. Before another "going out" could occur through the birth of a grandson to E_4, the brothers A_1 &c., would certainly be all dead, and the first cousins B_1 &c., would be the heads of divisions. It would next be B_1's turn to go out, and he would be succeeded in the headship of the indfine division by B_2 as the cousin next in seniority; and B_2 being succeeded by B_3 and B_3 by B_4 all the seniors would be promoted as before. By the fourth occurrence of such an occasion it would be D_1's turn to go out; if, indeed, before then the organization had not collapsed through the extinction of divisions and the want of men to re-form them.

The second branch of the case pronounced upon by the lawyers (see *ante*, p. 359) is more easily construed than the first. It points out that the men of a division shared equally the divisional property, whencesoever it came; that the common law of succession, by which a man might have the whole of any property coming to him from his father or brother, was overridden by this law of the organization. It thus is indicative of the organization operating a departure from ordinary succession law, and we shall see reason for believing that it was primarily a device designed to have such an effect.

The somewhat enigmatical terms in which this branch of the case and opinion is couched present little difficulty in the light cast on them by the interpretation of the first branch which I have suggested. If it be asked, for example, how could a member of one of the "families" have a father or brother in another, we see that that would happen were A_2 to become head of the indfine, for there would then be in the iarfine his brother A_3 and his son B_2. Were A_2 to be thereafter the last survivor of the indfine, three-fourths of his property would come to the iarfine division, and then, according to the opinion, his son B_2 would get but "a man's share" of it, and no more. Again, on the view that the words "from another place, from a family outside," point to a family outside the organization, observe that there is but one son of any father in a division. If A_1 had a fifth brother, younger than A_4, and that brother were to die, leaving property, and without a son, his estate would fall to his brothers, and a share of it to each of the divisions; and, in that case, the opinion of the lawyers says that the brothers would have to share their shares of it with their co-divisioners. On the same view, the case of a man within the organization having property left to him by a father outside of it would have to be regarded as a case of adoption into the organization.

It must be felt that our interpretation of this leading passage in the *Book of Aicill* still leaves this family arrangement mysterious and unintelligible. Grant that we have now a correct conception of the composition of a division, of the self-acting principle that promoted the seniors, of the reason for there being four men in each of three of the divisions, and a fifth man in the fourth, the questions remain, Why were such organizations formed at all? What were their functions? Were they really formed within the family as composed of the descendants of a surviving ancestor, and if not, within what species of family were they formed?[1]

Let us see whether we cannot obtain answers to some of these questions.

That the divisional organization was one of the divisions of the Fine, or Sept,[2] appears from a curious passage in the *Book of Aicill* (vol. iii. p. 489), which discusses the question from whom a forced exaction, as in payment of a penalty or fine, might lawfully be levied. Here the "seventeen men" are several times referred to as specially liable to such an exaction if levied on account of the crime of any man *connected* with them, in terms which seem to imply that every tribesman had, necessarily, a connection with a divisional organization which was liable for his defaults. In one place, the text, which as it stands reads as nonsense, must have been intended to indicate that the distant relatives of the criminal were liable for him only when the divisional organization was incomplete, or had collapsed—a reading which is confirmed by the text: "The four nearest tribes bear the crimes of each kinsman of their stock: geilfine and deirbfine, iarfine

---

[1] It is obvious that in the Irish code the words "family" and "tribe" have the most various significations, whether the confusion be due to the text or to the translators.

[2] I agree with Sir Henry Maine in regarding the Fine as the whole clan, or tribe of descent, holding together and deriving their descent from a common progenitor, known, or believed, to have existed in the remote past.

and indfine." (*Senchus Mor*, vol. i. p. 261.) Here the connection is disclosed between a tribesman, himself not the member of a divisional organization, and the organization responsible for him. It is sameness of stock. As the seventeen men were all of one stock, being brothers or brothers' descendants, the question arises, Who were with them within the bond of a recognized consanguinity? If we can answer this question, we can define the sub-group of the Fine which a divisional organization specially represented.

The editors of the second volume of the *Senchus Mor* remark (p. xlvi.) that the system of fosterage appears to have been connected with the "geilfine" tribe relationship. "It is mentioned," they say, "that the relations who were within this degree were those who received the children in fosterage." It plainly appears from this that "geilfine" tribe relationship—which we saw was defined as in the direct *and* in what was called the reverse line—was a general term for the relationship of the men in the organization; and in this, if not in a more extended sense, we find the term used in the *Corus Bescna* (vol. iii. p. 41), where "ten sons"—not necessarily sons of the same parents—are spoken of as being in "the geilfine relationship," the limiting term "tribe" being omitted. We may be sure that fostering did not take place between families that were in the direct lines of this relationship; the families would belong to different generations, and be unable to render fostering services to one another. It took place, then, between families in different lines. But if it were limited to the families represented by the seventeen men, no one beyond a third cousin could be required to foster a child. All the evidence we have goes to show that fostering had a wider range than this; and in the *Senchus Mor* (vol. ii. p. 285), we find that the limits within which fostering might take place are declared to be the same as the limits of recognized consanguinity. "By consanguinity, *i.e.* the person who is so near him of his tribe as to foster the children which descend from him, if he should require it." We have thus an inference that geilfine relationship, in its broadest sense, was co-extensive with recognized consanguinity, and hence that the "geilfine tribe" was a term of double meaning—in one sense denoting the youngest division of a divisional organization, in another, denoting the whole group of persons connected with such an organization, and who, in a special sense, acknowledged themselves to be kindred. The latter group was, I believe, the true "geilfine tribe," over which presided the geilfine chief—a person always of much importance, and who might even be the king of a territory.

Recurring to the hypothetical case of the lawyers, and assuming the two organizations which, according to the lawyers, would be formed among the descendants of the father, to have been completed as already described (*ante*, p. 359) after the death of the father and his two sons, we see that kinship must have been recognized as far at least as sixth cousins and the eighth descent from the father or common ancestor;[1] for the sons of the youngest members of the geilfine divisions, whose birth, while the organizations still existed, is contemplated, would be sixth cousins, and necessarily, as connected with the organizations, within the limits of the recognized consanguinity. Whether the lawyers were right or wrong in the opinion that there would, in the case supposed, be two geilfine divisions, this conclusion may be legitimately drawn from their opinion. The same conclusion is even more unequivocally indicated by the fact that the old Irish named their relatives, as far at least as sixth cousins, in the third collateral line. (Morgan, *Systems of Consanguinity*, &c., p. 45.) It seems certain, then, that all the descendants of a common ancestor to the eighth descent, holding together on the same lands, were counted of one stock—to be, in a special sense, kindred. But the conclusion cannot, I think, be avoided that all connected with a common ancestor within nine descents were, in such a sense, kindred. The geilfine divisions connecting men of five generations, a man counting above him four generations of ancestors, would almost necessarily count below him four of descendants; so that his own generation counting as one, there would be nine generations of relatives whom a man would think of as his kindred. This view, if it be adopted, presents the Irish "kindred" as corresponding in all respects with the Welsh.

The terms in which the excellent editors of the third volume of the *Senchus Mor* state the old Irish law as

---

[1] See *Manu*, chap. iii. v. 146.

to fines and compensations are word for word applicable as a general statement of the old Welsh law. "The compensation and honour-price," they say (p. cxv.), "awarded in respect of any injury, were primarily payable by the wrong-doer, and received by the person injured; but there existed a solidarité between persons standing in certain relations to each other, whereby parties [the family or kindred] strangers to the transaction might be required to pay, or entitled to receive, a portion of the award." Who the "kindred" of any criminal or injured person were in the Irish case, they think unascertainable. Who they were in the Welsh case, we know; and it will be more readily credible that the limits of consanguinity recognized in Ireland were truly those we have mentioned, if it be found that those were the limits recognized among the Celts of Wales.

The question, who were counted to be of the same stock with a criminal or injured person according to old Welsh law? is discussed in the *Ancient Laws, &c., of Wales* (vol. ii. p. 21), where the matter is introduced as follows: "Torwaith, the son of Madog, says that the right meaning of inquiry as to a stock is this—namely, when a relative is a refuser to the murderer of his share of the galanas [corresponding to the Irish Eric], and asking 'Whence the stock I am related to thee?' Then it is necessary for the murderer to explain to him the stock from which he is derived, and his consanguinity." Here "stock" is equivalent to "common ancestor," as may be seen in the plaints of kin and descent (*idem*, p. 45), where the common ancestor is called "the holding stock." How far removed this ancestor might be appears (*idem*, p. 569) from the text, which says: "The parentage of a man includes his father, his grandfather, and his great-grandfather, and thence unto the ninth degree and descent they are called 'gerni'—*i.e.* relatives." This is confirmed by passages too numerous to be cited. "The chief of kindred" is, for instance, described as "the oldest efficient man in the kindred to the ninth descent" (*idem*, p. 517); a description recalling that of the geilfine chief given in the *Senchus Mor*,—"that every one who is head or chief of the 'geilfine' tribe be of the people of the tribe—the person who is most experienced" (*Senchus Mor*, vol. ii. p. 281). But while, in Wales, the kindred thus comprised all descendants of a man to the ninth descent, it is noticeable that the only example given of the details of a "dispersed galanas" represents the levy, in payment of the galanas, as assessed on the kinsmen rateably as far as sixth cousins only (*Ancient Laws, &c., of Wales*, vol. ii. p. 21); which would indicate a common ancestor in the eighth generation. Sixth cousins were, of course, as entering the divisional organizations, in Ireland assessed for fines on account of kinsmen of their stock. The Irish and Welsh cases are thus at all points parallel, even to the doubt, in both cases, as to seventh cousins, in the ninth descent, being, for practical purposes, within the kindred.

In Wales, the "kindreds," with their chiefs, appear

everywhere as the constituent units of the population. They were assessed to pay fines for their kinsmen's crimes, and they shared the compensations paid for injuries to their kinsmen, as we know the Irish kindred did. It appears to me that we must believe that the " geilfine tribe," as an extended group, including divisional organizations, answered in every respect to the "kindred" of the Welsh; and its chief—the geilfine chief—to the "chief of kindred" among the Welsh.

It is obvious that within the same Fine, or Sept, all the men of which derived a real or supposed descent from a very remote ancestor, there might be several "kindreds," or "geilfine" tribes, with common ancestors no farther removed than the ninth [or eighth] generation. There might be as many divisional organizations, then, at the least within the Fine, as there were such kindreds. The hypothetical case, so often referred to, indicates that there might be more than one such organization within a kindred; and assuming that there might, we see a meaning in the word *nearest* in the text which says that the four nearest tribes bear the crimes of all the kinsmen of their stock. In the kindred derived from the father mentioned in the hypothetical case, the descendants of each son of the father would be those for which the organization formed in *his* family would be specially liable. In one place, however, there is a distinction drawn between a *middle* kinsman and a kinsman in general, which shows that this meaning of the word, nearest, is doubtful. Kinship, in its widest sense, was co-extensive with the Fine; middle kinship was that of the geilfine tribe or the kindred, and the "middle kinsman" was the man for whom "the seventeen" were liable. (*Senchus Mor*, vol. i. pp. 259 and 273.) At any rate, we have the conclusion that, within a Fine, there might be at least as many divisional organizations as there were "kindreds" or geilfine tribes.

The difficulties of levying on the Fine an assessment for the crime of a kinsman in general would be very great, if not insuperable; and there would be an obvious convenience in arrangements for replacing the ancient tribal liability by that of kindreds, and even in imposing, within a kindred, the liability on a small assortment of families, which bore it in respect of their possessing property specially liable for it, such as the ancestral lands. But it can hardly be believed that divisional organizations were designed primarily, or solely, to bear the crimes of kinsmen. It is much more probable that the organization was (primarily) a device for regulating the possession of, and succession to, the property itself; and this view is indeed forced on us by the case pronounced upon by the lawyers, which one can hardly read without perceiving that the commencement of an organization must have been accompanied by a sharing of property. Mr. W. F. Skene, with an instinct for the truth in that field of ancient history which he has most studied, seems to me to have come near the mark when he says, in the four lines he has published on this subject, that these organizations were designed to regulate the succession of the Flaith, or chieftain class, to their *orba*, or inheritance lands.[1] The numerous texts which indicate that all the Septmen, and not merely those of the chieftain grades, had their place in " kindreds," or " geilfine tribes," represented by divisional organizations, make it impossible to believe that these organizations were known only to the Flaith, and affected only succession to landed estates. But it may well have been that such organizations had their origin among the Flaith, and had reference, at first, to the succession to landed estate only. It is not difficult to imagine that arrangements of such obvious convenience, as defining and limiting the liabilities of kinsmen for one another, if once successfully established among the superior classes, would, in time, be imitated by the inferior; and the peculiar settlement of property, worked through a divisional organization, as may easily be seen, is nowise, in its nature, inapplicable to movable estate. Thus much at least is certain, that the most striking effect, if not the primary purpose, of a divisional organization, was the regulation of succession to property.

The rights of succession established between the divisions were as follows :—

(1.) No such right opened to the property of any

[1] Mr. Skene has stated no grounds for this opinion, and I am unaware of his views of the composition of the divisions themselves. When he wrote, the third volume of the *Senchus Mor* had not yet appeared : he was ignorant that there were four divisions, and mistook the indfine for the commonalty of the tribe. What he says is, " The law which regulated the succession of the Flaith to their own *orba* is somewhat intricate and obscure, and for this purpose they were grouped in three classes, called the geilfine, deirbfine, and iarfine." (See Fordun, article on "Tribe Communities.")

division so long as any member of it lived. "All the 'indfine' division became extinct in this case; but if any one of them had been in existence, he would *take* it [the property] when the other three divisions should not share it between them" (vol. iii. p. 333).

(2.) When a division became extinct through the death of all its members, its property was divided into sixteen parts. If it was the "indfine" that became extinct, 12 parts went to the iarfine, 3 to the deirbfine, and 1 to the geilfine. If it was the "iarfine," 12 parts went to the deirbfine, 3 to the geilfine, and 1 to the indfine. If it was the "deirbfine," 12 parts went to the geilfine, 3 to the iarfine (next nearest ascending), and 1 to the indfine. If it was the "geilfine," 12 parts went to the deirbfine, 3 to the iarfine, and 1 to the indfine. Thus, as regards succession, the "deirbfine" was the favoured tribe—if any can be said to have been favoured. It got 12 parts in two cases and 3 in one. The "iarfine" was the next most favoured, for it got 12 parts in one case and 3 in two cases; the "geilfine" the next, getting 12 in one case, 3 in one case, and 1 in one case. The "indfine," least favoured, got only one share in each of three cases.

The law farther contemplated the simultaneous extinction of two divisions, and divided their property between the other two on the same principles. On the failure of the geilfine and deirbfine divisions, three-fourths of their property passed to the iarfine, and one-fourth to the indfine; on the failure of the indfine and iarfine, three-fourths of their property passed to the deirbfine, and one-fourth to the geilfine; on the failure of the deirbfine and iarfine, three-fourths of their property passed to the geilfine, and one-fourth to the indfine; on the failure of the geilfine and indfine, three-fourths of the property of the geilfine passed to the deirbfine, and one-fourth to the iarfine, while of the property of the "indfine" three-fourths passed to the iarfine, and one-fourth to the deirbfine. For two possible cases of two divisions becoming extinct together there was no provision made—the cases apparently not having been thought out. In none of the cases of two divisions failing did the distribution, according to this law, take place unless there were forthcoming men of the family to complete the organization. If that condition could not be complied with, the property went to the next of kin.

How the property of a division was apportioned between its members we are not informed; but I have inferred, from the hypothetical case, that it was shared equally among the members of the division, which shows again that the geilfine was the least desirable division to be in. The common senior, on his going out "into the community," left behind him his share (see *Senchus Mor*, vol. ii. pp. 283–287), and when a man died, his share must have been equally divided among the survivors.

The most simple way of regarding the rules established for the fourfold organization, in order to see how they operated as a succession law, is to conceive the organization to be started by four brothers, A_1, A_2, &c. (see table, *ante*, p. 364), on the death of their father, leaving to them ancestral lands, which had come to him as next of kin, and which, at common law, they were entitled to divide equally between them. Thus regarded, the arrangement operated, in the first instance, as a settlement of the respective shares of the brothers on their heirs of line, the survivors or survivor of them, as far as great-grandsons. When a son B_1 appeared, A_1 shared the division lands with him; when a grandson appeared, they were shared again between the father, son, and grandson; and they were finally redistributed on the appearance of a great-grandson. After that, there were redivisions as the men in turn died, till, they being all dead, the land was shared, in the proportions specified, between the remaining divisions. The chief peculiarities of the system, it will be seen, are (1) that it stopped succession in the direct line, except in the geilfine division, at great-grandsons; (2) that the principle of primogeniture appears in the formation of the groups of co-inheritors and parceners; and (3) that a life-tenancy only was given to any heir. To comprehend the working of the system, we must think of the four brothers as having had one or more brothers who shared with them the lands on the death of their father, but remained outside the organization. These, I conceive, were the men of the family who, with their descendants, or whose descendants, if they were dead, might, on the extinction of one or more divisions, enter the organization by forming new divisions. If the indfine, for example, became extinct, the iarfine would become the indfine in the re-formed organization, the deirbfine the iarfine, the geilfine, dropping the fifth man, would become the deirbfine, and the next eldest brother to A_4, with his descendants, would become the new geilfine division. The new division would enter with a share of the ancestral lands equal to that possessed by the others, except so far as the others had their shares increased by the distribution between them of the lands of the indfine. And thus the organization would continue, confining the lands to great-grandsons, till it collapsed through the extinction of two of the lines and the failure of men of the family to re-form it. The succession law acting no longer, the lands of the extinct groups would then go to the next of kin, and be subject to the common law of succession, whatever that was, till the lands were again re-settled by the formation of a divisional organization.

It will diminish the surprise one may naturally feel in considering such an arrangement as this, to remember that, by the common law of the Irish tribes, the land which made up the Tuath, or possession of a tribe, consisted of two distinct allotments,—the fechtfine, or tribe land, and the *orba*, or inheritance land. The fechtfine land, when arable, was distributed at stated intervals among the ceile, or free members of the tribe, a redistribution taking place as fresh claimants for a share appeared; and when pasture, was pastured in common. (See Skene, Fordun, vol. ii. p. 444.) The *orba*, or inheritance land, belonged as individual property to the men of the chieftain grades, and most probably came to exist as such, solely through being continually reserved to particular families in the periodical distributions of the tribal lands. It would follow, from such reservations having been often made, that the families in whose favour they were made—whose chiefs, indeed, *made* them—should come to regard the reserved lands as their special family property. On the first rise of such property, they would be without rules for regulating the succession to it, would be put to contriving such rules, and would almost certainly import into the rules they devised the principle of sharing to which they had been habituated in regard to the community lands—the fechtfine. Thus the share of the land coming to A_1 came to be shared by him with his first-born son, grandson, &c., to the fourth generation. When on the death of the co-tenants in tail, so to speak, it left his family, it was shared with his brothers and their sons, grandsons, &c., the bulk of it going to his next younger brother's family. The portion going to any family was again shared among the members of that family. That the brothers of B_1, or his sons other than C_1, should have no interest, or right of succession, in the lands, should not surprise us who are accustomed to entails and primogeniture. These men were at least better off than younger brothers among ourselves, for, as free men, they would be entitled to their shares of the fechtfine.

The Welsh laws of succession to ancestral lands (tir gwelyawg) ignored any right of primogeniture, as, indeed, we must believe the Irish common law did—the divisional succession law being strictly of the nature of a settlement. When a ŭchelwr died, his hereditary land was divided equally among his sons; on the death of the sons it was divided equally among the grandsons (first cousins); on the death of the grandsons it was divided equally among the great-grandsons (second cousins). On the death of the great-grandsons, however, there was no division among the great-great-grandsons (third cousins), but each family of them took between them the share that, under the last division (that between the great-grandsons), had fallen to their father. (*Ancient Laws, &c.*, vol. i. p. 169.) The co-inheritors were thus, to the fourth generation from the man who left the lands, sharers on a principle which applied no farther. Here the equal sharing between the sons, grandsons, and great-grandsons of the common ancestor, and the limit set to it, exhibit brothers and their sons and grandsons as groups of co-inheritors, according to a law which was as powerfully, though differently, affected by the principle of sharing applicable to the tribe land (tyr cyvriv), as the Irish divisional law itself.

But more curious and interesting, as bearing on the Irish divisional law, were the rules of succession to ancestral land in Western India. On the death of an owner of ancestral estate, his sons divided the land between them equally. When the sons died, the grandsons did not divide the land again between them equally, as in Wales; the grandsons in any family shared between them the share that in the first division had fallen to their father. But the peculiar feature of the law was, that succession, according to some authorities, stopped at grandsons. The great-grandsons were not heirs at all to their fathers' shares of the ancestral lands, so that when a grandson of the original owner died, the land he had inherited went not to his own sons, but to the sons or grandsons of *the brothers* of the original owner. In default of persons entitled to inherit in the families of these brothers, it went to persons entitled to inherit in the second collateral line, and so on. According to other authorities, especially the author of the *Vivada Chintamani* and the author of the *Mitakshara*, this peculiar stoppage of the right of lineal succession took place not on the death of grandsons, but of great-grandsons. (*Vivada Chintamani*, Calcutta, 1863. Table of succession prefixed, and see pp. 237, *ff.*) On the latter view, this old Indian law arrested the right of succession lineally at the very point at which the Irish divisional law arrested it; and, so far as it provided that the lands should, on the death of a great-grandson, go to the sons, grandsons, &c., of the brothers of his great-grandfather, it was the same law as that of the Irish divisional organization—the same, that is, apart from primogeniture as a feature of the latter, and the limitation of the number of divisions to four. And as regards this limitation in Irish law, it must be observed that its effects were only temporary; that it was a rule of the Irish settlements that ultimately, before the collapse of an organization—and, indeed, this was a condition of such collapse being averted—all the brothers and their descendants might enter the organization, and have the prospect of becoming heirs to the family estate.

Recurring, for the last time, to the opinion of the lawyers, from which the view I have given of the divisions of the Irish family has been spelled out, I ask whether, in the light that has now been thrown upon it, the interpretation I have given does not seem a sound one? It presents the case of a man—probably an only son, to whom inheritance land has come as next of kin —settling the land on his descendants. Had he four sons, or more, the case would present no difficulty; but he had only two; there were, however, four sons to each of his sons, so that the peculiar customary settlement had become possible—possible, obviously, for his sons, at his death, when his property had been divided between them; and, in the opinion of the lawyers, possible for him to make in his lifetime, upon conditions essentially the same as would have arisen had the settlements been made by the sons. A simple arithmetical calculation will show that it was immaterial to the father whether there should be two divisional organizations or one only—except so far as there being one such organization only might involve leaving half of his property unsettled. In either case—the divisions getting equal shares of the land—he would be reserving to himself one-fourth of the whole land. It was material to his sons, however; and indeed I do not see how, without violation of principle, the two sons could enter the same organization. From the opinion, assuming its soundness, we learn that principle did not restrict the father to forming in his family one divisional organization only, that, viz., which would be formed through the grandsons descended from the elder of his two sons as its basis—the younger son getting at common law, on the father's death, an equal share with the elder, but not subject to settlement. As the partition and settlement were voluntary acts of the father, we may believe that he would have been free—there could be no hindrance except in custom—to make two settlements or one, as he chose; but if he wished to settle his whole property, and had fewer sons than four, it would seem that he had no choice but to form as many divisional organizations among his descendants as he had sons. That a man should share the inheritance lands with his sons and grandsons in his lifetime need not surprise us. The Indian law as to partition of inheritance land by a father in his lifetime shows that the partition, usually made with sons, might extend even to grandsons.

I think it will now be felt that the Irish divisional system is no longer so mysterious or exceptional as it at first appeared. The view I have taken of it may be familiar to Irish scholars. Except so far as has been disclosed, I have written in total ignorance of the literature of the subject, if there is any—which, from the recentness of the publication of the *Book of Aicill*, seems improbable. What attracted me to it was its appearing to connect itself with the classificatory system of relationships, but with that, I am now satisfied, it has nothing to do. That the description of geilfine tribe relationship remained true, while brothers shifted from division to division, was the chief hint of classification; but this feature was temporary, and in the geilfine division never showed itself, for in that the members, necessarily, always were a father and his heirs of line to the fifth generation. And this may be the reason why the relationship of the whole group was named from the geilfine division.[1]

[1] I may here, in a note, insert an explanation of the fact of the geilfine tribe, represented by "the seventeen men," being called "the hand-family" which I have some time fancied, or somewhere seen. If the reader, turning down the palm of his hand, will look at the back of the hand, holding down the thumb, he will see in the five joints nearest to him the geilfine division; and in the next two series of joints and the tips of his four fingers, the deirbfine, iarfine and indfine divisions respectively! Of course the suggestion is that some humorous or fanciful Celt early observed this correspondence, and that thence came the name, which, after many centuries, has been lately adduced, with the support of much high Celtic scholarship, as a proof of the former existence of the patria potestas among the ancient Irish.

THE END.

RICHARD CLAY & SONS,
BREAD STREET HILL, LONDON,
Bungay, Suffolk.

www.ingramcontent.com/pod-product-compliance
Lightning Source LLC
Chambersburg PA
CBHW030552300426
44111CB00009B/950